Alternative Modernity

Alternative Modernity

The Technical Turn in Philosophy
and Social Theory

Andrew Feenberg

UNIVERSITY OF CALIFORNIA PRESS
Berkeley · *Los Angeles* · *London*

University of California Press
Berkeley and Los Angeles, California

University of California Press
London, England

Copyright © 1995 by
The Regents of the University of California

Library of Congress Cataloging-in-Publication Data

Feenberg, Andrew.
   Alternative modernity : the technical turn in philosophy and
social theory / Andrew Feenberg.
      p.   cm.
   Includes bibliographical references and index.
   ISBN 0–520–08985–5 (c: alk. paper). — ISBN 0–520–08986–3
(p: alk. paper)
      1. Technology—Social aspects.   2. Culture.   3. Democracy.
I. Title.
HM221.F384   1995
303.48′3—dc20
                                                                    95–8666
                                                                    CIP

Printed in the United States of America

1   2   3   4   5   6   7   8   9

Contents

PART II. TECHNIQUE AND VALUE

PART III. POSTMODERN TECHNOLOGY

Preface

This book concerns the emergence of a new radical critique of technology in philosophy and culture since the 1960s. I reinterpret various theoreticians, including Herbert Marcuse, Jürgen Habermas, Jean-François Lyotard, and major Japanese thinkers, in terms of their relation to this trend.

In an attempt to avoid mere abstract talk about technology in general, the inquiry proceeds in part through case studies. Each of the four sections contains one essay on a philosopher and another on a concrete literary, cultural, or technical phenomenon that illustrates the problems raised in the philosophical discussion. Each chapter is relatively self-contained, although they are intended to illuminate each other usefully.

The case studies discuss the early image of nuclear disaster in post–World War II science fiction, dystopian themes in the popular spy films of the 1960s, the impact of AIDS on medical experimentation on human subjects, the suprising success of the Minitel in France, and the Japanese reponse to modernization as illustrated by Yasunari Kawabata's famous novel *The Master of Go*.

Throughout these investigations, my theme is the inextricable intermingling of scientific-technical rationality and culture. I argue from this constructivist premise to the possibility of reshaping the technical world around us. Technophobic ideologies of the sort that emerged in the mass culture and politics of the 1960s underestimate the potential for reconstructing modern technology. This potential is most clearly exemplified by the history of the computer. Social institutions that appear to rest on solid technical foundations, such as medicine, turn out to incorporate values in their very structure, and to be not so very solid after all. Modernization itself, I argue, is a contingent combination of technical and cultural dimensions subject to radical variation. Aesthetics, ethics, and culture can play a role alongside science and technology in the emergence of alternative modernities.

Although *Alternative Modernity* is strongly influenced by the Frankfurt School, in chapters 2 and 4 I explain why I think the Critical Theory tradition must now be revised. I attempt to overcome the frozen opposition, to which the Frankfurt School contributed, between those who are "for" and those who are "against" technology. At the same time, I am not willing to abandon the whole critical tradition of technology studies in postmodern resignation or celebration. The essay on Lyotard explains my reservations about this trend. The concluding chapters on Japan attempt to come to terms with the new multiculturalism in a way that avoids both positivist universalism and ethnic relativism. Here I draw provisional conclusions regarding the reconciliation of the often conflicting claims of reason and culture.

Both the philosophical and the political tradition need to be studied anew in the light of the growing importance of technology in modern societies. These essays make a start on this neglected task. However, my focus on technology is meant to bring it back into the critical discussion, not to eclipse the many other, equally important dimensions of modern societies that have begun to receive attention in recent years. In the hope of adding another thread to the discussion, I offer models here of a new kind of social criticism, mixing cultural hermeneutics, sociology of technology, and ethical inquiry, that is, I believe, urgently needed today.

Most of the essays collected here are based on earlier publications, heavily reworked for this book. With the exception of chapter 3, which belongs too fully to its time to be brought entirely up to date, they have all been updated wherever possible. The original versions appeared in whole or in part in the following sources: "Technocracy and Rebellion: Spy Films and Social Criticism," *Telos*, Summer 1970; "An End to History: Science Fiction in the Nuclear Age," *Johns Hopkins Magazine*, March 1977; "The Bias of Technology," in R. Pippin, A. Feenberg, and C. Webel, eds., *Marcuse: Critical Theory and the Promise of Utopia* (South Hadley, Mass.: Bergin and Garvey Press,

1987); "A User's Guide to the Pragmatics of Computer Mediated Communication," *Semiotica*, July 1989; "From Information to Communication: The French Experience with Videotex," in M. Lea, ed., *Contexts of Computer Mediated Communication* (London: Harvester-Wheatsheaf, 1992); "On Being a Human Subject: Interest and Obligation in the Experimental Treatment of Incurable Disease," *Philosophical Forum*, Spring 1992; "The Critique of Technology: From Dystopia to Interaction," in J. Bokina and T. Lukes, eds., *Marcuse Revisited* (Lawrence: University of Kansas Press, 1993); "The Technocracy Thesis Revisted: On *The Critique of Power*," *Inquiry*, Spring 1994; "Playing the Japanese Game of Culture: Kawabata's *Master of Go*," *Cultural Critique*, Fall 1994.

I would like to thank the following friends and colleagues for sharing their ideas and helping me to formulate mine: Yoko Arisaka, Hal Barwood, Catherine Bertho, Jean-Marie Charon, Peter Dale, Gerald Doppelt, Anne-Marie Feenberg, Peter Fitting, Marc Guillaume, Linda Harasim, Ruth Heifetz, Sharon Helsel, Martin Jay, Nobuo Kazashi, Douglas Kellner, Illana Löwy, Marie Marchand, Ted Melnechuk, Ryosuke Ohashi, Robert Pippin, Mark Poster, Richard Smith, and Morton Söby.

CHAPTER ONE

Introduction

Technology and Freedom

DEMOCRATIZING TECHNICAL CHANGE

A new understanding of technology has emerged from several decades of public controversy over technical issues. Debate has spread from ecology to nuclear energy to medicine and genetic engineering, and even, in less visible forms, to theoretical fields such as artificial intelligence and the human genome project.

Some of these controversies brought about significant technical improvements as a direct result of public participation. For example, in the early 1970s, as a generation of baby boomers had their own children, expectant mothers demanded changes in obstetrics and large numbers joined organizations promoting natural childbirth to get their way. They challenged the overemphasis on medical technology in the hospitals they frequented; some of their gains have become routine, for example, reduced use of analgesia and anesthetic, and the admission of husbands or coaches to labor rooms (Charles et al. 1978). In this case, a major technical institution—for, have no illusions, medical care today is technical—adapted under pressure to public demands.

But some public interventions do not have such a happy ending. At about the same time women were joining movements for natural childbirth, rising public concern over the safety of the nuclear industry prepared the collapse of one of the major technological projects of modern times. Nuclear power promised to free industrial society from dependency on the bottleneck of fossil fuels. But the nuclear industry

1

became fixated on unsafe designs in the 1960s and was unable to adapt to the standards of the seventies and eighties. In the head-on confrontation with public opinion that followed, technology lost (Morone and Woodhouse 1989). Today conversion initiatives multiply as the owners of old nuclear plants switch back to fossil fuels.

I could multiply such examples at length, but the main points are clear. First, we are entering a new era characterized by pervasive technology that affects us in the most unexpected ways; and second, it matters what we do about technology because, perhaps for the first time in history, public involvement is beginning to have significant impacts on the shape of technological change. This is a book about the philosophical implications of this unprecedented situation.

Philosophy of technology is adjusting gradually to the emergence of technical politics. Until recently it polarized around two contrary positions: we were obliged to choose between uncritical acceptance of the claims made for technology or uncompromising rejection of its dystopian power. This dichotomy depended in turn on the sharp distinction between technology and society that used to be shared by both advocates and adversaries of technical progress. Today this distinction has broken down.

For some that breakdown signals the end of history, the collapse of all resistance to alienation in postmodern celebration of a brave new world that fuses human beings and machines in a harmonious totality; for others the same shift renews hope in radical change, contrary to the dystopian projections of those like Martin Heidegger, Theodor Adorno, and Jacques Ellul who despair of technological society. From this standpoint, we are "enframed" in Heidegger's terms, but not helplessly so because in drawing us into its orbit the system has exposed itself to new forms of resistance. *Alternative Modernity* reflects the latter approach. It argues that modern technology is neither a savior nor an inflexible iron cage; rather, it is a new sort of cultural framework, fraught with problems but subject to transformation from within.

As I explain in Part I, the popular dystopianism of the 1950s and 1960s was the original breakthrough that created the space for a critical politics of technology in the United States. Every chapter therefore responds to that breakthrough in attempting to understand the new conditions of critique and agency in a technological age. Anticipating, I conclude that indeed it is possible to reconcile technology and freedom, however, not within the framework of the currently dominant technical culture. That culture supports a rigidly hierarchical conception of the technical order. In chapter 2, I argue that a very different world can emerge from the gradual democratization of technical change. But public participation in technical politics is often dismissed as symptomatic of irrational fears or hopes that are at best a nuisance, at worst a serious threat to progress.

An astonishing blindness is revealed by this commonplace reaction to environmentalism, the antinuclear movement, the struggles of AIDS patients, and similar activities. Understanding these initiatives requires change in the accustomed view of technology. Much of this book argues for that change, both theoretically and through case histories. But can we reasonably demand the generalization of democratic initiatives, with the expectation of sociotechnical transformation as a consequence? In the remainder of this introduction, I will consider that question in its relevance to the essays collected here.

UNDERDETERMINATION AND PUBLIC INTERVENTION

To begin, I would like briefly to describe the results of my own recent book, *Critical Theory of Technology* (1991), which reflects several current trends in technology studies. This book attempted to establish three principal points: (1) technological design is socially relative, contrary to deterministic arguments or theories of technical neutrality; (2) the unequal distribution of social influence over technological design contributes to social injustice; and (3) there are at least some instances in which public involvement in the design of devices and systems has made a difference. (This last point is developed much further here in chapters 5 and 7.)

These points form the necessary foundation for a theory of democratic technical change. Indeed, were any of them false—were technology determined or neutral, were the unequal access to the design process without consequence, or were there no examples of constructive public involvement—the idea of democratic technical change would make no sense.

The simplest way to explain my position is in terms of the thesis of underdetermination, the so-called Duhem-Quine principle in philosophy of science. This principle refers to the inevitable lack of logically compelling reasons for preferring one competing scientific theory to another. In the realm of technology, the thesis holds that technical principles are insufficient by themselves to determine design. Of course, it remains true that some things really work and others do not: successful design respects technical principles. But often several different designs can achieve the same or similar objectives with no decisive technical reason to prefer one design over the others. *Technical choices are thus "underdetermined," and the final decision between alternatives ultimately depends on the "fit" between them and the interests and beliefs of the various social groups that influence the design process* (Feenberg 1992).

Typically, technological designs are negotiated achievements involving many partners, not rational inspirations that spring full blown from the mind of an individual genius or pure laboratory research. The design process is the place where the various social actors interested in a developing technology first gain a hearing. Owners of businesses, technicians, customers, political leaders, and government bureaucrats all qualify as actors. Their variety guarantees that design represents many interests. They wield their influence by proffering or withholding resources, defining the purposes of the devices they require, fitting them into existing technical arrangements to their own benefit, imposing new directions on existing technical means, and so on. Technologies, like other rational institutions, are social expressions of these actors. This argument, on which my earlier book rests, is also central to recent constructivist sociology of technology, and to Axel Honneth's reconstruction of Critical Theory, discussed in chapter 4.[1]

I have proposed the term "technical code" to describe those features of technologies that reflect the hegemonic values and beliefs that prevail in the design process. Such codes are usually invisible because, like culture itself, they appear self-evident. For example, tools and workplaces are designed for adult hands and heights not because workers are necessarily adult, but because our society expelled children from the work process at a certain point in history with design consequences we now take for granted.

Technical codes also include the basic definition of many technical objects insofar as these too become universal, culturally accepted features of daily life. The telephone, the automobile, the refrigerator, and a hundred other everyday devices have clear and unambiguous definitions in the dominant culture: we *know* what they are in principle sim-

---

1. For the constructivist position, see Bijker, Hughes, and Pinch (1990) and Bijker and Law (1992).

ply because we are acculturated members of our society. Each new instance of these standard technologies must conform to its defining "code" to be recognized and accepted by people like us. Constructivists sometimes call the establishment of such codes "black boxing" because one does not question what is "inside" the technology once its definition is generally accepted.

If all this is true, we need to take seriously Langdon Winner's (1992) proposal that technology is a new kind of legislation shaping our way of life, not so very differently from law in the proper sense. Technical codes reflecting particular social interests decide where and how we live, what kinds of food we eat, how we communicate, are entertained, healed, and so on. As technology becomes central to more and more aspects of our lives, its legislative authority increases. But if technology is so powerful, then surely it should be measured by the same democratic standards as other political institutions. By those standards the design process appears outmoded and unfair. Owners of corporations, military bureaucrats, and the professional organizations of technologists have far more influence over it than ordinary citizens. For the most part it is they, not we, who determine technical codes. I will return to this problem of the "operational autonomy" of elites in chapter 4.

At this point a clarification is in order: I do *not* argue that these currently dominant groups obstruct technical progress to further their own interests. It would be more accurate to say that they channel progress in a particular direction compatible with those interests. Nor do I mean to imply that they wield an arbitrary dictatorship over technology. Clearly, under the influence of the market, they represent a wide range of needs and achieve many important goals. However, it is important not to confuse this sort of responsiveness with democratic control of technology. While markets in many goods are surely desirable, they lack the public character, the element of debate and conscious coordination, that we associate with democratic action. With rare exceptions, such as the French videotex case discussed below, there are rather narrow limits to what can be done by isolated individuals acting on the market. To call such a system consumer "sovereignty" is a pathetic exaggeration of the actual power consumers wield in advanced capitalist societies. Even with the help of state regulation they usually cannot break through the modern corporations' imposing facade of fiscal power and technical resources. In fact, the issue of control over technical decisions rarely surfaces in the context of the market. Thus, however responsive they may be in other respects, those in charge of our technical destiny meet few serious obstacles to reproducing their technical power in their relations with consumers.

In my earlier book I followed the lead of the many historians and sociologists for whom the assembly line exemplifies the biasing of design by powerful interests. The history of the deskilling of the labor process under capitalism, which culminates in a production system in which workers are controlled by machines, points to the essential role of design in providing an objective basis for the class structure. According to this hypothesis, alienation is due not so much to the pursuit of efficiency as to the struggle for managerial power. Here is a clear case where *undemocratic design procedures have substantive consequences through the attempts by powerful players to preserve their technical initiative and control in the systems they create.* Their interest in maintaining that power is a kind of bottom line inscribed in all their technical decisions, biasing those decisions in the direction of centralization and hierarchy.

The resulting inequalities are by no means transcended in contemporary capitalism, despite profound changes in technology and management. On the contrary, while some sectors of the labor force clearly benefit from recent advances, others stagnate or fall behind in a pattern that promises to reproduce a class-divided society into the foreseeable future, and perhaps to intensify the conflicts to which it gives rise. I take up these problems in chapter 6 in relation to the computerization of society.

Here I will also introduce other examples that stretch democratic concerns well beyond these classic problems of control of production. In chapters 5 and 7, I offer case studies in medicine and computer design that show a few privileged actors obstructing the expression of important interests in ways not generally recognized by political economy. The technical code of medical experimentation defined it exclusively in terms of scientific research and industrial product testing. That code offered human subjects basic protection from exploitation, but it ignored terminally ill patients' demands for experimental participation. In the case of French videotex, a computer network installed on the scale of an entire nation through the distribution of millions of free terminals (the famous Minitel) was intended primarily to give access to information; users' interest in communicating with each other was ignored. In each case public interventions, by AIDS patients in one and network users in the other, significantly altered the systems to accommodate excluded interests. Now Food and Drug Administration regulations and experimental designs are in flux as medicine gropes toward a new approach that recognizes the demands of dying patients. Similarly, in France, the Minitel was transformed when users hacked the system and introduced new communications applications that had not been planned by the designers.

These experiences reveal ideological blind spots in the design process. They show, furthermore, that technical systems cannot be considered finished until they have withstood social tests that expose them to a wide range of public influences and concerns excluded in the design phase. The fact that, in these cases at least, the technical systems underwent major changes after release suggests a flawed process. This observation is confirmed by other experiences with new technologies and argues for democratizing design.

LEGITIMACY AND RATIONALITY

Democratization of technical change means granting actors who lack financial, cultural, or political capital access to the design process. There is no reason of principle to think that their participation would be detrimental, since nontechnical actors are already involved; democratization would simply increase their number and variety. Indeed, far from impeding progress as is sometimes supposed, it might help avoid problems of the sort which currently plague clinical research and nuclear power. At the same time, it would ensure adequate representation of interests that are currently undervalued because they conflict with centralized, elite control of design, such as the interest of workers in an outlet for their skills. The long-term implications of more democratic design are earth-shaking, given the significant imprint of elite control on so many aspects of our society.

Typically, democratic interventions are the work of activists caught up in a local problem or crisis. This localism should not be surprising, as technical issues are usually of interest only to those directly affected by them and therefore willing to devote the time needed to form what Donna Haraway (1991) has called a "situated knowledge." In some cases, active minorities select themselves on the basis of common social attributes such as neighborhood, race or gender, hobby or illness, and then try to influence public opinion by provoking technical controversies (Cambrosio and Limoges 1991). AIDS patients, for example, attacked regulatory procedures, demanded hearings, and negotiated changes. In other cases public involvement in the design process takes the form of what I will call "reappropriations," that is, modifying technologies through innovative applications. The example of the French videotex system shows the effectiveness of such a posteriori interventions by users.

The reigning common sense still discourages exploration of these democratic potentials of technological society with three objections. First, centralized authoritarian administration is a "technological imperative" of industrial production which every modern society must respect if it is to be successful. Second, while protest groups may occasionally be right, even against the opinion of experts misled by professional biases, there is no easy way to know if their views are representative. Thus there is no special reason to call their interventions democratic. Third, political activity in the technical sphere represents a step backward from experts' hard-won freedom from lay interference. The general public would likely disapprove of such interference if it knew the true cost.

The counterargument in favor of the democratization of technical change must (a) show the *possibility* of democratic control of technology; (b) establish the *legitimacy* of informal public involvement; and (c) reconcile public involvement with the *rationality* and *autonomy* of professional technical work. I cannot respond adequately to these objections in this brief introduction; the essays collected here offer some starting points for reflection.

(a) To refute this first objection we need at least a sketch of a theory of the exercise of power through technique. (For a fuller treatment, see *Critical Theory of Technology.*) Every technology has an operator and an object, and a specifically technical power arises where both roles are played by human beings. This is the case, for example, with medical and production technologies, and, more generally, wherever a way of life is imposed through the choice of technical systems. This type of power is central to the organization of advanced societies, which necessarily require management to coordinate the activities of their members in contact with complex technical systems. However, it is important not to prejudge the issue of technical democracy by simply identifying operator and object with rulers and ruled as though the structure of technology determined the social system. There is a choice between technical elitism or democracy, between a system in which these two roles are distributed between different classes and another system in which they are different institutional expressions of the same class. In the latter case, management is chosen and ultimate policy decided by those subordinated to the system in the usual democratic way. This is not a trivial choice, a point to which I will return in the next section.

(*b*) While it is sometimes difficult to tell whether the outcome of a technical controversy corresponds to a public will, there is another sense in which public involvement in technical change is intrinsically democratic. Democracy includes not only voting on political issues but also acting to reform the procedures of government, business, education, and other social spheres in order to enhance participation and agency. I follow C. B. Macpherson (1973) here in claiming that a democratic society should offer opportunities to develop human capacities and powers. All forms of public activity and participation should be sanctioned as democratic so long as they respect civil rights. *As more and more of social life is framed by technical systems, cases increasingly appear in which public interventions into technology determine the conditions of agency. If agency is a value in itself, its enhancement may provide a basis for calling certain technological controversies and reappropriations democratic despite the fact that they do not appear political at first sight.*

Such activities foreshadow a world in which technical "legislation" will emerge from new types of public consultation. For example, in the Minitel case not only did the users exercise an unaccustomed agency in the technical sphere by significantly modifying the system, but they enlarged the realm of public discourse for many others by creating a new virtual space of public discussion, thereby indirectly enhancing democratic agency in general.[2] This and many other cases show that technical politics, in the form of minority protests or reappropriations, does not stand in unmediated opposition to democratic community as skeptics contend, but actually realizes important democratic values.

(*c*) Nevertheless, democratic values are not our only concern. We also want to know if wider participation has unacceptable costs and diminishes the efficiency of our society. This brings us to the problem of the rationality of public intervention.

This problem is relevant to one of the major contemporary approaches in democratic social theory, Jürgen Habermas's theory of communicative action, which I consider in chapter 4. Habermas (1984, 1987) defines modernity in terms of the differentiation of cognitive, normative, and expressive spheres to which correspond facts, values,

---

2. For a parallel account of reappropriation in the AIDS case, see Epstein (1991).

and feelings. What makes a society modern is the institutionalized distinction between these spheres reflected in different rationalization processes that support the progressive development of knowledge and technology, on the one hand, and political and personal freedom, on the other. This differentiation is apparently threatened by public involvement in technology because political opinions and situated knowledges are less differentiated and methodically disciplined than specialized scientific-technical knowledge, and mix values and facts. Habermas's theory thus could provide the basis for rejecting technical democratization as a regressive movement running counter to the main trend of modernity.

However, in his early work, Habermas (1991a) introduced another important concept, the notion of a "public sphere" as an informal institutional foundation of democracy. The public sphere and formal democracy are distinct but mutually dependent aspects of democratic political life. The extension of this dual system to technology promises an enrichment of public life, an advance in what Habermas calls the "communicative rationality" of the society. Environmentalism can be seen as a model for this new "technical public sphere." Once again, it is the underdetermination of technical decisions that leaves a space for public intervention.

Habermas emphasizes the importance of consensus in the legitimation process. But this aspect of his theory is particularly unconvincing in the case of technical politics. Technocratic authority is based on the most effective machinery for building consensus in modern societies— the mystification of technical choices by deterministic notions of development. Politicizing technology is all about dissensus, not consensus. I find support for this argument in Jean-François Lyotard, the postmodern theorist whose work I discuss in chapter 6. His concept of "paralogic legitimation" offers an alternative way of thinking about communicative rationality.

The rationality problem appears in another guise as the fear that the politicization of technology will destroy the autonomy of the technical professions (Florman 1981). This fear is based on an illusion specific to technical change. Successful protest or reappropriation modifies the technical code to reflect interests excluded at earlier stages in the design process. As these new interests are internalized in the code, it masks their source in public protest. The waves close over forgotten controversies and the technologists return to the comforting belief in their own autonomy, which seems to be verified by the conditions of everyday technical work. Who today, even in the hospitals where women once struggled to change procedures, recalls the sometimes fierce resistance to admitting husbands to labor rooms? How many nuclear engineers remember the history of radiation exposure standards (Caufield 1989)? How many architects know the story behind emergency exits?[3]

The notion that technology is apolitical is thus a misleading consequence of the very success of past protests; it reappears with each new phase of public involvement in technology as a defensive reaction on the part of professions and corporations that want no interference with their technical initiative. But in reality the autonomy they claim was violated long ago in the course of earlier controversies the outcomes of which they now unwittingly endorse in defending their traditions. Informal democratic procedures are thus already an implicit part of the design process despite the illusions of technologists.

The historical rhythm of public and professional dominance in technical fields parallels Thomas Kuhn's famous distinction between revolutionary and normal science, with, however, a significant difference. As it professionalizes, natural science wins ever more independence from direct expressions of public opinion and democratic interventions become rarer and rarer. Of course, this does not mean that mature science is independent of politics and culture, just that their influence reaches it indirectly through established administrative channels and scientists' personal vision. However, the constant involvement of the population in technical activity, if only as an object of technical systems, generates ever renewed situated knowledges that can become the basis for public interventions at any stage in the development of a technical field.[4] In these cases social initiatives influence technical rationality without destroying it. This is possible because *the autonomy of technical professions has less to do with their separation from politics than with their capacity to translate politics into rational technical*

---

3. The skeptical reader is referred to John Burke's (1972) excellent study of the origins of the mundane boiler code in early nineteenth-century struggles over steamboat safety.

4. The boundaries between science and technology are increasingly blurred; in some fields the distinction must be replaced with the hybrid category "technoscience," which applies, for example, to medical experimentation, discussed in chapter 5. However, it is premature to dismiss the strategically significant distinction made here: theoretical physics and General Motors testify to its continuing, if reduced, validity.

terms. In this context, public intervention may actually enhance technical rationality by bringing significant issues to the surface early in opposition to vested interests entrenched in the design process.

VALUE, CULTURE, AND TECHNOLOGY

The argument so far has established the design consequences of struggle over the democratic value of agency. But agency is a formal value. One can still ask, agency in the name of what, for what higher purpose? To put it bluntly, if technical design were to privilege agency rather than centralized power, would anyone care (Pippin 1995)? Alasdair MacIntyre (1981) argues that the thrust toward ever-expanding technical power over nature is rooted in the breakdown of traditional normative consensus and the substitution of productive efficiency for it as the only shared value of modern societies. Hence the democratic objection to elitist design does not really address the underlying problem of modernity, which is the never-ending spiral of technical power satisfying ever-escalating demands for material goods.

I have two criticisms of this diagnosis of the problem.

First, even if it is true that modern societies are committed to an unending spiral as MacIntyre claims, it makes quite a difference whether the demands of the population can be satisfied only by an authoritarian technical system or whether an alternative democratic system is possible.

It is obvious that there will be different substantive consequences for subordinates in either case, such as more or less control over health and safety, hours, skills, or convenience and fairness of administrative procedures. *Critical Theory of Technology* argues that in the long run technical design would evolve differently. The differences are even clearer in the relations of the First to the Third World; all too frequently, developing economies are restructured around advanced technical means to centralize control and to yield products for the world market. Often effective subsistence economies are shattered and no viable alternative is put in their place. Modernization then has catastrophic consequences for the indigenous population. Surely even the most acquisitive individual would care about these matters, and they depend directly on who controls technology.

I have a second objection. Is it really true that modern culture lacks any resources for achieving normative consensus? In fact consensus is commonplace; only its manifestations are unexpected and therefore overlooked by philosophers who assume that it must take the discursive form of agreement on legislation or doctrine as in the lost utopias of early parliamentarism or the medieval church. Today, on the contrary, consensus is materialized in various social and technical codes. At any given time, we do "know" such things as that the victory of the Union in the Civil War was good, that Paris is a beautiful city and should be preserved, that medicine should serve the interests of patients, or that lowering labor costs is socially more desirable than protecting workers' skills. Such normative propositions are not mere opinions but, as I will argue in chapter 4, are institutionally "delegated," for example, to textbook standards, zoning codes, professional regulations, technical designs, in sum, the real foundations of modern life. That each such value is both unfounded and contested merely proves that we are living in the modern world; it is no warrant for hasty relativism or cultural despair.

This point is important, because it shows that technology embodies the fruits of normative consensus in the aesthetic, ethical, and cultural domains and not merely pure efficiency or a consumerist delirium of acquisitiveness. To fail to see this is to accept positivistic claims at face value and to exaggerate the difference between premodern and modern societies. Whether such a position is taken up in criticism or celebration, it blocks a concrete grasp of actual social life.

Thus it is necessary to broaden the range of values involved in technical decisions. The issue is not just elitism versus democracy but concerns the whole cultural field that is embodied in one form or another in technical codes. Why is this not obvious to us today? Why do we tend to see modern technology as "pure" and contrast it with values as with an alien sphere? A view of technology I will call "Weberian" seems to have such a grip on the modern mind that we can only free ourselves from it with difficulty. According to this view, technology is based on knowledge of causal processes in contrast with values, which express merely subjective preferences. Even if ethical norms are granted their own specific rationality, as in Habermas, they are still safely separated from technology.

This Weberian prejudice is deeply ethnocentric; it excludes the very possibility of a fundamentally different modernity based on another technological dispensation. Several chapters discuss challenges to the Weberian position from a variety of thinkers, including Herbert Marcuse, Axel Honneth, Bruno Latour, and Donna Haraway. In one way or another, they all reject the sharp separation of value and fact in modern thought and treat technology as relative to a framework of social practices. Technology no longer exemplifies pure rationality but is embedded in a value-governed action system. From this standpoint, the technical order appears in its contingency as a possible object of political critique and action.

The chapters on Japan in Part IV confront similar problems historically, building on earlier discussions of ethics and aesthetics to argue for the possibility of an alternative modernity based on national culture. They challenge the invidious comparison of non-Western and modern societies the Weberian view assumes. That assumption was called into question before World War II in the work of the Japanese philosopher Kitarō Nishida, discussed in chapter 8. Like Marcuse, Nishida was strongly influenced by G. W. F. Hegel, whose dialectic he applied to show that cultural alternatives haunt the scientific-technical achievements of Western capitalism.

This argument is continued in chapter 9, which explores the relation of rationalization to culture through an example from Japanese literature, Yasunari Kawabata's *Master of Go*. Kawabata's novel concerns the modernization of Japan as exemplified in a championship Go match. The match symbolizes the confrontation between the old Japan and the new. From the constructivist standpoint the match is emblematic of the cultural specificity of Western modernity. It turns on a single move which, like a scientific fact or technical device, appears to be purely rational. But that move can be intepreted at many levels—strategically, but also socially, historically, aesthetically. In fact, the whole content of the novel unfolds around it. The novel reveals the bias of the modernization process represented in that move. Kawabata's challenge to the false universality of Western rationality suggests the possibility of an alternative modernity based on certain distinctive values of Japanese culture.

CONCLUSION

This introduction has argued that the democratization of technical change reflects potentialities contained in the nature of technology itself. Coupling the technical design process to aesthetic and ethical norms and national identities through new and more democratic procedures is no utopia. Modern technologies open not only possibilities internal to the particular world they shape but metapossibilities corresponding to other worlds they can be transformed to serve. Technical change is not simply progress or regress along the continuum so far traced out by the West; it may also come to include movement between different continua.

As the postmodern age struggles to make the transition out of the technocratic heritage of the twentieth century, this project will appear increasingly as a practical task. Only if we can concretize the issues on the technical terrain will that transition succeed. Only then will we find out what it really means to live and create in a technological society.

PART I

Dystopian Enlightenment

Klaatu/Mr. Carpenter (Michael Rennie) and Gort (Lock Martin) in *The Day the Earth Stood Still*. ™ and © 1951, 1995 Twentieth Century Fox Film Corporation. All rights reserved. Used by permission.

CHAPTER TWO

Marcuse and the Critique of Technology

From Dystopia to Interaction

The task to be accomplished is not the conservation of the past, but the redemption of the hopes of the past.
—*Max Horkheimer and Theodor Adorno 1972: xv*

PROLOGUE: OBSTINACY AS A THEORETICAL VIRTUE

Karl Marx considered any merely moral critique of capitalism to be arbitrary. Whole societies cannot be condemned at the whim of the individual critic; they must be measured by the values they effectively strive to realize. Marx therefore judged capitalism by reference to an immanent criterion, the unsatisfied needs of the population. The argument was persuasive for its time but no longer relevant once capitalism proves itself capable of delivering the goods. Then the (fulfilled) needs of the individuals legitimate the established order. Radicalism means opposition not just to the failures and deficiencies of that system but to its very successes.

From what standpoint can society be judged once it feeds its members? It takes astonishing nerve to persist in radical social criticism beyond this point. Herbert Marcuse is important because he faced this challenge and struggled to rebuild the critical tradition in the "affluent" society of the 1950s and 1960s. Was this not merely an obstinate refusal to admit the failure of Marxism? Perhaps, but as Marcuse (1968: 143) himself once wrote, "obstinacy [is] a genuine quality of philosophical thought." To be obstinate means to reject the easy reconciliation with society, to keep *a sense of reality* based on longer time spans, deeper tensions, higher expectations and goals.

Marcuse's solution to the problem had two parts. First, he believed

19

that the historically evolved ideals of peace, freedom, and happiness still provide criteria in terms of which to measure the existing society. These ideals are not merely subjective but have roots in nature itself. They drive the historical process forward through the formation of new needs reflecting as yet unrealized human potential.

New needs are not arbitrary because—and this is the second part of Marcuse's solution—the unrealized technical potential of advanced industrialism provides a basis on which to concretize them as historical projects. Advanced society, Marcuse argued, is capable of "pacifying" existence but artificially maintains competition and violence as the basis for domination and inequality. That society is, in a certain sense, *technically* outmoded by its own achievements. As he put it in a late speech on ecology, radical political struggle today consists in "existential revolts against an obsolete reality principle" (Marcuse 1992: 37).

In this chapter I would like to explore Marcuse's contribution to the question of technology, which he, more than anyone in the last thirty years, placed on the agenda of political discussion. He wrote his most influential works in the 1960s. In the third chapter of this book I explore the roots of the popular dystopianism of this period in science fiction, films, and advertising. Marcuse contributed and responded to this new mood in terms of the rich philosophical tradition of the Frankfurt School, to which he had belonged since the 1930s. That heritage enabled him to transform the existing dystopian critique of society into the basis for radical opposition.

However, he was unable to elaborate a strategy that went beyond the gestures of revolt that animated the New Left. The formulation of such a strategy is perhaps possible today, now that critique of technology is no longer the purely theoretical scandal it was in 1964, when Marcuse published *One-Dimensional Man,* but has become increasingly a matter of concrete practice. In the course of this chapter, I would like to sketch a new approach, linking the tradition of radical critique with a new "interactivist" perspective that is illustrated by concrete examples in later chapters of this book.

THE PROTEST AGAINST PROGRESS

What made Marcuse's critique of technology so different from the usual complaints about the hidden costs of progress? For the most part these protests are conservative and recommend moderation in the application of technology, or even retreat to pretechnological social arrangements. With Marcuse we are on different ground. He argued that progress up to now has been inextricably bound up with domination and that that link extends to scientific-technical rationality itself. Emancipation therefore requires not just social change but a radical transformation of Reason as well. "As a technological universe," he wrote, "advanced industrial society is a *political* universe, the latest stage in the realization of a specific historical *project*—namely, the experience, transformation, and organization of nature as the mere stuff of domination. As the project unfolds, it shapes the entire universe of discourse and action, intellectual and material culture. In the medium of technology, culture, politics, and the economy merge into an omnipresent system which swallows up or repulses all alternatives. The productivity and growth potential of this system stabilize the society and contain technical progress within the framework of domination. Technological rationality has become political rationality" (Marcuse 1964: xv–xvi).

It is true that Adorno and Heidegger held similar views, but it was Marcuse's work that had explosive impact because these earlier sources were eclipsed in the 1960s and in any case did not address a specifically American audience. This Marcuse did to tremendous effect, with the result that his radical critique of technology had a significant influence on the New Left.

Today many of his scandalous paradoxes have been so thoroughly confirmed that he would no doubt feel right at home in contemporary discussions of technology, far more so than in the atmosphere of the 1960s when his ideas were often rejected as irrationalist. Marcuse would agree, for example, with the now commonplace view that despite its grandiose achievements, scientific-technical rationality has endowed us with an extraordinarily destructive way of life. And he would surely applaud us for losing our confidence in expertise and progress. These developments made possible public debate about technical issues just as Marcuse hoped.

But the recent news from the East seems to close down the debate before it begins: if in fact there is no alternative to capitalism as we know it, then, for better or worse, technology is destiny and social critique is as outdated as alchemy. History, in the words of one recent commentator, is over. In fact, history is in better shape than the theories with which we try to understand it. Although old assumptions about progress are losing ground, no equally convincing new ones have replaced them. This situation is not merely a function of events, discouraging though these are, but reflects deeper problems in the very foundation of modernity, the project of building a rational society. Today that project is in crisis in all its various forms—political, economic, technological.

Formerly, the distinction between modernity and tradition was supported by a naive faith in reason. Modernity was said to be rational in the strong sense that its cognitive foundations—science and technology—were superior to those of any earlier society. According to positivism, rationality was universal, independent of social and historical conditions. To question or criticize it was not only to challenge the legitimacy of the modern age but to undermine the only reliable standpoint from which to make judgments about the world.

But in recent years that legitimacy has appeared more and more doubtful, and rationality is increasingly explained as an effect of culture. New social interpretations of science and technology flourish today amidst the shattered technocratic illusions of an earlier generation. Tradition, insofar as it supports cultural variety against the "false universality" of the West, is now granted a dubious reprieve. Differences of race, religion, and gender recover an importance they had lost in the melting pot of rational universality.

To understand Marcuse, we must abstract from this startling breakdown of enlightenment assumptions and transport ourselves back in thought to an earlier time when rationality went practically unchallenged. His position comes into focus set against the background of those assumptions and the sparse and necessarily eccentric attacks on them of marginal thinkers like himself.

RATIONALITY AND DYSTOPIA

At the core of the old confidence in reason was the belief, shared by all but a few cranky social critics, that humanity was in control of technology. I will call this consensus view the instrumental theory of technology, or instrumentalism for short (Borgmann 1984: 9). Instrumentalism holds that technology is neutral: like a transparent medium, it adds nothing substantive to the ends it serves but merely accelerates their realization, or realizes them on a larger scale, or under new conditions. Because technology is neutral, the decision to employ it can be made on purely rational grounds, that is, measurable improvements in efficiency.

This view has political implications. Rationality has always been considered a basis for truly free association; where common goals emerge from debate and argument, people cooperate without coercion. As we saw in the last chapter, modern life has taught us how difficult it is to share goals, but efficiency is a universal value and as such subject to rational agreement. And as concern with efficiency spreads to more and more domains, its constraints supply a framework for social life. Technology, as the sum of efficient means, acquires an emblematic relationship to reason, and the effective command of it is increasingly identified with the project of societal rationalization. In a technological society, the argument goes, consensus can be reached over means despite the undecidable contention over goals characteristic of the modern world. That would at least make for a well-ordered society in which the areas of disagreement were reduced to manageable proportions. Instrumentalists therefore hold out the hope of general reconciliation— social integration—in an advanced society.

The proposal sounds innocuous in this form, but projected to the limit, it describes a technocracy in which political order is based on expertise rather than citizenship. The idea has been around for over a century in one form or another, but only in the 1960s did it become the legitimation of actually existing states. Ideology was supposed to be exhausted; the emerging "Great Society," proclaimed by Lyndon Johnson, was to be justified by its success in delivering the goods. At that point, the critique of technocracy, already adumbrated in Fëdor Dostoevsky's *Notes from Underground*, was transformed from a conceit of a few literary intellectuals into a mass cultural phenomenon.

Science fiction had long articulated the fear of technocracy in stories depicting the horrors of life in a perfectly rationalized society. At stake in "dystopias" (negative utopias) like Aldous Huxley's *Brave New World* or George Orwell's *1984* is the destiny of the human spirit in a world based on scientific enlightenment. The issue is not simply the destructive misuse of scientific discoveries but the fate of individuality in a scientized world. The successful integration of modern mass society provokes a nostalgic backward glance toward lost freedoms. The isolated individualistic hero of these tales stands for the human values inevitably ground underfoot by the march of Reason.

From this dystopian standpoint, technical progress is not just a value-neutral increase in efficiency but a whole new way of life. This is also the view of philosophers such as Heidegger who propose what I will call substantive theories of technology. They reject the notion that technology is neutral and argue that it is actually a distinct cultural framework embodying its own particular values. This critique forms the background to Marcuse's work, perhaps not accidentally, since Heidegger was Marcuse's teacher. Indeed, Heidegger sounds indistinguishable from Marcuse in certain passages such as the following: "The outstanding feature of modern technology lies in the fact that it is not at all any longer merely 'means' and no longer merely stands in 'service' for others, but instead . . . unfolds a specific character of domination" (quoted in Zimmerman 1990: 214).

The grounds for substantive critique vary; some social critics claim that technology as such is biased by its Promethianism or abstraction; others argue that technology is neutral in its own sphere but distorts essentially noninstrumental domains such as the family or the public sphere. Heidegger, Ellul, and Ivan Illich are the most prominent representatives of the first view. They are joined by those feminists who criticize modern technology as an inherently "masculinist" enterprise. Habermas, to whose work we will return in chapter 4, is the best-known defender of the second view.

All these critics agree that technology fundamentally transforms activities hitherto regulated by tradition and human values, so much so that its specific accomplishments in these domains matter little by comparison. The content of the choices made under the rule of efficiency is less important than the fact that efficiency criteria play a role in making those choices. That in itself creates a new kind of society which is not merely a streamlined version of the old.

The flavor of these various theories can best be gathered from Heidegger. Let us look, for example, at his formulation of the distinction between traditional tools and modern technologies. Instrumentalism holds that means operate not on the substance of desire but on the pace, scale, and conditions of its fulfillment. But beyond a certain point, changes in pace, scale, and conditions transform means into contexts independent of the particular ends they serve. Heidegger (1977: 135) calls this the "giganticism" of modern technology.

A city traversed by freeways is not the same place as the old pre-automotive urban center. This obvious fact indicates the limits of the neutrality of technology. Of course, the automobile is indifferent to its driver's destination, but not to the infrastructural preconditions it requires to be operated at all. Supplying those preconditions actually reshapes the world in which destinations are chosen, transforming fields and neighborhoods into roadbeds. This example is characteristic: what in modern societies we call progress in "efficiency" is precisely the employment of means with such massive impacts (Berman 1982: 166–

168).[1] Our world is in the grip of them, "enframed" in Heidegger's terms.

Now it is true that premodern artifacts are occasionally "gigantic" too, for example, late medieval architecture. But they usually leave nature as they found it and their social reach depends less on technical than on symbolic power. Today the sheer pervasiveness of our machines makes it impossible to confine their effects to particular applications. Devices that were supposed transparently to realize preexisting ends have become so intrusive that they assault the natural landscape and impose their own requirements on the human beings they were made to serve. The grand traditions of the past can flourish in the shadow of a Gothic cathedral, but not under a freeway overpass.

In sum, modern means already change the world "immanently," independent of the purpose for which they are employed. Our tools have become a life environment; increasingly, we are incorporated into the apparatus we have created and subordinated to its rhythms and demands. Heidegger calls this the "peril" of the age.

RADICAL CRITIQUE OF TECHNOLOGICAL SOCIETY

Dystopian literature and the substantive critique of technology opened the cultural space within which today we speculate about the meaning and nature of modernity. From them we learn that we are *inside* the machine, that technology is not merely a tool extending our capabilities. This realization is a necessary condition for understanding contemporary culture.

Traditional Marxism, if not Marx himself, appears hopelessly beside the point in this context. However, radical social criticism does not disappear as technology advances; on the contrary, it becomes ever more uncompromising and eventually inspires resistance to the dystopian universe it denounces. The Frankfurt School, and especially Marcuse, enjoyed real popularity in the one-dimensional society that, it charged, had made critique all but impossible. Both the American and German New Left were influenced by its dystopian perspectives. Somewhat later, after the events of May 1968, French social theory too turned dystopian in the work of Gilles Deleuze and Michel Foucault

---

1. Note that giganticism is not merely a question of physical size but more importantly of scope and effect. Thus biotechnology is gigantic in Heidegger's sense even though it works at the microscopic level.

and in that form had a considerable political impact on the "new social movements" of the 1970s and 1980s.

Although strongly influenced by substantive critique, Marcuse rejected Heidegger's fatalistic resignation to technology. Rather, he argued that technological domination is a political issue. This approach, which Marcuse shared with much of the New Left, marked a sharp break with traditional Marxism. Where, formerly, Marxists had denounced capitalism as inefficient, the new radicals rejected the authoritarian consequences of the successful pursuit of efficiency. Modern societies, they claimed, are involved in a devil's bargain: their increasing order and prosperity is invariably accompanied by new forms of control from above. That control does not depend on traditional social distinctions in status, wealth, age, or gender, but employs social technologies of management, administration, training, therapy, medicine, and advertising. The new authority system is rooted in the power the operators of these technologies gain over their human objects.

This nexus between efficiency and authority suggested to Marcuse a new interpretation of Marxism as a dystopian critique of rationality.[2] This in turn led him back to the work of Max Weber, the great theorist of rationalization, whose conception of modernity was influenced by Marx but who probably did more than anyone to dash socialist hopes.

Weber defined modernity in terms of the spread of markets, formal law, democracy, bureaucracy, and technology. He called these "rationalized" institutions in contrast to traditional ones because they share certain qualities which we normally associated with reason: they appear more abstract, more exact, more value- and context-free, better grounded in scientific knowledge and more efficient.

Weber's concept of rationalization is ambiguous. On the one hand, he frequently wrote as though modern societies were *in fact* more rational than their predecessors. This is the Enlightenment view according to which modern methods are better than traditional ones and modern individuals free from the ancient prejudices of their ancestors. On the other hand, Weber (1949: 39) seemed to say that "real" rationality attaches more to the sociologists' "ideal type" of modern society than to its messy realities. And he worried that bureaucratic rationality be-

---

2. Foucault's critique of dystopian rationality concluded that industrial alienation is a variation on a more general cultural theme, the emergence of a "disciplinary" society. In that society science and technology are not simply instrumental, but play their part in the institutionalization of new forms of social hierachy (Foucault 1977: 221). For a comparison of Foucault and Marcuse, see Feenberg (1991: chap. 4).

comes increasingly ritualized with time. Weber (1958: 182) concluded that we are headed not toward enlightenment but toward "mechanized petrification" interrupted periodically by charismatic convulsions.

Weber founded an influential sociological tradition in which the notion of rationality has continued to play a central role, but without his critical edge. In the work of Talcott Parsons (1964: 61–63), for example, history culminates in the substitution of "universalistic" for older "particularistic" values as science and democracy replace traditional forms of belief. In the postcolonial era, modernization theory extended the range of such arguments, cheerfully predicting the passage to Western style modernity on a world scale. In Part IV of this book, I will discuss the Japanese critique of these ethnocentric assumptions which, along with the Soviet challenge, represented the only significant alternative to the orthodox concept of modernization in this century.[3] With the defeat of these alternatives, the orthodox view, suitably modified to take into account neoliberal economics, has become the world-political common sense of the West and the passionate hope of the East.

The stress on "rationality" as the distinguishing trait of modernity suggests a pejorative evaluation of the "irrationality" of tradition. Of course, inequality and injustice have hardly disappeared, but liberals and most Marxists split with dystopian radicals over the cause: is it the incomplete rationalization of modern societies, or might it be a consequence of such rationalization as has occurred? Marcuse defended the latter view and in the process called attention to an important aspect of Marx's thought that had been largely forgotten, his critique of capitalist rationality.

Traditional societies do not hide the substantive consequences of the exercise of authority, the inequalities it inevitably creates, the favoritism that is its prerogative. But modern formal rationality serves similar social purposes under an appearance of neutrality. No longer does the monarch decide fates by tipping his fan toward this or that subject. Instead, purely objective criteria, such as examinations, hearings, or measurements, discriminate between the individuals. Markets know no persons, only commodities and money. Scientific and technological discovery depends on objective proof, not subjective preferences. Yet these institutions form the basis of a new type of social hierarchy in which new inequalities in the distribution of social power replace the traditional order.

3. For the Marxist critique of modernization theory, see Amin (1989).

It was Marx who first discovered how to construct an effective critique of this new hierarchy. He argued that markets are not merely neutral mediators between those who have and those who need; their generalization subjects society to a new type of power, the power of capital. What is true of markets is equally true of the labor process, although it has been more difficult for the Marxist tradition to accept the implications of Marx's arguments in this domain.

External supervision of work first emerges when ownership and management are separated from the work itself in early manufacturing. Capitalism begins to reshape production to reinforce its control of workers. Eventually discipline is tightened through deskilling labor, that is, replacing skilled workers performing traditional crafts with unskilled workers each performing a tiny fraction of the whole job. In the industrial era, control functions are transferred to machines, the design of which is determined by the preexisting division of labor and authority. Mechanization finally perfects the hitherto clumsy, personalized techniques of industrial discipline by objectifying the split between conception and execution. Marcuse concluded that the capitalist *technical* system is not universal but reflects particular class interests. "The machine," he wrote, "is *not neutral*; technical reason is the social reason ruling a given society and can be changed in its very structure" (Marcuse 1968: 225).

The traces of these social origins can be seen in Weber's theory of rationalization. Weber never questioned the extension of efficiency criteria from technology to administration. It did not occur to him that human relations might be rationalized other than through technical control. In this regard, he uncritically adopted the capitalist point of view. Marcuse (1968: 212) concluded: "The highly *material*, historical fact of the private-capitalist enterprise thus becomes . . . a *formal* structural element . . . of *rational* economic activity itself." Weber smuggled a whole system of domination into his definition of rationality. Today, what Marcuse called a "one-dimensional" society extends the same sort of mystification to ever more rationalized spheres, including leisure, education, sexual life, and so on.

This thesis carries us well beyond Marx, for whom capitalism is still subject to criticism on the grounds of technical inefficiency. He argued that, since private property is an obstacle to the personal fulfillment of the producers as well as to the growth of productive forces, the normative goal of socialism is in conformity with the technical goal of increasing economic productivity. The critique of capitalism can therefore emphasize technical considerations that command wide consensus in the expectation that further advance will also achieve its normative goals.

Marcuse concluded that this Marxian position had been invalidated by the progress of contemporary capitalism. Technical rationality no longer demonstrates the inadequacy of capitalism but instead legitimates the society. The "universe of discourse," public and eventually even private speech and thought, increasingly limits itself to the posing and resolving of technical problems. "When technics becomes the universal form of material production, it circumscribes an entire culture; it projects a historical totality—a 'world'" (Marcuse 1964: 154). The universalization of technique undercuts the development of oppositional consciousness. The normative dimension of Marxism is therefore forced to the surface. It can no longer hide behind the demand for a liberation of the productive forces to full development.

Here we have the intuitions that lie at the origins of Habermas's critique of Marx's "latent positivism" and his theory of the "colonization of the lifeworld." Modern societies are threatened by the measureless expansion of technically rational means, a process which is not itself rational because it obliterates the all-important distinction between the normative and the technical dimensions of human experience. But, as we will see in the fourth chapter, unlike Marcuse, Habermas is no critic of science and technology per se, but rejects only their institutionalization as the foundation of a *total* social order. He argues that this totalization of technique is irrational even though science is true and technology neutral (Habermas 1970).[4]

Marcuse himself went considerably further than this. He argued that science and technology—indeed, all the formally rational, supposedly neutral structures of modern society—are politically biased not just by the specific demands capitalism places on them in the application, but in themselves, essentially. This, Marcuse's most radical critique of technology, anticipates current feminism and environmentalism and justifies a renewed interest in his thought today.

4. Habermas's position on the neutrality of technology has by now worn pretty thin. But when he first proposed it, so strong was the prejudice in favor of instrumentalism that a number of critical theorists followed him in beating a hasty retreat from Marcuse's daring call for a reform of scientific-technical rationality. Recent work in social constructivism, described in chapter 7, finally brings this episode to a close by removing any reason to concede the autonomy of scientific-technical rationality.

THE ONTOLOGICAL CRITIQUE
OF TECHNOLOGY

I will call this second strand in Marcuse's critique of technology "ontological" in the sense that it goes to the essence of its object. That essence is civilizational insofar as current technology grows out of the specific conditions of class society in which it has developed over thousands of years.

In this critique scientific-technical rationality is therefore not just an epistemological category but a civilizational one as well. The complex formed by modern society and its technology is no more neutral than Gothic architecture or Egyptian pyramids but embodies the values of a particular civilization, Western civilization, the civilization of "reason." The critic's task is to articulate and judge these values and in the course of doing so to uncover the bias of reason itself. It is in this context that Marcuse proposed his most controversial thesis, the claim that there is an intrinsic a priori connection between scientific-technical rationality and domination. According to this thesis, "science, *by virtue of its own method* and concepts, has projected and promoted a universe in which the domination of nature has remained linked to the domination of man" (Marcuse 1964: 166).

Here Marcuse challenged the traditional view of science as disinterested knowledge. He argued, on the contrary, that the subject of knowledge must be conceived first and foremost as an active being, and therefore as a being engaged with reality for essentially interested reasons. From this point of view the objectivity and detachment associated with scientific-technical knowledge appears as an ideology hiding undisclosed existential involvements. Thus it is no accident that science issues in technology, and this is not simply because, as Francis Bacon claimed, "knowledge is power." Rather, if science yields power over nature, this is due to an a priori orientation toward power characteristic of its most basic methods and concepts. Ultimately it is not knowledge which is power but certain types of power which are forms of knowledge. Formal classification under universals and laws, cause-effect reasoning, and especially quantification are the epistemological expressions of the interest in instrumental control underlying the pursuit of scientific knowledge.

This is one aspect of Marcuse's position, argued at great length with the aid of citations from Edmund Husserl, Heidegger, Adorno, and Horkheimer. However, for Marcuse, merely pointing out the internal link between science and instrumental control is insufficiently criti-cal. Habermas shows, for example, that the theory of science as instru-mental reason can be worked out in complete abstraction from all po-litical content. Science can be founded on an instrumental interest of the human species without actually toppling the "idol" of objectivity because, as Immanuel Kant demonstrated long ago, such generic at-tributes can be treated "as if" they were univerally true for all practi-cal purposes. Indeed, if science represents a *human* interest in control, it is detached and neutral with respect to all particular interests, that is to say, all really historically existing interests such as we know them. What more can one ask in the way of disinterestedness?

Marcuse's ambition went beyond the demonstration that science is linked to instrumental control of nature to claim further that it is pre-destined to serve the domination of some human beings by other hu-man beings. That controversial point derives from Horkheimer and Adorno's famous *Dialectic of Enlightenment*. They argued that the structure of reason is essentially marked by the heritage of class soci-ety to which it belongs.

Reason emerges as a separate faculty in the struggle for survival under conditions of scarcity. The separation of human beings from na-ture and the split between reason, imagination, and feeling go hand in hand as tribal life is left behind in the pursuit of ever greater power over their environment. The price of power is suppression, first of the individuals' own inner impulses, and second of each other. In this context, faculties that do not serve immediate survival needs are con-signed to a derealized realm of fantasy and compared unfavorably with the seriousness and effectiveness of rationality. The stage is set for the emergence of Enlightenment as domination and, correlated with it, of a utopian domain of ideals, most especially the ideal of an impossible return to unity with nature.

Marcuse developed this critique of Enlightenment under the influ-ence of Heidegger and Husserl's phenomenological project of founding theoretical reason in practice. According to phenomenology, the theo-retically purified concepts of science have their source in the *Lebenswelt*, the lived world of everyday practice and perception. Marcuse added that not only are scientific concepts founded in everyday practice, they carry up into their theoretical heaven the lowly conditions of their birth, including the narrowing of perception occasioned by class conflict in a ruthless struggle for existence. Technology too is fundamentally marked by these origins and projects the same power drive as science. With these reflections Marcuse established a link between the Frankfurt School's general social critique of rationality and concrete analysis of the technologically structured way of life of advanced societies.

Alongside this critique, Marcuse developed a theory of art as a kind of negative counterworld in which what has been lost in the discipline of civilization is conserved in imagination. This is what Marcuse called the "affirmative" function of art. Adorno and Horkheimer identified it with the myth of Odysseus and the Sirens. Tied to the mast, Odysseus hears the dangerous music of a lost utopia while his sailors labor at the oars with their ears stopped. The division of society into classes is also a division into those whose elevated social situation effectively renders the dream of regression harmless and those who must be denied dreams altogether because their humble station offers insufficient compensation for their sacrifice as members of a civilized society.

This historical account of rationality suggests a possible resolution of the contradictions of civilized life. If civilization could advance beyond the struggle for survival, then it might also release nature from its most aggressive assaults and reunite the faculties, rejoining the various spheres of existence in a harmonious whole and recovering what was lost in the passage out of tribal origins. Marcuse argued that today this is *technically* feasible, but advanced societies perpetuate the struggle for existence in the second nature they have created and intensify the alienation of human beings from nature and from themselves. And they do this in the shadow of an ever more imminent possibility of total liberation, reflected in new forms of discontent and resistance they must repress.

Marcuse's argument had to lead to some such eschatology of reason. If class society has given rise to the split between the faculties, then the end of class society will see their reconciliation. The theory leads to the conclusion that the derealized dimensions of art and the imagination must now be rejoined with real life through a completely new kind of scientific-technical theory and practice. The two worlds must become one through a final reconciliation of essence and existence, real and ideal: "Technique would then tend to become art and art would tend to form reality: the opposition between imagination and reason, higher and lower faculties, poetic and scientific thought, would be invalidated. Emergence of a new Reality Principle: under which a new sensibility and a desublimated scientific intelligence would combine in the creation of an *aesthetic ethos*" (Marcuse 1969: 24).

What would be the content of this new form of technical practice?

Obviously, it would have to continue to provide food, shelter, and other necessities. But the *form* in which it did so would be determined by aesthetic needs that express tendencies in nature which come to consciousness in and through human beings. Marcuse (1972: 66) suggested the "outrageous" concept of a "liberation of nature" to describe these tendencies, not in the sense of a natural teleology, but rather to refer to "forces in nature which have been distorted and suppressed—forces which could support and enhance the liberation of man."

In a free society the realization of these tendencies would operate not alongside or over and above ordinary technical practice, as in the marginalized world of artistic production today, but in the very practice of transforming nature to make it serve human needs. The result would be a reconciliation of human beings and nature, not a return to nature, but a harmonious coexistence in the framework of a lightened and adapted technology.

Marcuse's theory of socialism draws together the Marxist aim of a disalienation of industrial society, the modern avant-garde's struggle for a radical desublimation of art, and the contemporary environmental and feminist critiques of productivist industrialism. At the core of the theory is a reevaluation of the aesthetic as the source of new needs and a new practice of freedom. "Aesthetics of liberation, beauty as a 'form' of freedom: it looks as if Marx has shied away from this anthropomorphist, idealistic conception. Or is this apparently idealistic notion rather the *enlargement of the materialistic base?* For 'man is directly a *natural being*; he is corporeal, living, real, sensuous, objective being' who has 'real, sensuous objects' as the objects of his life. . . . This is . . . the extension of Historical Materialism to a dimension which is to play a vital role in the liberation of man" (Marcuse 1972: 67–68).

This passage harks back to Marcuse's early attempt to synthesize Heidegger and Hegel in an ontological conception of revolution. That early Marcusean synthesis depended on the phenomenological idea that the ultimate nature of reality must be understood through the structures of our human involvement with the world and not in terms of the abstract nature of the sciences. The living, "sensuous" nature of concrete human experience to which Marcuse refers here is thus foundational, irreducible to a naturalistic substratum. The forms in which that subject apprehends and deals with the world can no longer be seen as merely subjective additions to raw sense data, nor are they transcendental constructions. Rather, these forms are revelations of being itself. Categories such as beauty, which emerge from our practical involvements, can then be redeemed as in some sense "objective" or at least not arbitrary. They supply revolutionary norms, the dialectical counterpoint to the given, in the Hegelian moment of the synthesis.

In later discussions of the prewar Japanese response to modernity, I will return to the problems posed by this approach to transcending scientific naturalism and technological instrumentalism. Japanese philosophers shared similar German sources with Marcuse and came to parallel conclusions. However, for reasons I will explain in chapter 7, they emphasized the preeminent role of national-cultural values to which they attributed an ontological status not unlike that which Marcuse attributed to aesthetics.

INTERACTIVE STRATEGIES OF CHANGE

Despite his success in reviving critical Marxism and undermining rationalistic justifications of social hierarchy, Marcuse lacked an adequate account of how radical change might be brought about. He advocated uncompromising opposition to racist violence and imperialist war, but nothing comparable makes sense in the technical sphere. Although sometimes accused of technophobia, he never called for the dismantling of modern industrial society. Rather, he argued that "if the completion of the technological project involves a break with the prevailing technological rationality, the break in turn depends on the continued existence of the technical base itself. For it is this base which has rendered possible the satisfaction of needs and the reduction of toil—it remains the very base of all forms of human freedom. The qualititative change rather lies in the reconstruction of this base—that is, in its development with a view of different ends. . . . The new ends, as technical ends, would then operate in the project and in the construction of the machinery, and not only in its utilization" (Marcuse 1964: 231–232). But how can this be achieved?

Marcuse's critique of capitalist technological rationality contained a promissory note on which he failed to deliver. We ought to be able to get an alternative theory of rationality out of it which would show us *how* human values can be incorporated into the very structure of technicity. Unfortunately, his gestures in this direction were so abstract and sketchy they cannot easily be linked to any concrete practice. And as practical attempts to grapple with technology in fact proliferate, this flaw seems more and more significant. In conclusion, I want to describe recent theoretical shifts that may help to carry the critical movement Marcuse did so much to initiate beyond the limitations of his own position.

The dystopian model inspired what Marcuse called a "Great Refusal" of advanced industrial society, but today the idea of such uncompromising opposition rings false.[5] Notwithstanding the growing distrust of technocracy, dependence on technology continues to increase. There is no disguising the alienation, but no getting away from the system, no psychic or political retreat in which to assemble and mobilize the disalienating energies of a subject of history. What is more, the breakdown of faith in rationality, already apparent in Marcuse, has proceeded much further in French theory with Jacques Derrida, Foucault, and Lyotard, and in recent social constructivist sociology of science and technology. Thus we are drawn to a different type of strategy that plays on the internal tensions in modern societies. The aim is not to destroy the system by which we are enframed but to alter its direction of development through a new kind of technical politics.

Such strategies have appeared both globally and locally. As I will argue in Part IV of this book, certain non-Western encounters with modernity—for example, the Japanese—involve attempts to incorporate Western technology into an ethnic culture through a mutual transformation. Something similar has appeared in the West itself, most obviously around environmental problems, but also in domains such as computers and medicine where the technocratic conception of modern life is increasingly contested by what I call an *interactive* politics of technology.

Foucault's critique of the social limits of rationality is a key theoretical innovation that sheds light on current technical struggles. Foucault suggested that the imposition of a rational order gives rise to particular, local standpoints from which the dominated perceive aspects of reality obscured from the universalizing standpoint of the hegemonic sciences. These "subjugated knowledges" offer a basis for progressive change (Foucault 1980: 81ff.). Thus like Marcuse, Foucault distinguished at least implicitly between a particular form of hierarchical rationalization, characteristic of modernity up to now, and a possible subversive rationalization adapted to a more humane and democratic society (Feenberg 1992). But where Marcuse's critique aimed at total

5. Marcuse also occasionally mentioned reformist strategies such as the "long march through the institutions" and working within the "interstices" of the system but never developed them in any detail or applied them to technology.

transformation, Foucault called for new forms of local action without any overall plan.

Although apolitical so far in its brief history, constructivism in sociology of science and technology offers support for Foucault's position by linking scientific-technical achievement to social backgrounds. Roughly sketched, the constructivist argument holds that the route from a bright idea to a successful application is long and winding, strewn with inherently viable alternatives abandoned for reasons having more to do with social values and interests than with the intrinsic technical superiority of the final choice.

This position marks a sharp break with instrumentalism, which assumes that technical development provides uniquely efficient solutions to clearly defined problems rooted in basic human needs. On this view, social factors intervene in the technical sphere only marginally, deciding, for example, the pace of development or the priority assigned different types of problems. Constructivism argues, on the contrary, that development involves negotiation and struggle between social groups with different conceptions of both problems and solutions. The choice of each gear or lever, the configuration of each circuit or program, is determined not just by an inherent technical logic but by a specific social configuration. At issue is not just the pace of technical progress or who benefits from it but the very content and meaning of progress itself.

Constructivism has developed in close association with "network" theories of technical development that expose the reciprocal relations between social actors and technical systems (Pinch and Bijker 1984; Latour 1992). These theories count among significant actors not merely inventors and engineers, but also managers, workers, government agencies, consumers, users, everyone involved with technology.[6] Networks are bound together by the very structure of the artifacts they create, which provide in turn a kind of platform for their further activities.

Technology is thus neither the neutral tool of instrumental theory nor the autonomous power of substantive theory; it is just as social as other institutions. It plays a central role in modern hierarchies which are supported by networks of technical artifacts and associated practices rather than by myths and rituals, or by ideologies and the exercise of coercive power, as in premodern societies. Constructivism is thus the ultimate refutation of what Marcuse called "one-dimensionality,"

6. Latour (1992) goes still further and treats material objects as actors as well.

the illusion that there is a unique form of technical rationality which sanctions domination under the rule of efficiency.

But most constructivist research is so narrowly focused on particular cases of technological development that it lacks any sense of the larger social context in which these cases may play a politically significant role (Winner 1992). And, as Haraway remarks, the history of science and technology studies is distorted by the now widely accepted view that the break with positivism was due to a purely scholarly evolution beginning with Kuhn, while ignoring the contributions of the various antitechnocratic struggles of the 1960s and, I would add, of radical thinkers such as Marcuse (Darnovsky 1991: 75–76). Ironically, the currently dominant social theory of science and technology seems to have no grasp of the social conditions of its own credibility.

Yet just because the rise of constructivism is so closely, if unconsciously, linked to increased resistance to technocracy, it sharpens oppositional thinking. Both Foucault and constructivism focus on what makes the "System" a system, on the manifold ways in which it integrates human beings into the technological conditions of their social reproduction. This approach suggests strategic possibilities Marcuse overlooked.

In the 1960s, the image of resistance was shaped by peak struggles, large-scale simultaneous political mobilizations such as May 1968 in France, the waves of urban rioting in the United States, or the national student strike against the invasion of Cambodia. In this context, the struggle against technocratic oppression was conceived in terms drawn from the history of political revolutions. For many on the Left, technology was the enemy in the way the state had been in an earlier era; to revolt was to reclaim humanity against the machine.

Today's political movements are dispersed across traditional boundaries between the political, the social, and the personal. Arguably, more people than ever before are actually influenced by the Left around issues of race, gender, and the environment. But simultaneous mobilizations have become few and far between in the advanced capitalist world. At the same time, we have learned to recognize politics in small interventions that modify the life environment without directly confronting the state. This approach is sometimes called "micropolitics," a situational politics based on local knowledge and action. It implements no overall strategy and offers no global challenge to the society; instead, it involves a multitude of potentially converging activities with long-term subversive impacts.

The larger question of the nature of micropolitics and its ability to provide an effective replacement for earlier forms of mobilization lies beyond my concern in this chapter. I will return to that question in chapter 6, where it is formulated in terms of Lyotard's concept of "paralogy." What interests me here is the emergence of micropolitical practices in the technical sphere where there used to be very little oppositional activity of any kind. Technical micropolitics involves forms of concrete political protest that aim to transform particular technologies or technical systems through pressure from users, clients, or victims. Such agitation lacks much of the armature of a political movement in the traditional sense; it may have no centralized coordination and only a vague consensus on a desirable direction, but it is able to go beyond earlier forms of technical politics that were handicapped by the hegemony of positivist faith in progress.

All this is rather different from Marcuse's view. He concluded that technologically advanced societies were so successfully integrated that opposition could only come from their margins, for example, from minorities, students, or the Third World. To this marginal revolt corresponded his quasi-Freudian notion of a psychic basis of resistance below the threshold of social struggle. These ideas are less persuasive as we enter a historical period in which the boundaries between the individual and the system are increasingly blurred. In this situation opposition must be "immanent," implied somehow in the very contradictions of the system. The way out must be a way through.

Several later chapters of this book discuss cases that reveal just how vulnerable technical systems are to such transformation from within. However, the movements I describe are so different from traditional political ones that they are easily overlooked. They are based not on ideologies or clienteles but on technical networks. Chapter 4 explains how technocratic hierarchies are founded on such networks by restricting and channeling communication. The stakes in these struggles are thus also unexpected, not wealth or administrative power, but control of the technical procedures and designs structuring communicative practices.

Let me briefly offer three types of examples here to make my argument more concrete. First, the environmental movement has had a major impact on the understanding of technology, transforming privately held, supposedly neutral "technical" information into grist for public controversy. "Right to know" legislation, leaks from concerned technical personnel, and the skillful use of public forums such as Environmental Protection Agency hearings have all opened access, and corporations and government agencies are gradually losing the veil of secrecy under which they escaped responsibility for their actions in the past. As a result, questions of technological design in such domains as nuclear power and toxic waste disposal are subject to public discussion. As individuals redefine themselves as potential victims of pollution, they close the political circle by claiming their right to control industrial processes in which they are unwittingly involved.

Second, the evolution of the computer offers a striking instance of new types of public participation in technical development. In the past decade, two large-scale computer networks have recruited millions of users. They are the Internet, an international research network, and Teletel, the French domestic videotex network, discussed in chapter 7. Both networks were intended by their creators to facilitate the flow of information such as research data and airline schedules. Both networks were hacked by their users and transformed into media of personal communication. These users have changed not only the meaning of the computer but also the type of society it is gradually creating. The strategy was not a "Great Refusal" but a subtle hybridization that gave an unexpected twist to the technical system.

Third, the medical field offers abundant examples of patients modifying medical practice and technique from within the medical system itself. As noted in the introduction, the revolution in childbirth education that occurred in the early 1970s significantly changed the role of women in childbirth, although its achievements have been eroded by a new technological offensive in recent years. From passive patients, isolated, anesthetized, and controlled, women became for a time active participants in childbirth. More recently, as I explain in chapter 5, AIDS patients have demanded improved access to experimental treatments and in the process have challenged the organization and rationale of clinical research. In both these instances, patients altered their roles in the medical system, demanding information and control in ways that temporarily subverted the established technocratic hierarchy of medicine.

From the standpoint of substantive critique, these movements seem merely to result in co-optation, since they do not extract human agency from the machine and restore its original autonomy. Certain values and spheres of life need to be saved from pointless technologization, but general hostility to technology is not only futile but disarms any less totalizing critique. The new interactive politics of technology, on the contrary, reveals the human implications of different technological designs and strategies of development. It defines us as moral and political subjects in the midst of the devices and systems that form our daily environment and shape our future. From that standpoint, the demand for communication these movements represent is so fundamental that it can serve as a touchstone for a concept of politics adequate to the technological age.

We have come a long way since Marcuse. His concept of marginality implied by contrast a strong notion of inclusion that seems less and less applicable to our experience. The emergence of technical micropolitics testifies to the fact that marginality is potentially an aspect of everyone's condition in a technological society. Although we are integral parts of a social machinery and cannot separate ourselves from it to challenge it through the classic gestures of revolutionary politics, we are not helpless: we are discovering how to perform as *inter-actors* in society's technical systems. The technical environment of our daily lives no longer appears as the inhuman oppressor we imagined it to be in the 1960s, but as a "soft machine," a loosely organized and highly vulnerable structure *that includes us.*

In sum, Marcuse was right to argue that technical networks of the sort constructed everywhere by advanced societies expose their members to new forms of control; what he overlooked was that these networks are themselves exposed to transformation by the human groups they enroll. Immanent resistances arising in the technical sphere are significant bearers of new values, imposing a new form on technical institutions. Perhaps these transformations can accumulate and build on each other, altering the direction of development and resolving the dystopian crisis.

CHAPTER THREE

Dystopia and Apocalypse

The Emergence of Critical Consciousness

CRITIQUE AS MASS CULTURE

The twentieth century has been a time of growing doubts about the viability of the modern project. So long as the pessimistic mood was confined to a few literary humanists, it had little impact. But since World War II, prophecies of doom have become clichés on everyone's lips. Social critical themes hitherto reserved for an intellectual elite are now mass political culture.

This chapter concerns one of these themes: the secularized myth of the end of the world, eschatology that no longer needs religion now that it has become a distinct technical possibility. The myth takes two forms, corresponding to the material and spiritual destruction of humanity by its own technology. Nuclear and environmental disaster promise the death of the human species, while future technologies of mind control are extrapolated from contemporary propaganda, advertising, and computers. In this chapter, I describe three significant moments in the process by which these apocalyptic and dystopian themes entered popular consciousness in the 1950s and 1960s.

I begin by tracing the rise of new doomsday myths inspired by the invention of the atom bomb. Scientists frightened by their own achievements were among the first to awaken to the posthistoric implications of technological advance. They tried to communicate their insight to the general public by writing both serious essays on public policy and science fiction. Although their hopes for nuclear disarmament were quickly dashed, they did manage to provoke increasingly worried reflection on the likelihood of nuclear war.

That worry left its mark on the popular imagination through a genre of science fiction that depicts natural disasters of planetary scope: the cooling of the sun, the awakening of long-frozen monsters from another era, collision with another planet (Sontag 1969). Like the threat of nuclear war, such catastrophic events suspend the day-to-day conflicts of human history; energies must suddenly be mobilized beyond mere political rivalries in the interests of species survival. Written up as science fiction, the making of the bomb would be just another example of the disaster genre, with the conclusion left up to the reader's imagination.

While one type of postwar science fiction spread apocalyptic fears, another played on emerging dystopian anxieties. Literary projections of totally administered societies offered an ever more believable description of America in the 1950s. Television and generalized bureaucratization, while perhaps not quite as efficient as the techniques imagined by Huxley and Orwell, applied intense conformist pressures. Dystopian fiction reflects a new society in which the principal social cleavage divides the masters of the modern technical system from those who work and live within it.

These early responses to the new society were soon overshadowed by anti-Communist hysteria. The dominant culture repressed open hostility to the technocratic trend in America and projected dystopian imagery onto the Soviet rival. Dystopianism became a mass phenomenon for the first time in this twisted form, replacing New Deal liberalism as a popular interpretation of history.

In the 1960s an attempt was made to cast the Vietnam War in the cold war mold, with disastrous results. Films provide a good index of the growing crisis, although surprisingly, few were made about Vietnam at the time. Instead, the real war films of the period were lighthearted spy adventures that enjoyed enormous popularity at the height of the conflict. The second part of this chapter analyzes the emergence of popular dystopianism in these films.

Their strangest feature is their vision of the Enemy: in most of them an underdeveloped society exemplifies technocratic dictatorship. The Enemy never employs the guerrilla tactics of the Viet Cong; instead, it possesses an antlike army supplied with technologically advanced weapons, helicopters, and nuclear devices. The hero—a Westerner—is captured and, working from within, destroys the Enemy's technology with his bare hands. Here underdevelopment represents the power of machines over men, while the West is the haven of humanism. The viewers are encouraged to identify with James Bond in a guerrilla war against Third World technocracy.

The absurdity of this projection and the war in Vietnam it justified soon became too obvious to deny. Other strands in the popular culture of the period focused on the technocratic threat in the advanced societies themselves. Dystopianism shifted targets and found a new focus at home. The rejection of conformity and expertise grew hand in hand in this period as more and more Americans began to see themselves as rebels against a rationalized order. Advertising capitalized on these confused feelings of revolt to market products identified with the new individualism. Meanwhile real revolt stirred in the rapidly expanding youth culture. The third part of this chapter traces these developments.

The concept of dystopia implies the impossibility of escape; in this period, social critique actually foresaw its own disappearance in the face of the mounting success of modern technology. Yet paradoxically, the notion of the disappearance of critique was a powerful stimulus to critique, and more than that, to action. Radical protest, banished along with communism as the cold war got going, returned in a new guise as the New Left was born from the mood of antidystopian resistance.

AN END TO HISTORY

I suppose there's no way of putting the mushroom cloud back into that nice shiny uranium sphere.
—*Isaac Asimov 1972b: 236*

SCIENCE FICTION IN THE NUCLEAR AGE

Science fiction, at least a significant fraction of it, is the literature of the "other" culture, the culture of science and technology. Its double audience has always included not only scientists and technicians but also the general public in search of diversion. It communicates the experience and speculations of the former to the latter, representing the scientists' worldview to those who participate only passively in an increasingly mechanized society (Bainbridge 1986: chap. 3). This was particularly true after World War II. With the invention of the atom bomb, the dilemmas confronting scientists and technicians became universal concerns.

The late forties and early fifties were times of unusual literary activity by scientists and engineers. John Campbell, editor of *Astounding*, began to encourage scientists to write science fiction prior to World War II. In the wake of World War II this participation increased dramatically, both in quantity and quality (Stover 1973). The war and its aftermath apparently struck some resonant chord that drew serious scientists and engineers like Fred Hoyle, Isaac Asimov, Arthur C. Clarke, and Leo Szilard into the world of the imagination. Indeed, many of the themes still treated in science fiction by nonscientists acquired their current forms in the postwar scientific community.

In the immediate postwar period American scientists were caught in a contradictory situation about which they had ambivalent feelings. American society was experiencing a quantum leap in the concentration of capital and the size of government. The trend toward "big science" organized on the corporate-bureaucratic model was greatly accelerated by the war; its ultimate implications had become visible to all at Los Alamos (Greenberg 1967: chap. 6).

The individualism of little science, in some ways comparable with artisanal status, gave way to mild forms of the corporate collectivism, conformity, and alienation already typical of the world of big business and government. The old ideal of the wise and gentle mathematical poet, incarnated for many by Albert Einstein, was replaced by the reality of the academic entrepreneur, the middleman between a more bureaucratically organized scientific community and the government that funded it.

Thus the creation of the atom bomb traumatized the scientific community by shattering its traditional self-image once and for all. Suddenly the detached and obsessive wise man of little science became the sorcerer's apprentice in thermonuclear power politics. As Robert Oppenheimer (1955: 88) put it, "In some sort of crude sense which no vulgarity, no humour, no overstatement can quite extinguish, the physicists have known sin; and this is a knowledge which they cannot lose."

Of course, some scientists gained an immensely increased power and sense of power from this change, while most others found their material situation dramatically improved. On the whole the new era was well received, and scientists felt their usefulness was recognized at last. But even so, increased influence implied increased dependency and top-down control, and traditional value systems and role models were subverted by the new organization of scientific labor. A widespread sense of "wrongness" in the scientific community was expressed in hostility to government control, the new security systems, worry over the bomb, the fate of Oppenheimer, and related issues. These concerns appeared metaphorically in the science fiction of the period, which can thus be viewed as a reflection of the problems confronting this social group (Kevles 1979: chap. 23).

The physicist Arthur Roberts captured the contradictory spirit of the times in satirical songs which were widely circulated among scientists in the late forties. The lyrics of one of them, quoted here, may take the place of volumes of sociological analysis.

> How nice to be a physicist in 1947,
> To hold finance in less esteem than Molotov or Bevin,
> To shun the importuning men with treasure who would lend it,
> To think of money only when you wonder how to spend it.
> Research is long and time is short!
> Fill the shelves with new equipment,
> Order it by carload shipment,
> Never give a second thought:
> You can have whatever can be bought.
> How nice to be a physicist in this our year of grace,
> To see the scornful world at last admit your rightful place,
> To see the senators defer to every wise pronouncement,
> To fascinate the women's clubs and star at each commencement.
> Research is long and time is short!
> Drink your fill of adulation,
> Glory in the new sensation.
> Never give a second thought:
> Sinatra holds a place that many sought.
> But have you sought a physicist and place for him to dwell,
> And searched the town in vain to find a vacant dungeon cell,
> Or tried to teach a thousand students who can't do a sum,
> The girls who'd like to be Greer Garson finding radium?
> Research is long and time is short!
> Board the thesis, drive the student,
> Physics was his choice imprudent.
> Never give a second thought:
> Brains are still a thing that can't be bought.
> Oh did you write a book on fission that you tried to sell,
> Or wonder while you lectured what you could or could not tell,
> Or try to get declassified some nuclear equations,
> Or wonder if the work you do was done at secret stations?
> Research is long and time is short!
> If you find a fact essential,
> Classify it confidential.
> Never give a second thought:
> The FBI's approval must be sought.

How nice to be a physicist in 1947 . . .
How nice?
How long do you think it would take to learn something about,
     uh, butterflies?

Like Roberts's song, much science fiction of this period expresses ambivalence, moral doubt, and anxiety in the face of the nuclear age. Of course, the new "scientific statesmanship" also addressed the issues of the day in articles and lectures on public policy. But the political leaders of the scientific community were willing to make major concessions to get what they wanted—increased funding, disarmament negotiations, and so on. Science fiction was freer to express the full depth of scientists' anxiety and even opposition. Judith Merrill (1971: 74) exaggerates only slightly when she says that in the McCarthy era, "science fiction became, for a time, virtually the only vehicle of political dissent."

Viewed in this light, science fiction resembles the positivist philosophies of Saint-Simon and Comte, which, at a much earlier date, also attempted to universalize the worldview of the new technical strata generated by nineteenth-century capitalism in opposition to the dominant values and institutions. The popular form of this new expression of science is clearly a ruse, like the borrowed voices of Szilard's dolphins through which alone scientists can convince others to listen to their views on world problems.

Leo Szilard's story "The Voice of the Dolphins" (1961) is in fact a metaphor for science fiction itself. It is a charming summa of the rationalistic approach to world problems that fascinated many scientists in the fifties. But the "voice" of science is ignored until a group of researchers pretend to have understood the language of the dolphins, from whom they obtain the solutions to all outstanding world problems, from hunger to disarmament. Szilard's dolphins are presented to the public—and accepted—as alien and superior intelligences, but there is irony in the fact that these intelligences walk among us incognito in the person of scientists. In science fiction too, science borrows a "voice" from literature in order to make itself heard and understood.

MONSTERS FROM THE ID

The building of the bomb was the most blatant transformation of knowledge into power in human history. Those who accomplished this technical feat believed themselves uniquely qualified to govern its applications. They, at least, could understand that a turning point in the human adventure had been reached. A "scientists' movement" arose from the bomb builders' realization that they had provided humanity with the means to destroy itself despite their personal dedication to the humanitarian mission of research.

In the postwar years a constant theme recurs both in serious essays on public policy by scientists and in science fiction: knowledge of man has lagged behind knowledge of nature, and the rift between the two explains the apocalyptic results of natural scientific inquiry. Man has the power; now he needs the wisdom to use it, even if he must surpass Newton in the discovery of new sciences and Socrates in the control of his own destructive impulses. The moment of truth has arrived in which humankind will fulfill its highest potentialities or disappear like the dinosaurs.

Soon after the destruction of Hiroshima, these sentiments motivated scientists to call for the transcendence of national rivalries. In 1946 Oppenheimer (1955: 12) spoke for the scientific community in arguing: "Many have said that without world government there could be no permanent peace, and that without peace there would be atomic warfare. I think one must agree with this."

This view achieved popular expression in Robert Wise's 1951 film *The Day the Earth Stood Still*. For once, Hollywood became the mouthpiece of the scientific community, reflecting its fears, regrets, and ideology. But even so, there is something ominous and inhuman about the story. This film was based on Harry Bates's novella "Farewell to the Master" (1940). In the original story, Gnut the robot and Klaatu, a man, arrive in Washington on a "space-time traveler" from a more advanced civilization than that of earth. As they step from their ship, Klaatu is immediately killed by a madman before he can explain their mission. He is later reconstructed by the robot from a recording of his voice. As Klaatu prepares to leave, the narrator, Cliff, asks Gnut to "tell your master" that humanity regrets his rude reception. "You misunderstand," the robot says. "I am the master" (Bates 1975: 815). With these words, the space-time traveler departs, leaving Cliff in awe and bewilderment at what is evidently the future fate of humanity in a world ruled by robots.

The film based on this story gives a specific historical content to the image of machines taking over. Klaatu now represents a galactic empire which demands a halt in weapons development on earth. The earth he visits is depicted in constant tension, mobilized without respite by technology and national rivalries. Klaatu briefly brings all engines on earth to a standstill in a "demonstration" of his power, following a policy many scientists recommended to the U.S. government as an alternative to dropping the atom bomb on Japan. After rejecting world political leaders and their "petty squabbles," Klaatu delivers his message to an international assembly of scientists and writers. His robot, renamed "Gort," is left behind, empowered by the empire to destroy aggressors. Gort represents the sort of "international control," exercised by a purely logical mind, which scientists see as the only alternative to war in the nuclear age.

But even Hollywood could not get through with Klaatu's message. A suspicious and hostile public saw the scientific community as a demonic force, untrustworthy and menacing. Frankenstein's experiments were child's play compared with this: Gothic romance now became mass consciousness. Scientists were, as Szilard (1961: 20) complains at the beginning of "The Voice of the Dolphins," "on tap but not on top." Their political ambitions were suspect. They were perceived in terms of the dominant metaphors of science fiction itself as "aliens" whose intervention had interrupted the continuity of history.

These conflicts of image resulted in the polarization of science fiction. The "mad scientist" of the movies reaches his classic peak in the "philologist" of *Forbidden Planet* (1956) who wants to make mankind too wise and powerful for its own good and dies of hubris. Scientists felt attacked by such caricatures that seemed to blame them not only for the discovery but also its misuse, not only for the light of knowledge but also for the "monsters from the id" that, in *Forbidden Planet,* govern its applications. The general public, however, was reassured by the film's moral that some things man was not meant to know—that our ignorance and weakness, our finitude, is safely guarded by our inherent limits as a species.

Although science fiction representative of scientists' own views rejected this condensation of knowledge, power, and evil in their person, it remained within the sorcerer's apprentice problematic of these movies. As scientists' hopes for disarmament and world government were disappointed, they too identified the source of the problem as "monsters from the id," the id of the crowd, of dictators, of politicians, in short, the irrationality of a species too powerful for its own good.

Eugene Rabinowitch (1960: 608), editor of the *Bulletin of the Atomic Scientists,* wrote that "human consciousness needs time to adjust itself to this new state of affairs in which no security exists." Jack

Williamson's *The Humanoids* (1949: 168) sounds like a *Bulletin* editorial when it finally gets to the point: "Technology had got out of step with mentality, the craggy man insisted. Don't you see? Technicians too busy to see the tragic consequences were putting such toys as rhodomagnetic detonators in the hands of mental savages. I made the humanoids, to put an end to that. Such technicians as yourself—with the highest possible intentions—had wrecked the balance of civilization, so that it was breaking up like an off-center flywheel. The humanoids simply made them take a holiday until the philosophers could restore a better equilibrium."

Isaac Asimov's most famous novel is built around this same theme. In the *Foundation* trilogy (1951–1953), Hari Seldon builds two planetary foundations to save something from the ruins of a dying galactic empire. The first is devoted to natural science but is destroyed by a mutant with a hypnotic power to mobilize irrational emotions. Then the second foundation, devoted to "psychohistory," intervenes and saves the day by taming the irrational forces which escaped the grasp of natural science.

In several novels by Arthur Clarke the problem is posed in terms of the ability of the human species to take its place in a universe of rational or even superrational minds. In *The City and the Stars* (1956) humans no longer seek to go among the stars where formerly they were at home. Somewhat as in the *Foundation* trilogy, civilization is divided into two mutually indifferent cultures, one based on a perfect mechanical technology, the other on the mastery of psychic powers. Only through the union of these two cultures can mankind discover the truth of its past, overcome its fears, and again participate in the great galactic adventure of Minds beyond imagining.

In these novels, the real-life extrapolation of nuclear power to the limit calls forth a desperate reflection on the possibilities and need for a similar moral and mental extrapolation. Intelligence, as a hierarchy of forms that may well extend beyond our present limits, is a key theme to which corresponds the projection of psychic capacities to the thermonuclear last degree.

DREAMS OF TRANSFIGURATION

The bomb stimulated science fiction writers to new speculations about the destiny of the human species and indeed of the universe itself. Jean Giraudoux (1935: 13) calls destiny "the accelerated force of time." Nothing has ever accelerated time like the atom bomb. In the bunker awaiting the explosion of the first nuclear device, Edward Teller recalculated the probability of the bomb fusing atmospheric hydrogen in a planetary holocaust. In the early days there was a strong conviction that nuclear war was coming and with it the end of history. The clock on the cover of the *Bulletin of the Atomic Scientists* moved ever nearer to the midnight hour of nuclear pandestruction. And *this* science has wrought . . .

At the end of the road to Bacon's New Atlantis lies not utopia but an insane world, heir to atavisms and social structures that drive human beings to produce and fight without respite in the midst of abundance. Modern technology has completed the work of history, has raised social labor to such high levels of productivity, has intertwined the fates of all peoples so thoroughly that the continued thralldom of mankind to the struggle for existence has become an obvious absurdity. In this context the question of the meaning of life is posed with new urgency. Surely several billion years of evolution and tens of thousands of years of human history are not for naught. There must be a point to it all, even if it is nothing more than the production of a spare part for an alien spaceship as in Kurt Vonnegut's *Sirens of Titan*. In any case, the end of history provokes new reflections on its meaning and especially on the place of science in its terrifying course.

Many contemporary stories approach this question through space travel considered as a symbol of the transcendence of human limits. The symbol is well chosen: space travel can be made to serve a literary function similar to that of nuclear war. Both are thought experiments become real, striking imitations of art by life.

The prospect of a galactic destiny gives a sense to the ideal oneness of the human species, as does the atom bomb. (Recall Tom Lehrer's song "We'll All Go Together When We Go.") Both devalue the traditional notions of historical victory and political power in the face of vaster goals. As Arthur Clarke (1956: 157) put it, "The illusions of our day cannot survive the fierce, hard light that beats down from the stars." The same could be said of the "fierce, hard light" that first shone in the deserts of New Mexico. The planetary perspective is that of a viewer who knows the truth about the bomb, that it abolishes human history as such. So too, rockets bring man face-to-face with destiny, which is beyond politics and national rivalries, essentially human and eternal, in a way that is structurally similar to the bomb.

Of course, space travel had been treated before in science fiction.

But the excitement lay in the conquest of space itself, the technical procedures, the astonishing discoveries of the first explorers. It was the adventure of lonely intelligence in the infinite spaces that so frightened poor Pascal. Stories like this continue to be written, but now they are old hat. The demystified space of the nuclear era requires new fantasies of exploration. As André Benedetto (1966: 58) has written, "Il y a longtemps qu'on a cassé / A double bang le silence éternel / De ces espaces infinis" (The eternal silence of these infinite spaces was shattered long ago by a double bang).

After World War II, with the first rocket to the moon less than a generation away, the technical difficulties were all dismissed with a cursory mention of "atom drive" or "hyperspace." By force of repetition technological exoticism has since acquired the everydayness of the electric toaster. The interesting problems concern the moral fitness of the human race for space travel.

Alfred Bester's *The Stars My Destination* (1956) describes a future in which teleportation has been extended to astronomical distances. At the climax of the book the hero selects people at random all over the world to receive a new fissionable material that can be detonated directly by human thought: not the politicians but ordinary people must choose between life and death, the stars and nuclear self-destruction. The dialectic of nuclear war and space travel could not be more clearly presented. The race to the stars is the moral equivalent for nuclear war, a domain in which to sublimate the will to earthly power.

In many other stories space travel is similarly treated as a test of human courage and wisdom, often in the face of irrational fears or prohibitions imposed by past generations or alien species. In Isaac Asimov's *The Caves of Steel* (1953) the population problem is solved by emigration to the stars, once fear of open space and hatred of robots is conquered. Arthur Clarke's *The City and the Stars* is also about overcoming the fear of space. Theodore Sturgeon's *More Than Human* (1953) is another novel that concerns the conquest not of technical obstacles to space travel but moral obstacles. In all these stories the question is less one of technical mastery in the service of a Promethean destiny than of space flight as a symbol of human self-mastery or self-transcendence. In several stories space travel forms the background to a veritable apotheosis of the species. The "lopers" of Clifford Simak's *City*, the Overmind of Clarke's *Childhood's End*, are images of its total transfiguration beyond the realm of history.

In *City* (1952) the explorers of Jupiter employ a device that converts them into "lopers" capable of surviving on the surface of the planet. As it turns out, it is much more fun being a loper than a man. "He had found something greater than Man had ever known. A swifter, surer body. A sense of exhilaration, a deeper sense of life. A sharper mind. A world of beauty that even the dreamers of Earth had not yet imagined" (Simak 1952: 117). Humanity deserts earth for Jupiter, leaving its old home to a race of intelligent dogs who narrate Simak's tale. The human form is cast off altogether and with it reason, mortality, and responsibility. In this novel the destiny of the human race is to become a sort of cosmic beatnik in flight from the intolerable burden of historical and individual existence. Here the human species does not transcend its limits; rather, the species itself is transcended.

Childhood's End (1953) reaches a similar conclusion. It begins with the United States and Russia about to conquer space: another step in the long march toward mutual conquest and destruction. Suddenly alien spaceships appear over every major city. The "Overlords" have arrived to save mankind from its own folly. Humanity is forbidden war and space travel ("The stars are not for man" [Clarke 1972: 137]) and united in prosperity under a world government. A golden age of peace, leisure, and creativity begins.

But all human hopes are cut short by a startling change in the children. More and more of them withdraw from reality into a dream world. The Overlords explain that above them all in the hierarchy of cosmic intelligence stands a being of pure mind which the children of humanity will soon join. The history of the species is over. The Overlords have served not as masters but as midwives for the birth of a higher form of purely mental life. The last surviving man witnesses the final transfiguration of what once were human children: "There lay the Overmind, whatever it might be, bearing the same relation to man as man bore to amoeba. Potentially infinite, beyond mortality, how long had it been absorbing race after race as it spread across the stars? Did it too have desires, did it have goals it sensed dimly yet might never attain? Now it had drawn into its being all that the human race had ever achieved. This was not tragedy, but fulfillment" (Clarke 1972: 205).

The concept of transfiguration in these novels revives some of the wildest dreams of nineteenth-century utopianism: Charles Fourier's reconciliation of man and nature; the young Marx's liberation of the senses; Kirilov's resurrection of nature in Dostoevsky's *The Devils*. Beyond the mere pacification of existence in an enlightened and rational social order—the goal of scientific enlightenment—appears a further horizon of joy and purposeless power, a Nietzschean transcendence of "the vermin man" and his humiliating divinities.

Why this recrudescence of romantic antirationalism in the very mainstream of a literature that always sought to rationalize the fantastic in the dreams of science? It is as though the failure of enlightenment as a social project also revealed the limits of scientific knowledge of nature. The modern concept of nature as an object of investigation and control is subordinated to an older idea of nature as a miraculous living thing of which the human race is merely a part. It is the return of *Natürphilosophie*, an outlook that could hardly be more alien to the mainstream tradition of science fiction up to this point.

TOTALITARIAN ENLIGHTENMENT

The social goal of science is ostensibly human liberation through progress in power over nature, and early science fiction often responded to these ideological pretensions of scientific rationalism with images of a world wisely governed by scientists and technicians. This was the literature of positivism in the nineteenth-century sense of the term.

After the bomb, however, this theme rang false for many writers and readers. The old fantasy of scientists and technicians in power became less attractive once science and technique were mobilized in the race for the ultimate weapon. Science was already, if not in power, near enough to the centers of control that its further participation in history no longer promised liberation. Following the reorganization of science, the white knight of reason turned out to be a cultured bureaucrat in Washington or Moscow.

The cold war intensified the moral pathos of such structural changes, for a tighter organization of science was not only efficient but a matter of loyalty as well. The security problems to which Arthur Roberts jokingly referred were deadly serious. Freedom was the watchword of the suppression of those who exercised it too carelessly: the defense of tolerance required measured intolerance. This situation complicated the political prose of scientists as well as the metaphors of science fiction. Scientists were suspect; only the expression of unconditional loyalty and obedience to Western ideals could allay public fears. Yet the Enemy was hated and feared precisely because it demanded unconditional loyalty and obedience. Thus in this period every image of a society of total administration was simultaneously a denunciation of the Soviet

Union and a more or less conscious expression of anxiety about trends in the West itself.

As a result, images of nonconformity and individualism were also ambiguous. On the one hand, the scientists wished to defend their freedom of thought, which necessarily made them nonconformists with respect to the increasingly repressive society around them.[1] On the other hand, most scientists accepted the ideological framework of a cold war that rationalized the demand for conformity and institutionalized it in the new bureaucratic administration of science with its secrecy and security systems.

The bureaucratization of science was a mild form of a much more thorough bureaucratization of economic life in this period. It raised the specter of the technological obsolescence of humankind in a world of machines and mechanistic social organizations. Thematic material of this type is treated repeatedly from Karel Capek's *R.U.R.* in 1920 down to the present. After World War II, as Western democracies were increasingly recast in the bureaucratic mold, the theme became more and more popular. Novels like Orwell's *1984* took up the prewar elegy for humanistic values in a world of total administration.

A whole genre was based on the thesis that progress in the power of the human species over nature goes hand in hand with ever more effective domination of some human beings by others. These dystopias of totalitarian enlightenment represent reactions in the name of a humanism which admits its defeat in practice. To the triumphant positivist utopia thus corresponds a humanistic dystopia which is its spiritual *point d'honneur*. In both genres history is portrayed as the destiny of reason: which of its two sides will prevail, that which is dedicated to wisdom, to the intelligent choice of goals, or that which is dedicated to mere domination, to the ruthless control of means, including a robotized humanity?

In the late forties and fifties a number of science fiction novels attempted to revise the increasingly popular dystopian genre. These novels did not ignore or minimize the threatening character of modern social trends as did positivist utopias. Yet reason for hope is always found in spite of the apparently successful dissolution of the old forms of individuality. It is as though the pressures of cold war conformism

---

1. As P. W. Bridgman (1948: 70) wrote in the *Bulletin of the Atomic Scientists*, "The assumption of the right of society to impose a responsibility on the scientist which he does not desire obviously involves the acceptance of . . . the right of the stupid to exploit the bright."

and the bureaucratic reorganization of the scientific community forced it to ponder the possibility that technology will indeed reduce human beings to mere tools of a mechanical system. And yet to accept this conclusion would be to abandon the ideology of science, the whole notion of progress through power over nature. The solution would have to take humanism's nightmare into account while saving the dreams of enlightenment.

Asimov's *The Caves of Steel* depicts an overpopulated world compressed by fear of open space into crowded cities. As robots replace workers, the mass of "declassified" laborers grows, and hostility between men and machines reaches a violent peak. But in the end the problems are all solved, and the policeman hero is even reconciled to his forced partnership with a robot. The cyborg destiny of humans and robots is to live in "a culture that combines the best of the two on an equal but parallel basis" (Asimov 1972*a*: 48).

Fred Hoyle's *Ossian's Ride* (1959) pits a scientist hero against a technoscientific enterprise suspected of evil intentions in spite of the useful products it has developed. The hero goes through harrowing adventures spying on the corporation but finally learns that its owners are benevolent visitors from another star system, come to earth to preserve the last remnants of their doomed culture. They will contribute through the corporation to the upward struggle of humanity and indeed of all intelligent life.

Novels like these can be understood as expressions of ambivalence within the scientific community about its own transformation and that of society at large. They are studied exercises in "generic discontinuities" (Jameson 1973). The reader is already familiar with novels of totalitarian enlightenment such as *1984* and *Brave New World*. Asimov, Hoyle, and writers of similar tales plunge the reader into a conflict typical of the genre. But the conflict is finally dissolved in a surprise happy ending, contrary to all the pessimistic expectations awakened by the clichéd "man versus machine" narration. The fruits of enlightenment are saved from the critique by the optimistic conclusion, but not until the "misunderstanding" on which the critique is based has been lived, suffered, and transcended.

Beneath the endless litany of praise to science in the late forties and early fifties, praise designed to justify the expensive integration of research and government, lay seeds of self-doubt. All the changes in scientific life and self-consciousness described above prepared a critique of the ideology of enlightenment on which scientific activity has traditionally been based. The pursuit of power over nature has reached an impasse. In popularizing the scientific community's increasingly troubled vision, these novels and stories contributed to the development of a new dystopian consciousness of history that gradually overshadowed traditional politics in the postwar period.

THE LAST HUMANIST

The longing to be primitive is a disease of culture.
—*George Santayana 1926: 19*

THE BREAKDOWN OF LIBERAL TECHNOCRACY

The period from 1964 to 1968 was one of the most remarkable in recent American history. Thirty-five years of American liberalism were tried and found wanting. Opposition movements were born, first on the Left, then on the Right, strong enough to shake the established political patterns. The spread of ill humor, intolerance, and personal cruelty spoiled the last traces of freshness and innocence in the American character. The temper of a nation was changed.

These changes corresponded with the apotheosis of liberalism, its transformation from a vaguely populistic movement, at least apparently opposed to established power, into a technocratic ideology of total social integration under the auspices of "scientific" expertise. The War on Poverty and the war in Vietnam were just two aspects of the final struggle to end the history of social conflict. Never was America stronger and more self-confident. Never was it engaged in a more hopeless task. Soon the failure in Vietnam became the prelude to the collapse of liberal technocracy in every sphere.

What went wrong? Herbert Marcuse's article "The Individual in the Great Society" offered a prescient explanation that demonstrated the significance of Vietnam for the technocratic project of pacifying human existence through total administration. Marcuse (1966: 15) saw in the advanced capitalist societies a "progressive transfer of power from the human individual to the technical or bureaucratic apparatus, from living to dead labor, from personal to remote control, from a machine or group of machines to a whole mechanized system." Personal life is now planned and orchestrated with the lives of others, from above, by the machine itself. The individuals "live in a society where they are . . . subjected to an apparatus which, comprising production, distribution, and consumption, material and intellectual life, work and leisure, politics and fun, determines their daily existence, their needs and aspirations" (Marcuse 1966: 15).

In this society, labor is still "alienated," that is, it is still production for an Other, and not for the individual's own needs or for those of his or her fellows. Although the society is rich enough to provide for all its members, "the individuals must go on spending physical and mental energy in the struggle for existence, status, advantage. They must suffer, service, and enjoy the apparatus which imposes on them this necessity. The new slavery in the work world is not compensated by a new autonomy over the work world" (Marcuse 1966: 15).

The individuals are bound ever more tightly to their society by what Marcuse calls a "libidinal attachment" to the goods and services it delivers. The very consciousness of alienation tends to be repressed as "individuals identify themselves with their being-for-others, their image" (Marcuse 1966: 15). "Under these circumstances, society calls for an Enemy against whom the aggressive energy can be released which cannot be channeled into the normal, daily struggle for existence. The individuals live in a society which wages war or is prepared to wage war all over the world. . . . The enemy is not one factor among others, not a contingency which the evaluation of the chances of the Great Society can ignore or to which it can refer to in passing. The Enemy is a determining factor at home and abroad, in business and education, in science and relaxation" (Marcuse 1966: 15).

These dystopian trends were reflected in and propagated by the mass media in the 1960s. This section discusses two popular expressions of the new consciousness. Spy mania swept the country after John Kennedy named Ian Fleming among his favorite authors. The first James Bond films had millions of viewers, and a new film genre was born in the instant. At about the same time, French and Italian films became quite popular among sophisticated audiences in America. Films like Federico Fellini's La Dolce Vita (1960) reflected discontents that found no voice in the usual Hollywood product. These films were more or less openly dystopian. They gained larger and larger audiences as cultural opposition spread.

These two types of films seem to represent diametrically opposed social attitudes. The Europeans rejected modern society and waxed nostalgic over the death of traditional humanistic culture, while the spies celebrated the pleasures of technological society and gloried in its triumph over malicious Third World peoples and criminal conspiracies. But close examination of these films casts doubt on this conventional contrast. As I will show, both genres depict resistance to an oppressive social machinery. In different ways, they exemplify a new popular dystopianism.

THE STRUGGLE AGAINST DYSTOPIA

Jean-Luc Godard's *Alphaville* (1966) is an ironic comment on the spy film. Godard's hero, Lemmy Caution, visits a city controlled by a computer called Alpha 60. In Alphaville "men have become the slaves of probability." The spy from the "outerlands" has come on behalf of "those who weep" to save Alphaville for human values which have been rooted out of the hearts and even the very dictionaries of the inhabitants. Caution eventually destroys the computer and escapes with the daughter of Alphaville's chief scientist, who is named, significantly, von Braun.

Alphaville is set in the Paris of the future, photographed in the most Americanized sections of contemporary Paris. The hero of the film represents values that are on the decline in modern technological civilization. That civilization includes not only the West but also its Soviet rival: Caution's alias in Alphaville is "Ivan Johnson, correspondent for Figaro-Pravda."

For Godard, evidently, the last surviving humanist is the spy, the detective, the newspaperman. As Caution says, "Journalism begins with the same letter as Justice." His credentials as a representative of Western culture are established through constant quotations from French poetry and philosophy. Paul Eluard's *Capital de la Douleur*, Ferdinand Céline's *Voyage au Bout de la Nuit*, Blaise Pascal's famous epigram about the eternal silences of the infinite spaces, lines from Jean Racine, and much else get into the act (Benedikt 1968).

Caution is the hero of a struggle against "technological time," the enemy of life and love, which Alpha 60 describes in the following terms: "No one has lived in the past; no one will live in the future. The present is the form of all life. Time is like a circle which turns ceaselessly, the descending arc, the past; the rising arc, the future." In a society of total administration, the individual has no need of past and future, both of which are taken care of by the computer. In such a society, only a Lemmy Caution can invalidate the apparent technological obsolescence of time. Only a man of action can follow the advice of the unfortunate criminal, executed for weeping at his wife's funeral: "It suffices to go forward to live, forward towards all that one loves."

A great many European films of the 1960s have a humanist hero of some sort, although none can compete with Lemmy Caution. In films of despair, like Fellini's *La Dolce Vita* and Michelangelo Antonioni's *The Red Desert* (1964), characters who represent resistance to society are doomed. In the former film, the aristocratic Steiner studies Bach and Sanskrit, entertains artists and poets, and eventually commits suicide. In the latter film, a similar function is filled by a neurotic woman lost in the industrial wasteland around Ravenna. In François Truffaut's *Fahrenheit 451* (1966), the humanist hero escapes from a world dominated by television to a region where a small fringe group conserves literary traditions.

In *Alphaville*, as in many spy films, the hero establishes his humanity and gains his victory through love, long since abolished in Alphaville as illogical and functionless. The girl is brought over from the enemy by being taught to love in a scene of extraordinary asceticism: there is practically no physical contact but only a sort of poetic interplay between the protagonists. Once obtained, the heroine's love serves to confirm the hero's humanity, to distinguish him from the cold, unlovable, and unloving computer.

But Godard goes even further and offers us a sadistic Lemmy Caution as well in order to sharpen the contrast with the benevolent computer, all of whose actions "serve the final good." Thus in one scene Caution purposely drives his car over an enemy agent's face. Godard grasps at any shred of evidence that human instincts of whatever sort still survive the reign of logic.

As the pure embodiment of what Marcuse called the "repressive rationality" of technological society, the computer exemplifies the System. It states, "In the capitalist and the communist world, there is no evil desire to subjugate men by indoctrination or money, but simply the natural desire to organize, to plan, to reduce the unforeseen." But the pursuit of total efficiency debases humanity itself. As Marshall McLuhan (1964: 46) put it, "Man becomes . . . the sex organs of the machine world." The threat of dehumanization dominates all these dystopian films, from *La Dolce Vita*, where it takes the form of mass culture, to *The Red Desert*, where the characters are sickened by the mere physical presence of factories.

The masses are portrayed in three different ways in this genre. The population of *Alphaville* is organized fascistically into an atomized and robotized collectivity. In *Fahrenheit 451* the population forms a large friendly family with a childlike wish to belong. This image appears to derive from a disparaging view of adolescent neotribalism in America. In *La Dolce Vita*, the portrayal of the masses is fractured along the lines dividing tradition from modernity in a society in transition. Marcello's fiancée, who longs for religion and family, stands for a dying way of life that still holds its attraction for the lower classes. But the truth of the present is represented by the swinging life of the Via Veneto, where advertising agents and their hangers-on manufacture new conformisms for an ever more modern society.

Correlated with the horror of these various collectivisms is a yearning for the simple country life of technological underdevelopment where spirit is not yet submitted to mechanism. But this alternative is never clearly localized. Lemmy Caution and his girlfriend escape Alphaville in a shiny Mustang to a destination unknown. A beautiful beach symbolizes an alternative in *The Red Desert*, while the smile of a simple country girl at the end of *La Dolce Vita* bears the same message. In *Fahrenheit 451*, the land of the "book people," a country retreat populated by refugees who have each memorized a favorite book, offers the most fanciful interpretation of the remaining possibilities of freedom. The restoration of human values is presented as an unrealistic utopia, and even, in *The Red Desert*, as a neurotic daydream.

THE HELICOPTER AND THE GUERRILLA

The contrast between these films and the spy films of the same period could not be more obvious. James Bond glories in the worst aspects of Western society, aspects which are unequivocally rejected by the social critique of a Godard or a Fellini. Rationalized collectivism in the Bond saga is exemplified in *Dr. No*'s (1962) island full of evil Orientals; nothing like it threatens back in good old England. Lemmy Caution takes no pleasure in the life of Alphaville, the joys of which are summed up by a vending machine that exchanges a "thank you" note for a coin. Bond is a vain and elegant hedonist.

Yet, despite the obvious differences, the two types of film have remarkably similar structures. Bond may not quote Racine, but he establishes his nonmechanical humanity in other ways. He always begins a film well provisioned with technical devices and weapons, the most spectacular of which is his car in *Goldfinger* (1964). And just as regularly he is stripped of these defenses by his enemies, captured, and exposed to their weapons. From then on Bond must depend on his courage, luck, and seductive powers to see him through. We are easily won over: his fumbling incompetence at disarming an atom bomb, his sheer physical strength, his search for pleasure in a world gone mad, the love of an enemy girl, all prove his humanity. Strength without machines and the test of love seem to be universal traits of the spy hero. These traits alert us to an underlying dystopian imagery.

Although constantly threatened, the spy hero is immune from harm, a characteristic that gives a black comic twist to the most frightening scenes. Under a laser beam or in a shark-filled pool, fleeing the guns of his opponents, or in bed with a beautiful counterspy, the hero always survives triumphant and unruffled. Not only is he immune from death, but, even more important, he is immune from fear, injury, and all the things which would cause him to lose his self-possession.

The Spy Who Came In from the Cold (1966), which refuses this pattern for the sake of "realism," ends up confirming it after all. The hero chooses death gratuitously as a protest against reality. He is thus *essentially* immune, but lets himself be killed at the last minute for the sake of human values sacrificed by a hateful world. But this film does not play by the rules; that in fact is what made it so interesting to viewers whose expectations were formed on the Bond films.

A good spy cannot have ideals or human attachments. He knows what to expect from life and never worries about politics. He is precisely not like the hero of *The Spy Who Came In from the Cold*, a normal mature adult capable of personal commitment and sentimental involvement. Instead he is a "cool" superadolescent, able to assert his humanity and individuality in a crazy world without assuming a tragic role. Scaled down, this "cool" is something like a *model response* to the threats present in the daily life of the audience. This trivialization of the problems of modern life was a constant refrain in the contemporary television series *I Spy* that gave Bill Cosby his start.

As in the dystopian film, the enemy in the spy film is collectivized and technologically sophisticated. There is an amusing scene in *Goldfinger* which points up the contrast between this new villainy and old-fashioned crime. Goldfinger has invited a number of gangsters to his house for a payoff and proceeds to execute them with poison gas. Chemical warfare rather than gangland heroics greets the "Little Caesars" of the films of the thirties and forties.

The original Bond novels are characterized by a rather old-fashioned imperialist demonization of Central Europeans, Russians, Orientals, and blacks, indeed, just about anyone who is not English. But, as many critics point out, Fleming's racism is not entirely sincere; his Manichaeanism takes on targets of convenience rather than reflecting a consistent ideology (Eco 1984: 161). The case is somewhat different with the Bond films. In them too, and in the many films they inspired, a Third World country or non-Caucasian race is cast in the role of villain. But the Vietnam era gives new meaning to the spy film's racism.

One might assume, given actual events in Southeast Asia, that the villains would employ the guerrilla tactics of the Viet Cong; instead, they usually possess a disciplined army generously supplied with high-tech weapons. The hero is always captured by his enemies, and working from within defeats their advanced technology practically unaided. Sometimes he gets a bit of last-minute help from his own side, armed with its advanced weapons, as at the end of *Goldfinger*, but the basic work has to be done by a lone man in enemy territory. Thus the real relation between Western imperialism and the underdeveloped world is reversed, the former basing itself on men and the latter on machines, the former on the principles of Mao Tse-tung and the latter on those of Lyndon Baines Johnson.

The struggle between man and machine is carried to the point of self-caricature in a film called *Arabesque* (1966). The story concerns a Middle Eastern prime minister who must be saved from the clutches of a group of evil Arab conspirators. At one point, the villains pursue the "good guys" across a field, riding a combine and a thresher. Just as Goldfinger attempts to have Bond crushed in a car by a scrap-metal machine, a picturesque image of the fate of the average American caught in a head-on freeway collision, so here the enemy catches the representatives of Western society in the situation of pedestrians in city traffic. The absurdities continue in the succeeding scene as the heroes find horses waiting to carry them away and are chased by a tank and helicopter. The West has somehow become the nineteenth century to the East's twentieth.

Here the technocratic threat present in our own society is projected onto the underdeveloped world. That threat is often represented by a helicopter, an image drawn from the Vietnam struggle. In *Fahrenheit 451* the hero is also chased by a helicopter, and in *La Dolce Vita* the triumph of technocracy over tradition is symbolized in the grimly ironic opening scene by a huge statue of Jesus dangling from a helicopter. In every case, we are asked to identify not with the helicopter but with its earthbound victims.

The concept of "underdevelopment" has a different significance for European and American audiences. The dystopian films were deeply anti-American, nostalgic for the European past prior to the invasion of American technology. The force of this ideology was such that a French cartoon strip, *Asterix*, became as popular as *Mickey Mouse*, at least in France, by glorifying the triumphs of primitive Gaul over sophisticated Rome.

In Europe dystopian imagery can be expressed through opposition to the great powers ("Ivan Johnson"). This theme forms the background to the amusing spy movie *You Only Live Twice* (1967). This film, made at a time of grave economic difficulties for Britain, reflects an unusual "third force" concept. Here James Bond takes a plunge into the ranks of the secondary powers. Although weak, they are justified by their humanity against the quadruple menace of the great powers, Russia and America, China and SPECTRE, the first two embodying blind mechanical automatism, and the latter two diabolical evil.

In this film Bond "dies," to be resurrected later in another identity. Bond's sacrifice for Little England corresponds with the decline of Great Britain itself, and the dream of its renewed appearance on the world scene. The film announces this death and transfiguration as the supposedly executed Bond is reborn in the torpedo tube of a submarine, from which he is launched to shore for his final mission. The new Bond, Sean Connery with fat cheeks and the paunch of a middle-aged businessman, is not yet the perfect expression of England's postimperial and overripe maturity. He must also ally himself with a non-Anglo-Saxon power, Japan, in order to save the world from the madness and stupidity of the great powers. To seal this alliance Bond's transformation must be total: he must become Japanese and even marry a Japanese girl.

Bond then learns *ninja*, the traditional Japanese art of stealth and violence, and goes to work for the Japanese secret service. In the final scenes, Bond's small helicopter outmaneuvers the great helicopters of SPECTRE, representing big-power high technology. How unromantic! Bond is no longer flesh and blood against mechanism; he has his own little technology. This reproduces the precise position of Europe in world politics, not fighting on the ground like the Viet Cong, but in an intermediary zone, surviving and even occasionally winning by cleverness and maneuverability.

This comparison of dystopian films and spy films reveals surprising convergences. In both the hero is a sort of guerrilla warrior, fighting an evil technocracy from within. In both his humanity is established by individual action against the machine, while the enemy possesses the helicopters. But the social functions of the two types of films are quite different. The dystopian film exacerbates the conflict of human values and technological society, while the spy film offers a mythic resolution. This explains their different treatments of underdevelopment, which, for reasons that must be analyzed, serves a particularly important symbolic function in advanced society.

AMBIVALENCE TOWARD TECHNOLOGICAL SOCIETY

Despite their differences, these films made a similar point: persecuted by a rationalized order, the viewers were asked to identify themselves as heroes in the struggle against technocracy. But there was an element of bad faith in this Manichaean identification. As Philip Slater (1970: 125) writes, "The impersonal, intricate, omnivorous machinery that threatens, benumbs, and bureaucratizes the helpless individual in Marcuse's *One-Dimensional Man* is not something external to the individual; it *is* the individual—the grotesque materialization of his turning away." The individuals play contradictory roles: they are both integrated participants in the society and alienated critics of its conformism and its technology. In the former role they pilot the counterinsurgency helicopters that keep the others in check, while in the latter role they fight a rear-guard guerrilla action for a more individualistic society. Not surprisingly, then, the system is both rejected and loved, feared and accepted.

The imperialism of the spy film was a coded expression of these ambivalences. In fighting a guerrilla war against a technologically sophisticated underdeveloped world, viewers projected the most unpleasant aspects of their own society onto others while establishing themselves as "individuals." The aggressivity generated by repression in the First World was unleashed on the Third World. What better solution to the dilemma of individualism and conformity than identifying regimentation with a foreign nation and defeating it with the perfect marriage of humanism and technology, as represented by James Bond?

This false resolution of the conflict between the individual and society fixated the population in a posture of defense against the social Enemy. Reconciliation with society implied war with the symbolic projections of secret and unconscious "subversive" tendencies. The demand for war became an urgent necessity, for only through it could the individuals ensure their ambivalent integration in the system. It was this psychic constellation that made both the spy film and real counterinsurgency warfare plausible to millions of people.

The dystopian film had a different impact. It idealized alienation from society without, however, identifying any real possibility of resistance to it. Viewers remained caught in the actual ambivalences of daily life, their critical consciousness awakened in contradiction with their social situation. The romantic image of cultured, humanistic, pretechnological society, even though it was not concretized geographically—Vietnam or Cuba was precisely not the place to go—nevertheless indicated indirectly a historical and personal possibility: "dropping out," the "Great Refusal" of advanced society. The dystopian film thus dramatized the symbolic meaning of underdevelopment, the real threat which it contained and the real possibilities of personal liberation it signified.

THE VANISHING CONSENSUS

May we not be justified in reaching the diagnosis that,
under the influence of cultural urges, some civilizations,
or some epochs of civilization—possibly the whole of
mankind—have become "neurotic"?
                                        —*Sigmund Freud 1961: 91*

MANIPULATION AND RESISTANCE

Popular dystopianism is present throughout the culture of the Vietnam era. In this section I will offer a sketch of changes in advertising that parallel the ones documented above in the case of science fiction and film. I will argue that in the 1950s and 1960s the mind managers were visibly struggling to keep ahead of an increasingly resistant public, more and more skeptical of corporations' claims, and that this resistance inspired new approaches not only to selling but to politics as well.

Advertising's dilemma lies in the very nature of persuasion that contains an implicit reference to the real interests and freedom of those to whom it is addressed. Persuasion claims to bring those interests to consciousness where they can be grasped by that freedom. The victims of all-pervasive advertising and propaganda thus find their own individuality constantly valorized even as it is redirected to alien purposes. At the same time, there is a very real sense in which the manipulated masses are free, free to appropriate and interpret the manipulation to which they are subjected in a variety of unforeseeable ways (de Certeau 1980). The resulting tensions between advertising and its audience are not so much resolved as masked by constantly changing techniques.

While there are no sharp breaks in the history of advertising styles, emphases do change. For example, there has been a long-term trend away from rational toward irrational appeals (Schudson 1984: 60). Ads from the nineteenth century look remarkably benign; they seem to consist primarily of information, usually accompanied by some restrained pictures and a modest slogan. The early twentieth century saw a new emphasis on crude "hard sell" ads pressuring individuals to enter the new consumer markets, followed by a post–World War II shift to "soft sell" image ads depicting conformist lifestyles (Riesman, Glazer, and Denney 1953: 100ff.). As these ads too began to seem old-fashioned in the 1960s, consumers were increasingly offered a self-contradictory *image of nonconformity* that flattered their individualism and originality (Ewen 1976: 218–219).

Whether many of these ads were really effective is irrelevant to my concern, which is the cultural logic they exemplify (Schudson 1984: chap. 4). But surely they had some notable successes. For having grasped the new logic early, Volkswagen took the lead in auto imports and Ronald Reagan became governor of California, and eventually president as well. The new ads were at the very least expressions of a new mood and of the growing centrifugal forces that nearly tore the society apart in the late 1960s and early 1970s.

The ubiquitous hard sell of early radio—we have all heard those rasping voices and inane ditties in old movies or on late-night TV—addressed individuals who yearned for success yet feared it. Robert Warshow's analysis of the contemporary gangster film reveals the mechanism of this ambivalence.

> At bottom, the gangster is doomed because he is under the obligation to succeed, not because the means he employs are unlawful. In the deeper layers of the modern consciousness, *all* means are unlawful, every attempt to succeed is an act of aggression, leaving one alone and guilty and defenseless among enemies: one is *punished* for success. This is our intolerable dilemma: that failure is a kind of death and success is evil and dangerous, is—ultimately—impossible. The effect of the gangster film is to embody this dilemma in the person of the gangster and resolve it by his death. The

dilemma is resolved because it is *his* death, not ours. We are safe; for the moment, we can acquiesce in our failure, we can choose to fail. (Warshow 1964: 88)

The gangster film enabled the individuals to live through their ambition in art and reconciled them temporarily to a mediocre existence. This same structure was repeated in the advertising of the period. The hard sell drew timorous consumers with their tiny savings into the new mass consumer markets to which they were not accustomed. Advertising bombarded its audience with visual shocks, disgusting melodies, and insistent voices. Consumers were not simply offered information about the product; they were pressured and bullied against their will. This approach left them fully aware that their freedom of purse and better judgment were being violated. But that violation would surely have failed if it did not appeal to a repressed and inadmissible ambition to rise above mediocrity, to enter the world of dreams, success, uniqueness. During this period, consumer goods appeared as temptations to be resisted. The hard sell allied itself with desire against the consumer's reason.

In the fifties, the increased comfort and security of conformist existence conferred a positive value on it. The desire to rise above the crowd receded before the glorification of mediocrity. As Eric Goldman (1961: 264–265) explains, "The unquestionable trend was toward a home in a suburb—the mushrooming miles of middle-class and worker's suburbs—where the prime virtue was adjustment to what the neighbors thought and did. Under these circumstances the urge was not so much for individualism as it was for getting oneself into the most profitable and comfortable relationship with some larger group or organization."

Perhaps the purest expression of this change was the television situation comedy (Hamamoto 1989: 43–45). There the cloyingly sentimental portrayal of the happy home life of Mr. and Mrs. Average became entertainment. The individuals identified themselves fully and joyfully with their roles. No Mom was ever so sweet and pretty, no Dad so strong and understanding. The work world scarcely appeared, for it was still a sphere of frustration and conflict. But the situation comedy seemed to say that these mild inconveniences were surely worth it in exchange for the joys of home. Thus where frustration and conflict appeared at all, they were not tragic but a source of gentle amusement.

Of course, this perfect reconciliation of the individual and the society was a myth, and the soap opera was there to give it the lie. The alienation of the individual in work was not funny; home life was not blissful; major appliances and planned leisure could not fill an empty life. The individuals had indeed achieved a sort of success in their conformist existence, but this success was accompanied by proliferating anxieties provoked by an economic and social transition that could not be criticized even in the privacy of the soul.

The individuals were required to give allegiance to the increasingly impersonal and mechanical system that, after all, provided them with a decent income. Social deviance, opposition, the desire for something better could cost them what they had already achieved. The unique individual was no longer merely imprudent, but threatening to others. Now all that was different became evil. With Senator Joseph McCarthy, the science fiction threat of the alien became real. The conformist mass lived in fear of Communists, intellectuals, and flying saucers (Condon 1969: 523).

In fact, so compelling was the fear of the alien that an advisory board of scientists warned the Air Force that American communications systems were vulnerable to massive overload if an attacking enemy chose to perpetrate a large-scale flying saucer hoax; they urged the Air Force to examine flying saucer sightings and, preferably, to debunk them. (The text of the scientists' report can be found in the appendices to Condon 1969: 905ff.) This was also the time of the great brainwashing scare, and doubts about the integrity and durability of human personality were expressed at a higher cultural level in the spread of Freudianism. John Frankenheimer's prophetic and scary film *The Manchurian Candidate* (1962) summed up these fears (Whitfield 1991: 211–213).

Unable to reject the source of their misery without losing the rewards they owed it, individuals modeled themselves on it to discharge the surplus aggression it generated. Their revenge took the form of possession of and control over mechanical power, automotive horsepower, power mowers, power boats. Meanwhile, ultimate security was available through building a bomb shelter. (There were even macabre debates about whether to let the neighbors in—the consensus was "No.") Mechanized, with a safe retreat in readiness, individuals could remain in conformity with social demands.

The advertising of this period reflected these changes. Confronted with the hard sell ad, the consumer experienced an external compulsion corresponding to an inner temptation. But now some consumers, particularly those with a better education and more money to spend, resented this imposition. They learned to defend the freedom of their purse against the crass bludgeoning of the hard sell and reasserted their liberty. Subtler soft sell ads promoted group identification, an identification that incidentally committed consumers to the purchase of the advertised product.

The soft sell worked better because it exercised no compulsion at all, but simply reflected the internalized limits on freedom which the individuals already accepted. Since it was assumed that they wanted to be like each other, the image ad was relatively straightforward. It might show a group of happy and attractive young people, a group to which any viewer would like to belong. Then the ad had only to point out some particular attribute of the members, their toothy Colgate smiles, their Coca-Cola, their clothes, to interest the consumer in the product. Ads of this sort strengthened the conformist pressure even as they played upon it. The ambivalence of the consumer before the hard sell, an ambivalence composed of desire for the product and desire to be free and rational, was resolved in the apparently spontaneous urge to belong to the group.

Perhaps without the war in Vietnam, the "conformist fifties" might have lasted another decade, but if we believe Marcuse, eventually such intense regimentation would have provoked irrepressible aggressivity and conflicts of some sort would have broken out. In any case, the war made it possible for this aggressivity to discharge itself on the Vietnamese along lines exemplified in the structure of the spy film.

During the Vietnam era, most people were afraid to assert their independent individuality, for that could lead to a break with society and a loss of its benefits; they did not want to "drop out" and become beatniks or hippies. But they also feared being swallowed up in the social machine. The greatest danger no longer came from individualism, as in the days of the gangster film, but from the overwhelming drive toward conformity. Thus it was conformity that had to be projected onto others, while individualism became the (mythic) characteristic of American society.

A similar illusory resolution of inner conflicts took place in domestic political life with the conservative resurgence. The right-wing leader was the domestic political version of the spy film and the equivalent of the release of societal tensions and aggressivity in Vietnam. Typically, he was identified with American individualism by his propaganda and his most widely touted actions, but in fact he did little to change things once in power.

Ronald Reagan's first term as governor of California set the pattern. The artful governor convinced most of his constituents that he was struggling to reduce the size of government by verbal attacks on students and welfare "freebooters." These "Enemies" were stigmatized for their primitiveness and animality, while also being identified with the technocratic state against which Reagan claimed to be struggling. But in fact the budget continued to rise, and the dismantling of the social and political structures for which Reagan called was never really an immediate goal of his administration.

Again, these changes were reflected in advertising. It did not take long for many people consciously to understand the workings of the image. The image ads of the fifties became transparently repressive once the individuals decided to assert their individuality. The yearning to join the group of attractive and happy young people began to give way before the desire to be distinguished from the herd. At this point, the ambivalent individuals responded to advertising not just as integrated conformists, fulfilling the rituals of group identification, but also as alienated selves. But the desire to be unique was not experienced as an irrational temptation as in the thirties and forties. Rather, it was precisely through their uniqueness that the individuals demonstrated their freedom.

Capitalizing on the desire for individuality is difficult, for if everyone really wants to be different, there is no way to organize them through advertising. Indeed the production process could hardly anticipate their needs. The solution to the problem lay in discovering the specificity of the various distinctions which established the new models of selfhood. These "segmented" types could serve as the basis of counterimages, not so much by showing the similarities between the individuals within each group, but rather by emphasizing the differences between groups.

These new ads presented not the integrated but the alienated individual. To them we owe the "thinking man's filter," brassieres for ladies who like modern art, cars the modesty of which signifies the conspicuous parsimony of their owners, and computers that challenge technocracy's marching minions. Eventually a point was reached where the ad no longer even presented an image, but strove to reflect the superior taste of the individual by making fun of advertising itself.

Consumers' self-consciousness had reached the point where the best advertising complimented them precisely in their freedom from the power of the image and its conformist definitions of individuality. But now there was no escape: conformist and nonconformist alike, the lover of ads and their passionate foe, both became advertising images. Personal freedom and economic necessity achieved an absurd reconciliation.

THE ENEMY WITHIN

This brief sketch of the history of advertising indicates the extent of the instability and contradictions of the early 1960s. The war in Vietnam was the catastrophe that brought the problems into focus. The price of fighting the enemy in Vietnam was too high to permit the simultaneous integration of excluded groups at home. But such groups tended in any case to be seen as and to become surrogate enemies, and the will to integrate them receded before the need for objects on which to discharge aggression. Technocratic liberalism was not able to follow this transition from imperialism to outright racism, and it fell before more conservative political trends. Meanwhile, new opposition movements showed the individuals the way to discharge aggression on its real source, the System.

Social contradictions were now reproduced at a higher level, for the enemy had appeared within the society itself. Intrasocietal struggle was again possible, although no longer on the basis of the class oppositions of competitive capitalism. But once opposition appeared within the system, the ideal of total social integration was shattered. The excitement of the struggle between the various social groups quickly outpaced their desire for peaceful coexistence. Divisive and fragmenting tendencies emerged to overwhelm the liberal vision. By the late 1960s, the system had notably failed to integrate itself in a "Great Society." The war in Vietnam fixed the media images of "underdevelopment" and "individualism" clearly in everyone's minds and made it possible for oppositional groups to move from a vague humanistic protest of the sort exemplified by "beat" poetry and dystopian science fiction to a political movement.

Students and blacks were the first groups to switch and therefore also the first to draw the practical consequences of their own refusal of the illusory resolution of conflicts offered by the system. They began by making new demands and soon confronted forceful repression. The inner limit on freedom—conformism—became an objective external limit, and as such an object of collective struggle.

So long as gestures in this direction were prudent and modest, the possibility of co-optation remained, but as the conservative press and politicians slandered the early reformist opposition, the alienated individuals appropriated the role thrust upon them with ever-increasing enthusiasm. The Left began to imitate the socially prevalent concept of the Enemy, the hated Other in whom all social evils are embodied. In accusing the Left of violence and communism, society marked out the path to a new identity. As the slogan went, "We are the people our parents warned us against."

The motives of opposition were present in everyone, but repressed through the dominant ideology. So long as the enemy was a foreign country, it was treasonous to switch sides. But once enemies appeared *within* the society itself, it became easy unequivocally to assert individuality against the system by joining them. And individuals chose this option in large numbers. By 1970 it was clear that the enemy had come home and that aggression seeking an object had no need to cross the seas to find it. Large-scale opposition and social struggle reappeared within the society in large part on the basis of the new dystopian consciousness.

Technocratic liberalism had asked the individuals to realize themselves through their social roles, through their cooperation, through their similarities. But as aggressive tendencies were reinforced by real imperialist warfare, individuals tended to identify more and more with the violence that enabled them to reconcile themselves with the system. It was in the relation to the enemy that the individuals became truly real for themselves, no longer in cooperation with their fellows. The psychic foundations were laid for an era of social strife. For an increasing number of Americans, the rising aggressivity became a concrete desire for blood and enthusiasm in police brutality, political assassination, and social persecution. In opposition to strident nationalism, more and more Americans sought release from responsibility for their society through performing and suffering violence in radical political struggle. The stage was set for a decade of bloodshed and cruelty.

PART II

Technique and Value

Doctor wearing plague outfit during the Middle Ages. The beak of the mask contains sweet-smelling substances meant to counteract the stench of decaying bodies. Colored engraving, 1725. Courtesy Germanisches Nationalmuseum, Nuremberg (HB 13157).

The Technocracy Thesis Revisited

Adorno, Foucault, Habermas

The difficulty, which Marcuse has only obscured with the
notion of the political content of technical reason, is to
determine in a categorially precise manner the meaning of the
expansion of the rational form of science and technology . . .
to the proportions of a life form, of the "historical totality"
of a lifeworld.

—*Jürgen Habermas 1970: 90*

DIALECTICS OF ENLIGHTENMENT

In Marcuse's work, Critical Theory combined with the dystopian
tradition in an explosive mixture that resonated with the emerging political movements of the 1960s. This was the first and only time that
the Marxism of the Frankfurt School reached a wide public and entered
history as a force. But the Frankfurt School had been moving in this
direction for many years. Long before Marcuse's *One-Dimensional
Man*, Theodor Adorno and Max Horkheimer's classic *Dialectic of Enlightenment* explored the intertwining of the domination of nature,
psychological repression, and social power. Marcuse's theory was fore-
shadowed in their interpretation of the authority system of advanced
society, the technologies that integrate it, and the art forms that resist
its hegemony.

Dialectic of Enlightenment was a profoundly pessimistic book that
offered no strategy for overcoming the evils it denounced. Despite Marcuse's extraordinary efforts to define a radical alternative, his work too
is most persuasive as a fatalistic philosophy of history that shows the
human species enslaved by the very technical apparatus that gave it
mastery of nature. Because the Frankfurt School rejected as metaphysical anything like the Heideggerian appeal to being, the link it forged

75

between scientific-technical progress and progress in social domination appeared indissoluble.

Habermas's revision of the Frankfurt School overcame some of its most serious limitations through the application of communication theory, but lost much of its critical edge. His sober acceptance of the general framework of both academic discourse and the welfare state suited the calm that followed the historical storms of the 1960s and early 1970s. But even in Habermas technology appears as an oppressive force rather than as a medium of human self-expression. As a result, he too ends up pessimistically decrying the rising tide of technocracy without providing a persuasive alternative.

This negative vision is contested by Axel Honneth in *The Critique of Power: Reflective Stages in a Critical Social Theory*. Honneth's discussion culminates a process of self-critique among contemporary social thinkers influenced by the Frankfurt School. In this chapter I will use Honneth as a foil for reviewing this development and extending it in the direction of a communication-theoretic approach to technology.

Although Adorno and Horkheimer thought of themselves as updating Marx's social theory, their emphasis on the critique of instrumental domination completely overshadowed the traditional Marxist problematic. They interpreted class struggle on the model of the conquest of nature as the instrumentalization of a passive human raw material. Lost is what Honneth calls "the social," that is, collective, interhuman struggle over identity, meaning, and value. Not only does this model obscure the sources of resistance, Honneth points out the difficulties it places in the way of understanding structures of domination that are rooted in consensually agreed on norms rather than instrumental control.

The idea that domination is primarily anchored in norms seems paradoxical at first, but it corresponds more closely with the realities of advanced societies than theories of instrumental mass manipulation such as Adorno's and Marcuse's. Indeed, effective manipulation presupposes a cultural context of identities and understandings elaborated by the members of society in the course of their spontaneous interactions. The flaws in that deeper cultural consensus are precisely what exposes the society to manipulation.

But far from recognizing the limitations of his approach, Adorno radicalized them in his later works. He argued that conceptual thought is itself a form of domination; the task of philosophy became the critique of concepts in view of recovering a nondominating relation to nature, which, Adorno believed, was also and indeed primarily the achievement of great art. Critical Theory had come a long way from its Marxist origins.

This distance can also be measured in Adorno's conviction that advanced industrial society is capable of containing all those oppositional forces on which Marxism had traditionally relied. Honneth blames his pessimism on a rather simplistic identification of the sphere of individuation with the traditional competitive market. On this assumption, bureaucratic capitalism and media manipulation signal the disappearance of individuality itself; society appears now as a smoothly oiled machine. But this is far too easy. As Honneth (1991: 80) writes, Adorno "could not perceive the patterns of group-specific value orientations and everyday interpretations that, as horizons of meaning, guide the individual in working through the flood of media information. . . . Therefore, he could not believe that the suggestive influence of the culture industry could find its limits in the fact that the process of cooperative production of group-specific horizons of orientation was itself not subject to manipulation." This interpretation of Horkheimer and Adorno forms the background to the second part of Honneth's book, in which Foucault and Habermas, the two leading contemporary social theorists, are contrasted with the earlier Frankfurt School and each other.

The problem of domination lies at the center of Foucault's later work, but for reasons different from Horkheimer's and Adorno's. Foucault's approach is based on a Nietzschean theory of the social as a network of shifting power struggles out of which temporary equilibria emerge. He does not attribute the alienation of the subject to instrumentality as such, but on the contrary, attempts to show how the subject is first constituted in the course of its instrumentalization as the object of a variety of social practices. Despite this difference in starting point, the end result is similar: a theory of total social integration.

Since Foucault has defined the subject as a derivative result rather than as an irreducible foundation of social life, he must now identify something more basic from which it can be derived. Neither theories of cultural values, nor ideology, nor psychodynamics can help him here since they presuppose the subject rather than explain it. Instead, starting with *Discipline and Punish*, bodily training by disciplinary techniques is shown to integrate society while simultaneously producing the human individual, the subject.

As in the Frankfurt School, science is associated with domination, but for different and more historically precise reasons. Science (at least social science) depends on the availability of institutional techniques of control of the body that expose the individual to representation in a discourse. Once established, science contributes new techniques that intensify that control. Thus here knowledge is related to social domination rather than to the domination of nature.

Honneth argues that Foucault's picture of a society submitted to an ever more effective and totalitarian rationalization process contradicts the Nietzschean strand in his thought. Once individuality is reduced to a reflex of bodily training, no locus of resistance to power supports the idea of social struggle from which he originally set out. The action-theoretic starting point is abandoned in a systems theory that treats power as a functional response to growing population and expanded economic reproduction. This shift takes place tacitly in *Discipline and Punish,* which also blurs the line between total institutions and civil society in such a way as to further obscure the autonomy of the social.

From Adorno's theory of introjected domination we have passed to an equally one-sided view in which social integration is achieved through bodily discipline. The domain of the social is lost in both because neither adequately conceptualizes the normative foundations of social life. Honneth therefore turns to Habermas, whose communication theory promises precisely to explain those foundations.

THE TECHNOCRACY THESIS

Habermas argues that both Marxism and the dialectic of enlightenment systematically reduce communication to technical control. This is the result of generalizing instrumentalization to embrace society as a whole, as do Adorno and Foucault. Instead, Habermas situates the social functions of integration and individualization in an independent communicative sphere.

Communicative understanding involves acceptance of the subjectivity of the other; it is regulated by norms of truthfulness and sincerity which, even though they suffer constant violations in practice, form the horizon of interaction. Communication presupposes not control but agreement, not prediction and mastery but a common world of norms and meanings, an identity. In this conception stable accomplishments rest not on force or manipulation but on shared commitments. Honneth (1991: 243) comments approvingly, "For the first time in the history of Marxism, communicative understanding is treated systematically as the paradigm of the social." But there are unresolved problems here too.

Habermas's theory was originally based on a sharp distinction between symbolic interaction and purposive-rational action. He later reformulated this distinction in terms of two "principals of societal integration": communicative understanding achieved through discussion and success-oriented action in "media" such as money and power (Habermas 1984: 342–343). In each case, the first term involves rational consensus regarding facts and norms, while the second is limited to practical control, power. Habermas thus saves the social by clearly distinguishing its communicative dimension from technique.

Honneth does not so much deny the usefulness of Habermas's distinction as object to the identification of its terms with actual institutions. Then the mutual exclusion of understanding and control tends to be transferred to the institutions with which they are identified. The result is an elaborate account of mere sociological "fictions," purified ideal-types of family and state, public sphere and economy, stripped of the inherent ambiguity of real social life in which understanding and control are inextricably intertwined (Honneth 1991: 298).[1] Honneth blames Habermas's error on his ambivalent critique of the "technocracy thesis," which takes over some of the functions of the dialectic of enlightenment in his thought. This is the belief, widespread at a formative period for the development of Habermas's views, in "an irresistible autonomization of technology and, hence, of a necessary subordination of social evolution to the causal constraints of technical operations" (Honneth 1991: 248).

For Habermas the technocracy thesis is a "false consciousness of a correct praxis" (Honneth 1991: 218). Thus he does not reject the idea of a self-expanding technical sphere (eventually called the System), but argues that it must be theorized in a conceptual framework that also includes a normatively regulated social "lifeworld." Habermas accepts the System's "neutrality," its claim to legitimacy in its own sphere. Accordingly, he "bid[s] a farewell to the notion of alienation" and abandons hope in a fundamental transformation of economy and state (Habermas 1992: 444). He strives instead to maintain the boundaries

1. See McCarthy (1991) for a persuasive statement of this objection. Habermas (1991b: 250ff.) contests this critique in Honneth and Joas.

between spheres not only conceptually but also practically. This boundary work is what Habermasian critique offers in place of traditional radical goals.

In Honneth's view, Habermas's critique concedes too much to technocratic ideology and so ends up in a reified functionalism. Habermas's early theory (developed in *Knowledge and Human Interests*) suggested a different path based not on the institutional correlates of the types of action but on social struggle. In that alternative the distinction between symbolic and purposive-rational action is merely analytic, crosscutting every type of institution whatever its function. The issue is not norms *or* power, but norms *and* power, as mutually complementary "double aspects" shaping every institution (Feenberg 1992: 311). This approach shatters the framework of Habermas's later theory and justifies a partial return to the more radical formulations of earlier Critical Theory.

To be sure, Honneth continues to frame many problems in terms of Habermas's theory of communicative action. For example, he relies on the notion of distorted communication, distorted, that is, with respect to an ideal of uncoerced agreement. But he applies this concept to aspects of modern life that Habermas had regarded as governed in principle by neutral instrumental rules. Honneth thus reinstates social struggle over meaning and value at the heart of the System. The issue now is not merely the System's range of influence, as in Habermas, but its specific normative biases.

Among the consequences of Honneth's new position, two are of particular relevance to the question of technology. First, the social model threatens the neutrality of technology, an essential Habermasian assumption from his early essay "Technology and Science as 'Ideology'" (1970) down to the present. Second, Honneth raises doubts about whether anything like a technocratic evolution is actually taking place. It is not immediately clear how to apply his social approach to the dystopian logic of expanding technical subsystems. But is not technical control an important source of power in modern societies even if Habermas has failed to explain it adequately with the distinction between system and lifeworld?

At this point, two alternatives emerge that are not necessarily mutually exclusive: (1) one might bracket the technocracy thesis and revive a more traditional account of class struggle or substitute a theory of social struggle based on determinations such as ethnicity or gender; or

(2) one might reformulate the idea of technocracy in social terms, showing how the dross of technical control is transmuted into the gold of hegemonic power in the course of social struggle.

This chapter addresses the second alternative. I agree with Habermas that modern societies are dominated by ever more powerful organizations legitimated by their technical effectiveness. But this outcome cannot be understood as the triumph of a disembodied "technical rationality"; rather, it is the way in which specific social groups gain control of society through their leading role in technical organization. The problem is thus to reconstruct the dialectic of enlightenment *inside* a theory of the social instead of substituting the one for the other.

FROM THE SYSTEM TO THE ORGANIZATION

Habermas's notion of "system," derived as it is largely from Niklas Luhmann, is peculiarly reified and depersonalized. As Honneth points out, this notion contradicts the findings of organizational sociology, which highlights the normative understandings that underlie functional groups and enable them to pursue instrumental goals. Neither mere command and obedience nor simple bureaucratic rule following are likely to be effective without background agreements on legitimate purposes, procedures, and human relations. Often informal networks based on these background agreements do the real work, supplementing official organizational forms that have become dysfunctional. Success-oriented action is thus never "differentiated" and "autonomous" to the extent Habermas appears to claim, but is inextricably embedded in a normative lifeworld even in the most thoroughly modernized society.

Habermas's categories are abstractions from this organizational complex. Thus if something like the technocracy thesis is to survive Honneth's critique, the rationalization of society must be treated as an effect of organizational expansion and control rather than vice versa. Honneth argues accordingly that social theory must explain not just the alternatives—technical control or rational consensus—but the intertwining of both in real situations and institutional complexes. "The institutional forms in which social labor or political administration is organized must then be grasped as the embodiments of a moral consensus formation that the social groups, in their interaction, have (as always) attained through compromise. That is, the apparently purposive-rational organizations are also codetermined by moral practical viewpoints that must be conceived as results of communicative action" (Honneth 1991: 274).

This looks like a promising approach, but there are several ambiguities to clear up before it can be applied to a revised account of technocracy. My first question concerns where Honneth intends to locate the normative aspects of organizational life: in extratechnical beliefs, or in the technical sphere as well? In the former case, where, for example, the organization is integrated by bourgeois notions of merit, religious faith, or national loyalties, the result is not technocracy but traditional ideological legitimation. The technocracy thesis requires that bias enter the process of consensus formation at least to a considerable degree through technical aspects of organizational life.

But here another ambiguity arises. A hermeneutic of suspicion would immediately seize on the rhetorical value of terms such as *technical* and *efficient*. Technocracy might lie in ideologically distorted claims and manipulations based on doubtful credentials, jargon and mystification, artifical monopolizing of information, and suchlike. While these are clearly effective strategies in the world we live in, it is hard to see how they add up to a catastrophe on the enormous scale claimed by the technocracy thesis.

No, for that, the "technical" and the "efficient" would *really* have to be biased. Here the "double aspects" reappear in deepest tension: the technical, as it is embodied in particular machines and systems, does not merely apply cognitive-instrumental understandings but is intrinsically normative and distorts the formation of consensus. This view diminishes the difference Habermas tries to maintain between a neutral instrumental sphere responsive to a generic project of control of nature and a communicative sphere distorted by inequality and technocracy. Technology would then have some of the characteristics of ideology, as Marcuse famously claimed. But doesn't this contradict our commonsense belief that some things *really* work and others don't?

Honneth suggests an answer, a technical equivalent of the underdetermination thesis familiar from philosophy of science. "Technical rules incompletely prescribe the respective form of their transposition into concrete actions. Possibilities for action are closed not by a repeated recourse to purposive-rational considerations but only through the additional application of normative or political viewpoints" (Honneth 1991: 254). If this is so, technology is not governed by species interests but is just another social battlefield. Hence one cannot simply hand over decisions about technical matters to experts and their bosses without risking an outcome biased by their self-interested choice between alternatives that are technically equivalent.[2]

With this application of the concept of underdetermination, Honneth opens the way to a *technical turn* which Critical Theory has so far resisted in the wake of disappointment with Marcuse's utopian proposals for a new science and technology. But Honneth does not himself take this turn. While enormously suggestive, his book shies away from technical issues as much as Habermas's communication theory. The reluctance to engage these issues is understandable but, I believe, misplaced. The last decade of research and political action has so undermined confidence in the autonomy of technology as to enable us to reopen the old debate on new terms.

This is what I intend to do in the pages that follow. I will try to explain how technical choices both presuppose normative choices and have normative consequences, how they function within groups, and how iterative group processes can take on qualities of self-expansion partially captured in Habermas's systems-theoretic reprise of the *Dialectic of Enlightenment*.

DELEGATION AND CONSENSUS FORMATION

Control over technique and control over society go hand in hand in the modern world. But that control cannot be identified without further ado with a normatively legitimate authority. The revised technocracy thesis must explain how one gets from one to the other, how the modern power system is legitimated without the traditional reliance on ideologies extrinsic to the technical sphere. This is where our approach must be validated by demonstrating the essential intertwining of understanding and control in the social, that is, more concretely, in an organizational context. We must show how normative consensus emerges not only out of the sort of social struggles Honneth discusses, but also out of the technical roles and tasks of the different groups that coexist in modern organizations.

The question might be phrased as how mechanisms can be normatively compelling as well as technically effective. Bruno Latour's (1992) concept of "delegation" suggests an answer. Latour argues that norms

2. Does this notion of "pure" technique reinstate Habermas's distinctions? Not really, because it refers to an abstract property of technical systems—measurable effectiveness at a task—and not to concrete technical objects, technologies, which possess many other properties.

are routinely embodied in devices that serve to enforce obligations of one sort or another. He offers the humble example of the automatic door closer, which substitutes for the deficient sense of obligation of those who go in and out. The moral imperative "Close the door" is materialized in the mechanism, "delegated" to it in Latour's sense of the term.

What is the evidence that technical devices embody some sort of normative consensus? Are their effects not better explained in purely strategic terms? When we "delegate" the privacy of property to a lock, we substitute a strategic intervention for an ethical appeal. But that is not the whole story. The lock also has a communicative content easily identified by those who see it: the affirmation of ownership, or perhaps of ownership asserted in all its seriousness rather than tacitly presumed. Similarly, the door closer signals the desired state of the door as well as closing it. Strategic interventions important enough to be embodied in techniques do not just change the world, they teach us how the world is supposed to be. In this respect they go beyond mere strategy and participate in the communicative processes by which social consensus is shaped.

The examples I have offered so far may seem trivial, but more serious issues are raised where the definition of social roles is at stake. As Latour (1992: 232) puts it, "I will call . . . the behavior imposed back onto the human by nonhuman delegates *prescription*. Prescription is the moral and ethical dimension of mechanisms. In spite of the constant weeping of moralists, no human is as relentlessly moral as a machine. . . . We have been able to delegate to nonhumans not only force as we have known it for centuries but also values, duties, and ethics. It is because of this morality that we, humans, behave so ethically, no matter how weak and wicked we feel we are." It would be a mistake to dismiss this position as purely verbal. There is a substantive thesis here, namely, the idea that the social bond is mediated by technical objects as well as by intersubjective communication. That mediation supports a *sui generis* form of normativity. In fact, Latour argues, the cohesion of society would be incomprehensible without technical mediations since traditions, laws, and verbal agreements simply could not do the whole job.

Delegation may not exercise the plenipotentiary powers in the moral domain Latour claims for it, but his explanation does suggest an interesting organizational application. The prescriptions contained in devices also define a division of labor with its distinction of white and blue collar, conception and execution, command and obedience. To the extent that a generalized consensus consecrates the roster of roles and especially the desirability of good performance in them, technical choices are normative choices. And, since power and obedience go along with membership, these choices also legitimate the organizational hierarchy. The value attached to the organization's products or activities is transferred downward to legitimate its structure and the individuals' place within it.

Latour's point can be reformulated in terms of Habermas's (1987: 183) version of Parsonian "media theory." Parsons had proposed a rather elaborate scheme in which a variety of nonlinguistic mediations such as prestige regulate different aspects of social life on the model of the market. Habermas strips Parson's original proposal down to two "delinguistified media of action coordination," money and power. These institutions simplify and integrate social life by replacing understandings arrived at through discourse with systematically objectified interactions. If the account offered here is correct, technology would be another such medium.

However, Habermas's media theory has a limitation that becomes obvious in the context of this discussion of technology. He objects to mediation only where it takes the place of communicative action, for example, in politics. This is the famous "colonization thesis," which criticizes the *intrinsically instrumental bias* of media that renders their application inappropriate in domains of social life where noninstrumental values are at stake. But this approach seems to imply that the only thing wrong with media is their application outside their "proper" sphere, and so it provides no basis for criticizing whatever is inside that sphere. At that level, a different discourse is needed which concerns itself with what I will call the *implementation bias* of technology. This bias results from the selection of one among a multiplicity of technically underdetermined designs in accordance with social norms or interests. The assembly line, which is further discussed in the next section, offers a classic example of an implementation bias. The problem with the assembly line is not that it exemplifies an intrinsic instrumental bias, but that its implementation bias is hierarchical.

This distinction makes for a more concrete critique of coordination media than the colonization thesis alone. In the case of markets, for example, one must add to the effects of the intrinsic bias of imposing a system of exchange of equivalents the specific implementation bias introduced by the property system (public or private ownership of capital), the responsibility for externalities, the role of discrimination by age, race, and gender in access to work and credit, and so on. A similar account of power is also needed. In any case, in considering technology, one would have to look beyond the generalized orientation toward success characteristic of all purposive-rational action to take into account the normative implications of specific technical decisions.

With this modification, the media theory begins to bear a certain resemblance to Foucault's genealogy of power and in fact suggests a way of correcting the latter's one-sided emphasis on bodily discipline, which, as Honneth points out, has a suspiciously behaviorist aspect. If the normative function of devices were recognized along the lines sketched above, then one could make better sense of the texts in which Foucault attempts to define his own double-aspect theory of power/knowledge, such as the following description of the Panopticon: "The exercise of power is not added on from the outside, like a rigid, heavy constraint, to the functions it invests, but is so subtly present in them as to increase their efficiency by itself increasing its own points of contact. The panoptic mechanism is not simply a hinge, a point of exchange between a mechanism of power and a function; it is a way of making power relations function in a function, and of making a function function through those power relations" (Foucault 1977: 206–207). What is this subtle presence of power in mechanism if not the shaping and invoking of a special type of nonverbal normative consensus?

To me this seems like a promising, indeed almost an obvious line to take. And yet the word "technology" does not even appear in the index of The Theory of Communicative Action (Habermas 1984, 1987). I suspect there is a deep reason for this reticence. What would happen to the structure of the theory if the most basic form of purposive-rational action were socially relative? Habermas would lose the sharp distinction between communication and technical control that insures the independence of the former and guarantees social theory against regression to a productivist labor myth of the Marxist sort.

Despite these legitimate worries, the price Habermas pays for his methodological caution is too high. We live in a world of ecological crisis, generalized computerization, emerging biotechnologies, new forms of electronic communication and military hardware. If Critical Theory does not address this world and its problems, it will soon become irrelevant. I will therefore continue to test the hypothesis sketched above.

THE TECHNOCRATIC TECHNICAL CODE

The technocracy thesis holds that human beings have become mere cogs in the social machinery, objects of technical control. Habermas's reformulation explains this condition in terms of the substitution of action coordination through objective media for living human communication in the pursuit of consensus. Honneth objects to these formulations on the grounds that the incorporation of human beings into technical systems implies certain normative conditions that are absent where the object of control is a thing. To this I would add further that these normative conditions can be at least partially delegated to technology and that that is what technocracy is all about.

The revised technocracy thesis agrees with Habermas that considerations of efficiency increasingly replace communicative interaction. However, it adds that technical design is not neutral but is normatively biased through delegations that favor the hegemonic interests. These most general delegations form a background of unexamined cultural assumptions literally designed into technology itself. I call these assumptions the "technical code" of the society (Feenberg 1992: 313–315). Under capitalism and its Communist imitators, this code biases technical design toward centralization and hierarchy, systematically diminishing agency and participation, hence also communicative rationality.

The emergence of a technocratic technical code appears most clearly in two types of cases. First, there is the substitution of automation for workers' skills. Deskilling reduces the initiative of workers associated with traditional craft labor in favor of ever more top-down control. While this is not new, its significance has changed with the weakening of traditional ideological justifications of capitalism such as labor and property rights. Today the delegation of human competences to machines not only changes the balance of power between workers and employers, but also changes the very meaning of what it is to *be* a worker. Where formerly the worker was conceived primarily as an individual economic agent, the owner of a commodity—labor power— today's workers are "human resources," integral "component[s] of a mechanical system."[3]

3. The quoted phrase is from Andrew Ure's prophetic *The Philosophy of Manufactures*, published in 1835. Ure (1835: 18) wrote, "By the infirmity of human nature it happens, that the more skillful the workman, the more self-willed and intractable he is apt to become, and, of course, the less fit a component of a mechanical system, in which, by occasional irregularities, he may do great damage to the whole. The grand object therefore of the modern manufacturer is, through the union of capital and science, to reduce the task of his work-people to the exercise of vigilance and dexterity."

Struggles to reverse the tendency toward deskilling and centralization of administration are usually one-sided since management controls the innovation process and selects options adapted to its needs.
Weaker parties usually have no technical alternatives to offer, and so it
appears that management's choices are the "one best way" to higher
productivity. Opposition to deskilling thus appears as opposition to
"rationality," the new dominant ideology.

But sometimes these struggles succeed in significantly modifying the
installation and application of new technologies, dramatizing the normative bias of what are usually taken for straightforward consequences
of progress. In the context of greatly weakened unions, management
itself sometimes chooses to return a certain amount of control to the
shop floor in the hope of solving motivational problems. This too illumi-
nates the arbitrary nature of the so-called "technological imperatives."

Second, organizations responsible for delivering public services restructure them around technical mediations that impose centralization
and control. Modern medicine has emerged transformed from such a
process in recent years. Vast bureaucracies now mobilize the labor of
physicians and through them patients' bodies; these bureaucracies draw
their power not from their role in healing, but from control of buildings, instruments, and financial tools such as accounting systems and
computers.

The redefinition of treatment as a form of technical intervention alters the roles of physicians and patients. The delegation of communicative or "caring" functions to drugs is a particularly significant consequence of these changes. In the past, when physicians could offer no
cure, they were expected to talk patients through their problems, to
help them understand their condition and how to cope with it, and to
assure them that everything possible was being done. Today, physicians in this difficult situation often prefer to give patients a technical
symbol of concern, a marginally effective or even ineffective medica-
tion. As a result, patients are disempowered, left with few resources
for understanding and managing their situation and no basis for further claims on medicine.

Chapter 5 discusses how the incorporation of thousands of incurably ill AIDS patients into this system destabilized and changed it. The
key issue was access to experimental treatment. Clinical research is
one way in which a highly technologized medical system can care for
those it cannot yet cure. But until quite recently access to medical experiments was severely restricted by paternalistic concern for patients'

welfare. AIDS patients were finally able to open up access. At the time their disease was first diagnosed, they belonged to social networks mobilized around gay rights that paralleled the networks of contagion in which they were caught. Instead of participating in medicine individually as objects of a technical practice, they challenged it collectively and turned it to new purposes. Their struggle represents a countertendency to the technocratic organization of medicine, an attempt at a recovery of its symbolic dimension and caring functions.

A common pattern emerges from these examples. Despite occasional resistance, such as that of AIDS patients, the technical mediation of work, medicine, and other social activities creates a society that disqualifies its members from meaningful social and political participation. The division of labor becomes the model for the division of society into rulers and ruled. As in the factory or hospital or school, so in society at large, expertise legitimates power, and "citizenship" consists in the recognition of its claims and conscientious performance in mindless subordinate roles. Habermasian "communicative rationality" is inhibited at the source by these conditions, which are not due merely to "colonization of the lifeworld," but also to normatively biased technical designs parading in the neutral cognitive-instrumental mask Habermas appears uncritically to endorse.

These examples indicate a way of revising the technocracy thesis to take Honneth's objections into account. The very same process that subjects the individuals to a technical apparatus also elicits a tacit normative consensus. In such cases delegation effectively suppresses public discussion. The assembly line not only forces workers to pace their work according to management's will, it also defines good work as keeping up with the pace it sets. A medical diagnosis and prescription not only holds out a certain prospect of healing, it also signifies the meaning of medical care. In such instances, controversies could arise that would be difficult to resolve through discussion: What is good work and who should control it? What claims can the dysfunctional individual make on society? Technocracy is all about the settlement of these controversies through delegation.

ACTION AND CONSENSUS FORMATION

Honneth insists not only on the normative dimension of technical institutions but also on the role of social struggle in the establishment of norms. But how to do justice to social struggle in this context without falling back into discredited approaches such as class essentialism? Honneth (1991: 275) suggests a starting point: "The collective actors that relate communicatively to one another need not be understood as macro-subjects; they can be understood as social groups whose collective identity itself is the fragile and always threatened product of a process of socialization carried out between individuals." The inner life of groups must then be studied as a hermeneutic process in which the articulation of situations, interests, and spontaneous action orientations establishes shared beliefs and projects.

While this is an attractive program, it implies far greater instability than advanced societies actually exhibit. Groups appear "fragile" to Honneth because of the fragility of the mechanism of group formation he identifies: interpretive understanding. As I will show, there are ways of shoring up this mechanism to achieve a more realistic account.

Honneth refers to Lucien Goldmann's genetic structuralism for support. Goldmann's theory derives from the early Marxist Georg Lukács. For both, class formation depends on the articulation of the implicit content of collective action in common understandings ("class consciousness"). Group identification involves generalization from everyday actions in particular local situations to a broader social conception that implies correspondingly broader (class) solidarities and actions. This is a special type of reflexive cognitive procedure which differs from theoretical reflection in that here thought is embedded in action and action is grasped metonymically as displacing a larger framework of social determinations (Feenberg 1988b).⁴ (Phenomenological sociology offers a similar approach.)

Two significant breaks with traditional Marxism are required to apply this reflexive theory of consciousness to the problem of technocracy: first, class actors must be reconceptualized in terms of their roles in the inner life of modern rationalized social organizations such as corporations and state agencies; second, the actions reflected in con-

---

4. The position of Lukács and Goldmann could be interpreted deterministically and teleologically as a theory of a latent macrosubject slumbering unconsciously like a fairy princess awaiting the kiss of Theory to awaken to life. Furthermore, since the class's boundaries and interests are defined by the very theory that claims to be its hermeneutic self-understanding, there is a risk of dogmatism. What, outside the theory itself, guarantees this identification? However, to avoid a crude theoreticist misinterpretation of the reflexive account, it is sufficient to keep in mind the specificity of the learning process in which class consciousness consists, namely, the articulation of originally unclarified local actions. The problems Lukács and Goldmann leave unresolved result not from Stalinist faith in the party, as some critics maintain, but from the failure explicitly to problematize the theoretical constructions that play the articulating role. Bourdieu's (1981) sociology of representation offers a model of a successful approach to this objective.

sciousness must include not only political and union struggles but also the gestures determined by technical choices. Naturally, these are not the only actions of significance in modern societies, but where technocracy threatens, they overwhelm class identity to such an extent that the organization remains the horizon of action, even oppositional action.

Given these assumptions, what are the consequences of adapting the reflexive theory to the case of technically mediated activities? If the self-understanding of groups articulates their actions, we can show the normative role of technique by reversing the terms of delegation theory and introducing it into the account of organizational consensus.

As discussed above, delegations are normatively rich. They define what ought to be in establishing frameworks for action to which all members of the organization are committed by their very belonging. Hence once a device has been successfully installed, the prescriptions it bears can be raised to consciousness as the concrete content of the normative consensus underlying the organization.

The technical code that shapes the design of artifacts is thus simultaneously the basis of a tacit organizational consensus awaiting articulation. Making that consensus explicit in a technocratic group consciousness stabilizes the group by giving it a firm basis for coordinated action. When problems and conflicts arise, management can often defuse them by reference to the technical requirements of the work process. This is one effective strategy for enlisting subordinates into a consensus concerning behavior and goals. The frequent, even predictable success of this strategy is due to its resonating positively with the evident facts of the case. This explains why, instead of the fragile and shifting allegiances Honneth predicts from a purely hermeneutic theory of group formation, relatively stable organizations structure modern societies.

UNDERDETERMINATION AND
OPERATIONAL AUTONOMY

These considerations take us far along the way toward reformulating the technocracy thesis in the social, but not quite all the way because we still need an explanation for the accumulation of technocratic power in a self-expanding rationalization process. This is the sort of problem in social dynamics that is frequently addressed with functionalist or deterministic models. Such models are reassuring: even if we do not like the direction in which the arrow of time is pointed, the process of development is rational, necessary, dictated by system or technological imperatives. Honneth charges Adorno, Foucault, and Habermas with substituting functionalism for an account of the social struggles in which the increasingly uneven distribution of power is actually decided.

I am sympathetic to this critique insofar as it restores the contingency of the social order and therefore also the potential for effective resistance. But Honneth fails to explain the obvious fact that control of technology serves as a power base in advanced societies. I believe this is because he overlooks another type of system effect that is neither functionalist nor deterministic.

Not all long-term cumulative social processes are responses to functional imperatives; some of the most important result from positive feedback cycles. Economic theory is full of examples: the workings of inflationary expectations, the self-fulfilling prophecies of currency markets, the snowballing effects of urban decline, and so on. I will argue here that technocratic power is of the same type, a foundationless, contingent, but nevertheless unidirectional developmental tendency.

The concept of underdetermination is once again useful for my purpose when given a Marxist twist. Marx notes that capitalism liberates the technical selection process from tradition. He shows how the replacement of traditional techniques and division of labor founds a new type of organization—the enterprise—and creates within it a new post in the division of labor—the entrepreneur. This process is the cumulative result of introducing methods and techniques that reinforce capitalists' control over the labor process. The deskilling and mechanization of work consolidates capitalists' power in the new organizations they have created. Rationalization theory and its various descendants— critiques of enlightenment, power-knowledge, technocracy—generalize from this model to explain similar concentrations of power wherever instrumental rationality mediates social activities.

Unfortunately, Marx's ideas about technical progress are vague and subject to contradictory interpretations. If, as is widely assumed, he was a technological determinist, the failure of proletarian revolution would irretrievably refute his theory. But, as we saw in chapter 2, another interpretation of his position is possible. *Capital* contains several passages in which Marx argues that the choice between technical alternatives is made on social rather than technical grounds. For example, he remarks that "it would be possible to write quite a history of inventions, made since 1830, for the sole purpose of supplying capital with weapons against the revolts of the working class" (Marx 1906: I, 476). Here the capitalist is said to aim not only at the accumulation of capital but also at control of enterprise; his technical decisions reinforce his power and maintain his ability to make similar decisions in the future. The implication is that he will introduce no new device, no matter how productive, that diminishes his control. This passage suggests a nonfunctionalist systems theoretic alternative to traditional Marxism. In this interpretation the possession of technical initiative builds on itself just like the possession of capital. Technocracy would not be the effect of "technological imperatives" but of the pursuit of class power under the special circumstances of advanced society.

This approach explains the role of social conflict in the technical sphere. If otherwise comparable technical alternatives have differential effects on the distribution of organizational power, it is not surprising to discover that the choice between them often becomes the object of intense struggle. This has been the case with deskilling and medicine on occasion, as discussed above. Similar conflicts over technical choices appear in education, transportation policy, mass communications, domestic telecommunications, and many other spheres. Here too the extension of organizational control is mediated by technical choices, and sometimes resisted from below. To the extent that our society is in fact technocratic, this is due to the formation of a technocratic consensus through the defeat of these resistances.

I use the term "operational autonomy" to describe the accumulation of power through the iterative selection among viable technical alternatives in view of maximizing technical initiative (Feenberg 1991: 28–29). The preservation and enlargement of operational autonomy lies at the heart of the capitalist technical code. Any society in which technical development is governed by this code will exhibit the chief traits of capitalism regardless of its property system or political arrangements.

This account of technocracy also helps to explain why it is often conceived outside the context of social struggle, as it is in Habermas. The concept of operational autonomy describes both agents and the social structures that empower them. In making technical decisions, capitalists operate relatively autonomously with respect to traditional codes; at the same time these decisions create a centered structure from out of which just such autonomous decisions can be made. When the organization is viewed sociohistorically, the focus is on capitalists' active role in introducing techniques favorable to their own growing technical initiative. But viewed structurally, the capitalists' place in the organization is laid out by the design of the techniques they employ. Which perspective is fundamental?

Since Communist systems are also based on operational autonomy, it has been suggested that a "new class" similar to the bourgeoisie has taken power in them. However, it is even more plausible to abstract altogether from the role of class agents, since their differing ideologies and property rights are irrelevant, and to focus primarily on the structural facts of the case. Technology, it appears, requires hierarchical administration whatever the political system. Here is the origin of many common formulations of the technocracy thesis which end up affirming the supremacy of the structure of instrumental action over the social. What is obscured in all these formulations, of course, is the essential role of agency and norms in any underdetermined system.

Foucault attempted to avoid the dilemma of class agency versus structure by basing everything on the structure of (disciplinary) practices conceived as founding for their agents and objects. For example, a technology such as the Panopticon is explained as a materialization of the practice of observation. Foucault describes the workings of such practices in great detail in modern organizations such as prisons, clinics, schools, and factories, but lacks a similarly concrete account of the dynamics of technocratic power, the "capillary" spread of disciplinary techniques from one institution to another. Honneth understands Foucault to argue that this development is a functional response to population and economic growth, but might it not just as well be due to the self-perpetuating imperative to preserve control and technical initiative? An iterative process of successive rationalizations would then explain the rather mysterious "subjectless" evolution of modern society in Foucault.

CONCLUSION: THE TECHNOCRACY THESIS REVISITED

Three aspects of a revised technocracy thesis emerge from this discussion: (1) the distortion of the process of organizational consensus formation by "delegating" normative understandings to devices, (2) the role of the articulation of action in that process, and (3) the role of operational autonomy in the accumulation of technocratic power.

Technocracy results from the systematic, long-term selection of those technical alternatives that favor hierarchical control. Devices that can be purchased and introduced at strategic times and places can also be used to transform the normative structure of organizations through technical delegations that embody a new normative consensus in the apparently unchallengable medium of technical advance.

The technocracy thesis can now be reformulated as the ever-widening use of technical delegations to consolidate and legitimate an expanding system of hierarchical control. The more pervasive large-scale organizations become, the more significant the operational autonomy associated with them. What were formerly rather specialized internal functions of institutions such as workplaces or prisons become general features of social life. Organizations are encountered at every turn busily seeking to resolve normative disputes through technical delegations that reinforce their power and legitimacy. To the extent that such organizations proliferate and grow, the technocracy thesis gains plausibility, justifying the dystopian projections of the dialectic of enlightenment.

The extrapolation of such a system into the future paints a gloomy picture indeed. Yet this is not quite the picture found in Adorno or Marcuse of a "one-dimensional" society lacking a space for social conflict. Operational autonomy is the result of practices that can be contested through the emergence of new groups and challenges. Delegations can be problematized, although with difficulty, as we have seen in a variety of struggles over work organization, medical policy, and the environment in recent years. Debate in the new *technical public sphere* brings the normative content of technical decisions to the surface far more frequently and systematically than in the past. Although the expanding technocracy is a real threat, it is not an irresistible force. An account of it needs to be incorporated into a contemporary "critique of power."

On Being a Human Subject

AIDS and the Crisis of Experimental Medicine

There is no ground for ontologically opposing the organic,
the technical, and the textual.
    —*Donna Haraway 1991: 212*

CYBORG MEDICINE

Social norms and technology belong to different realms in the world
of everyday common sense, meeting only when the goals of a technical
intervention are set. Goals thus resemble the Cartesian pineal gland
that allowed mind and body to enter into an impossible but necessary
communication. Value and nature are joined externally in the techno-
logic of efficiency.

In this framework, medicine combines objective knowledge of the
body, understood scientifically as an elaborate biological machine, and
the subjective value invested in health. Objectivity and subjectivity confront each other across the institutional gap that divides practitioners
from patients, and medicine is a compound of the two with carefully
prescribed roles for each. Medical *authority* derives from mastery of
technical knowledge, while patients have *rights* reflected in physicians'
professional obligations. But of course these rights do not extend to
interference with medicine's technical side, any more than physicians'
authority cancels the social norms under which medicine is practiced.

Or so it is widely believed, especially by physicians. But there is reason to doubt the accuracy of this simple picture of the healing arts.
Recent struggles by AIDS patients attempting to influence the organization of research and treatment have challenged it more openly and
effectively than any earlier patient protest. These struggles demonstrate
practically that medicine incorporates norms in its technical structure,

in the design of tools and procedures. And from these struggles one also learns that patients' understanding of healing, and of the obligations and rights it prescribes, is itself relative to the state of technique in a variety of ways.

The idea that the body is a machine is a model, not a reality, and like all such models it has its uses but also its limits. An endless stream of studies shows the role of depression in health, of authoritative communication and explanation in the control of pain, of social support in survival after cancer, of superstition in excess mortality, and so on. Here the supposedly distinct realms of objectivity and subjectivity are fused in unexpected combinations that defy common sense. Now, it is possible to explain such cases as exceptions and to dismiss the boundary problems they raise as trivial. On the other hand, the growing visibility of these "exceptions" suggests a more radical critique of the whole framework within which they appear as such. That framework is a certain conception of the human body.

The body is the site of medical knowledge and action. It enters medicine as both object and subject insofar as it is both the thing on which medical technique operates and the bearer of the person who commands medical services. This coincidence of two bodies in one person is normalized by reference to the distinction between nature and culture. As object, the body is a mechanism, just as René Descartes defined it centuries ago. As subject, the body is a moral-legal entity that makes claims in discourse. The two bodies are distinct, like the two bodies of the king in medieval political theology, one natural, the other spiritual. Psychology, which is supposed to account for the anomolous impact of subjective experience on health, hovers uncertainly between them.

But the artificiality of the two-body conception is already apparent from these historical references. Descartes' notion of the body arose with the new mechanical worldview, a vision of nature transparently related to the social changes that accompany early capitalist development. Supposedly nonsocial mechanism is thus as social as the machines that supply its model of the universe. Similarly, the humanistic definition of the legal-moral subject is indebted to a theological concept of the soul in which it is increasingly difficult to believe. Attempts such as Habermas's to save the substance of this view through defining a transcendental basis for values have not on the whole carried conviction.

Once the soul dissolves in the acid of modernity, the two bodies collapse back into one. Mechanism has recently made a comeback on this basis as neurobiological speculation. Consciousness can be reduced to the brain *in principle,* without remainder, but unfortunately this is an empty boast from a medical standpoint, as current neuroscience can scarcely begin to understand the manifold involvements of what we are still obliged to call the "mind" in health and sickness.

Meanwhile, postmodern arguments against the universality and objectivity of science inspire an organicist discourse of the embodied self. Skepticism about science leads to a fideism of immediate experience, much as doctrinal skepticism once justified Protestant faith in the inner light. Instead of addressing the claims of the person indirectly, through objectifying the body, medicine is now supposed to treat the person directly, to participate in the immediately given world of the self. While this view at least recalls medicine to the realities of patients' experience, it cannot explain the obvious effectiveness of scientific treatment. Thus neither of these approaches is satisfactory and we are forced to look elsewhere for a solution.

Perhaps what is needed is neither a monistic reductionism nor a dualistic doctrine of separate spheres. Both views hypostatize the objects of the incommensurable discourses in which medical knowledge and experience are expressed and then attempt to reconcile those discourses in one way or another. Instead, we need to reverse the perspective in which medicine is seen as compounded of two separate types of objects—science and society, body and norms—and reconceptualize those dimensions as products of a system of practices I will call "cyborg medicine" following Donna Haraway's suggestive metaphor. For Haraway, the cyborg is a useful symbol because it joins soul and machine in a social, and hence promiscuous, combination without the convenient mediation of a naturalizing psychology or a transcendental constructivism, two versions of the Cartesian pineal gland, joining mind to body, that we must now learn to live without.

In cyborg medicine, nature and culture no longer function as primitive terms. Nature is already social, both in the metaphors and models that define it in scientific discourse and in the practices and procedures by which knowledge of it is constructed. The special epistemological privilege accorded the objective medical body, as mechanical nature, is withdrawn. But at the same time, Haraway also rejects the humanistic ideology of the moral-legal person transcending empirical conditions or, in romantic formulations, rooted in an ideal of lived nature. The self too is constructed socially, and so cannot judge science and technique from a nonalienated beyond. The solution is neither naive faith in the objectivity of science nor return to a natural unity prior to culture.

To emphasize the practical production of body and mind, Haraway describes the objects of science and lived experiences as texts rather than as substantial things. The textualization of nature brings it into closer proximity to culture, indeed, makes of it a kind of culture called "nature." At the same time, Haraway is careful not to *reduce* nature to a free self-expression of human actors. That postmodern move risks obscuring the conditions of our own finitude, our continuing incapacity to incorporate the world around us into our projects, the unexpected "tricks" it plays on us, and the ways in which our understandings of it both illuminate and obscure the context of our lives and actions.

How then can we reconceptualize the unity of a body on which two very different kinds of writing are inscribed? How does scientific writing coexist with the writing in which identity consists? What translations between the two are defining for medicine? These are the new questions suggested by Haraway's reflections. In what follows I will argue for the central importance of ethics in answering them.

The cyborg image is ambivalent and indicates two evolutionary possibilities of advanced societies: either the total incorporation of all aspects of subject and object into textual technologies of control such as genetic engineering and computerized automation, or the "friendly" coexistence of technology and body in a prosthetic prolongation of developing human capacities (Haraway 1991: 178). "The machine is not an *it* to be animated, worshipped, and dominated. The machine is us, our processes, an aspect of our embodiment. We can be responsible for machines; *they* do not dominate or threaten us" (Haraway 1991: 180).

This ambivalence is apparent in medicine, where it determines different images of the physician-patient relationship. Where the patient is simply the bearer of a mechanical body, medicine applies its techniques to passive objects. Where, on the contrary, patients succeed in encompassing medicine's bodily text within strategies of identity, a very different picture emerges in which medical technique mediates a collective subject of knowledge and healing that includes physicians, scientists, patients, and others involved in research and treatment.

Medical research is a privileged site for studying this ambivalence. In research it is difficult to maintain the sharp separations that comfort common sense. Science is obliged, as always, to follow the mechanistic paths that have been opened to it by its tradition. Yet at the same time, human subjects have recently begun to subvert the mechanistic view by dramatizing the medical implications of their own concrete experience of research. The paradox issues in ethical demands for innovations in research design which patients, especially those with AIDS, have attempted to reconcile with the requirements of scientific objectivity. The result is a remarkable breakdown of accepted institutional roles (Epstein 1991; Treichler 1991). In this chapter I will explore this fruitful starting point for a theory of cyborg medicine as a collaborative healing practice.

CARING AND CURING

The nature and function of medicine has gradually shifted over the past century. What was once a largely communicative activity aimed at *caring* for the sick has become a technical enterprise able to *cure* them with increasing success. While few would want to renounce these technical advances and go back to the past, medicine's traditional caring functions have been eclipsed by the new dispensation, and it is criticized now for losing the human touch that made it so helpful to patients even before it knew how to cure them.

The issue looks simple: human communication versus technique, Habermasian lifeworld versus system. We seem to be back in the dystopian framework, and indeed there is something dystopian about a certain vision of medicine as a purely technical activity in which patients are little more than specimens.

But there is nothing simple about medicine. As noted above, research on medical practice shows that patients' physical condition is often affected by the quality of the medical communication that contextualizes treatment. Even such elementary forms of care as explaining the likely effects of a procedure can have an impact on outcomes. What is more, techniques such as surgery or prescription drugs are themselves symbols of care, not just more or less effective cures, and so the style of technical intervention matters to patients in a way physicians do not always suspect. Paradoxically, medicine as a purely technical activity is *already* a form of communication, and communication has what would normally be considered technical effects.

These complexities usually lie safely in the background, where they are only dimly perceived by the doctor and patient, but in certain cases it is impossible to ignore them. These are difficult cases where medicine still does not have effective cures, and where, therefore, the need for old-style care is particularly strong. Here the inextricable intertwining of body and mind, technique and norms, in modern medicine raises ethical issues to a new prominence.

Physicians cannot simply shrug their shoulders when confronted with patients whose condition is difficult to understand. Instead, they must enlist the patients' cooperation in elucidating obscure symptoms, undergoing tests or procedures, trying a variety of treatments, perhaps even including experimental treatments, and so on. To give up is to fail the patient, to press forward to expose an already sick person to expense and risk. A whole vocabulary of rights and duties arises around the mutual obligations of physicians and patients in this situation.

This context resonates with Haraway's (1991: 199) demand for "the 'activation' of the previously passive categories of objects of knowledge." In medicine, of course, those objects include ourselves, and the pursuit of knowledge and healing in the clinical setting is therefore as much a normatively regulated communication in which we are involved as it is a technical enterprise. Ethics and, as we will see, even politics are thus constitutive of medical knowledge from the very beginning, and are not humanistic afterthoughts. "Accounts of a 'real' world do not, then, depend on a logic of 'discovery,' but on a power-charged social relation of 'conversation'" (Haraway 1991: 198). That conversation must be carried on at the intersection of ethics and technique.

Medicine's difficult cases have acquired a new and disturbing visibility in recent years with the urgent demands of AIDS patients for participation in medical experimentation. AIDS has only dramatized a longstanding conflict between incurably ill patients and physicians. These patients often wish to participate in clinical research, yet opportunities to do so are scarce. As the *Report of the National Commission on Orphan Diseases* (1989: xiii) concluded, "A majority of patients and families are willing to use investigational drugs but find it difficult to locate information on research projects in which they could participate." As a result, they feel driven to unsupervised self-experimentation and often enroll in unconventional treatment programs. In their eyes *experimentation is a legitimate form of care* for incurable disease even though they know that the prospects of success are quite poor, a form of care from which they feel arbitrarily excluded by the medical community and the Food and Drug Administration (FDA). Until recently, most physicians and ethicists dismissed this view of experimentation as irrational, a consequence of false hope. But AIDS patients have nevertheless significantly weakened the regulation of research on human subjects.

In what follows, I attempt to justify this trend in terms of the concept of "participant interests" in clinical research, which I distinguish from the rights of human subjects. But before turning to these matters, I would like briefly to survey the evolution of regulatory politics in the domain of clinical research. It was only in the context of that evolution that the recognition of participant interests finally dawned.

THE REVOLT AGAINST ETHICAL REGULATION

Ethical regulation of human experimentation is supposed to prevent drug company profiteering and to protect patients from researchers more concerned with science than humanity. Codes of ethics are designed to guarantee the patient's right to refuse to lend his or her body for use by others, the right to information about risks, the right to withdraw at any time, the right to treatment for complications arising out of experimental participation, and so on.

In 1966 the FDA issued strict regulations on human research, and since then the ethical climate has in fact changed for the better (Curran 1969). These regulations were designed to achieve both ethical goals and consumer protection, the first by codifying the rights of human subjects and the second by preventing the sale of drugs lacking scientific proof of safety and effectiveness.

The negative emphasis on rights is understandable given the origins of our current ideas about legitimate clinical research in the post–World War II revulsion against the abuse of patients and prisoners. In that context, experimental participation appears primarily as a sacrifice of the individual to society. Patients' desire to enlist is therefore prima facie evidence of a misconception on their part. After all, it is frequently said or implied, only desperation can explain why a sick person would want to join a scientific experiment he or she cannot understand and which probably will not work anyway (Ingelfinger 1972: 466; Mackillop and Johnston 1986: 182–183). Hans Jonas (1969: 239) writes that "everything connected with his condition and situation makes the sick person inherently less of a sovereign person than the healthy one. Spontaneity of self-offering has almost to be ruled out; consent is marred by lower resistance or captive circumstance."

Yet in recent years, these "desperate" patients have provoked a crisis of experimental medicine that promises to change it as radically as did the earlier reaction in favor of ethical procedures. The AIDS patients who are bringing this about entered the medical arena at the height of a major political organizing drive in the gay community that equipped them fortuitously to resist paternalism better than any previous group of patients. Energies mobilized around social and political rights during the preceding decade were turned on the medical system, and networks of patient education and support arose on a scale never before seen in connection with any other disease. They quickly won expanded access to experimental drugs and weakened the shield of protections enforced by the FDA and other medical institutions with such pride until quite recently.

The collapse of barriers to the use of unproven drugs occurred gradually under intense political pressure from 1987 to 1989. At first the FDA proposed accelerated administrative reviews of AIDS drugs (the "1AA review process") and an expanded program of "compassionate investigational new drug exemptions," or "treatment INDs," to make it possible to sell as-yet-untested drugs to dying victims of AIDS. The FDA also announced publicly the legality of importing unapproved drugs for personal use.

Although the new regulations were not in fact very effective in opening access to new drugs, they did tend to shift the burden of proof from drug manufacturers to the FDA, a change noted with concern by Senator Edward Kennedy (Marwick 1987: 3020). Kennedy was not wrong about the implications of the new policy. In June of 1989 the agency caved in completely and, in conjunction with the National Institute of Allergy and Infectious Diseases, instituted a new "parallel track" drug testing system. Under this system, physicians were authorized to prescribe unproven drugs that had passed toxicity tests just as they would a licensed drug, even before the results of regular controlled studies were in. "'It's a great step forward," said Dr. Mathilde Krim of the American Foundation for AIDS Research. "It represents a new consensus on how to handle drug development for AIDS and life threatening diseases in general"' (Kolata 1989: B5).

These measures contributed significantly to resolving the political crisis over AIDS drug testing, but Dr. Krim was unrealistic to invoke a new consensus. Many researchers are concerned about the harm the rules may do both to patients and to the scientific evaluation of new drugs (Marwick 1987: 3020; Reidenberg 1987: 599–560). They ask: How can patients be recruited to studies with placebo controls when they can obtain the very same experimental drug directly through their physicians (Goyan 1988: 3052–3053)? How can drugs be compared when patients can obtain and use all of them at the same time? And how can the results of the rather informal parallel track be rigorously assessed?

These questions are still unanswerable today, but the new rules are probably less to blame than they appear to be. In fact, controlled trials were already breaking down before the rules were changed (Barinaga 1988: 485). Unruly actors, AIDS patients and their community organizers opened all sorts of illicit channels to promising drugs. In the long run, that trend would have had the same consequences as the liberalized rules. The problem is thus not really a regulatory one but is due to a shift in the public perception of the balance between the scientific and the caring functions of clinical research, and correspondingly, between the passive and active roles of patients and physicians.

That shift will force the research community to rethink the relation of research and treatment. Up till now, researchers have been able to rely on the absence of alternatives to recruit incurably ill patients to controlled trials. These most rigorous trials may be used less frequently in the future, and more reliance may be placed on clinical experience and historical controls. But for certain purposes it will always be necessary to have the cooperation of patients who agree to be controls and to take only the medications approved by the clinician.

If experimental drugs are available outside the research framework, new ways must be found of recruiting participants to controlled trials. Two alternatives beckon: exporting research to poor countries where Western ethical restrictions can be evaded, or establishing a new framework for patient education and treatment within which recruiting for controlled trials can compete with the parallel track. The latter option is obviously preferable, but it can succeed only where medicine recovers some of its traditional responsibilities toward patients with incurable diseases.

Medicine has been forced by the AIDS crisis to recognize the desire for experimental participation as an interest of patients which can no longer be paternalistically dismissed. Science will have to find new ways to adjust to the problems posed by this moral advance, just as it adjusted to earlier limitations placed on research out of concern for patients' rights. Then and only then will a new consensus truly emerge.

PARTICIPANT INTERESTS

The intrusion of politics into medical policy provokes very different reactions. Those who continue to dismiss patients' demands condemn their political successes as demagogic intrusions into "science," identified with the established code of experimental medicine. The already social nature of that code is simply ignored. This way of responding to new demands is unfortunately typical. On the other hand, some argue for rejecting professionalism altogether in favor of the absolute right of medical "consumers" to select whatever treatment they desire (Illich 1976: 252–253). If this were the only alternative to the present system, the case for reform would indeed be weak, given the very real differential between the knowledge of physicians and patients.

But there is another possibility: to preserve professionalism while changing its technical codes to enhance knowledge sharing and patient initiative (Ladd 1980: 1128). As Paula Treichler (1991: 69–70) writes, "The strongest challenge to current conditions comes not from those who dismiss or denounce technology, but from those who seek to seize it for progressive political purposes and for the deployment of science and scientific theory in everyday life."

This is by no means a utopian project. There are many examples of medical practice changing for the better under public pressure. Sometimes new norms reflect patient demands in defiance of the division of roles supposedly constitutive of medicine as a technical field. In recent years obstetrics and gynecology have accepted childbirth training, the presence of spouses or coaches in labor rooms, and breast feeding, all under pressure from social movements of women. In these cases the technical code was modified to take into account the new demands, and now it hardly occurs to medical personnel to go back to earlier practices that used to seem so rigorous and scientific. After changes such as these enter official practice, their popular origin is lost and the illusion of technical autonomy is restored. The arduous work of establishing new norms is forgotten once they have been effectively incorporated into a technical code.

I will argue that the existing regulatory framework and technical code ignore important benefits to patients of experimental participation. It is this oversight that is responsible for the current challenge to professionalism. I will call the specifically health-related incentives for patients to accept the role of human subject "intrinsic" or "participant" interests.[1]

---

1. Medical ethics would classify these overlooked effects as incentives to participate in research. The literature generally treats incentives with great caution because of the difficulty of distinguishing between positive benefits and subtle forms of coercion (Freedman 1975). In fact, I do not believe these concerns to be relevant, but they must be mentioned because it is sometimes claimed that the hope of cure is a "reward" sought by the sick on the same order as payment by a volunteer. This identification is confusing. To treat cure as a mere extrinsic reward overlooks the tragic dimension of the patient's

As we have seen, achieving recognition of these interests is in part a political process. We take it for granted that all interests are represented to some degree in the public debates that determine social policy and law in a democratic society. But in fact the demands of social groups are not automatically credited as "interests," but become so only through an authorized interpretation of some sort. In the case of clinical research, the wishes of millions of citizens were systematically dismissed for lack of such an interpretation. These citizens were not so much judged to be wrong as incompetent.

In technical fields such as medicine, client interests must be embodied in a technical code to carry any weight. That code translates between the two discourses of the cyborg body and represents the moral-legal person to science. Ethics is thus central to medicine, not simply insofar as it posits goals or controls abuses, but more fundamentally, in the way it shapes devices and systems to adapt them to a specific conception of its mission. Delegation of norms, in Latour's sense, is thus at the heart of medical technology.

What I am proposing, therefore, is a new *sociotechnical* interpretation of medical ethics. Like other branches of professional ethics, medical ethics is usually formulated to offer rules for deciding individual cases. Ethical questions are treated against an unexamined background consensus concerning procedures, physician-patient relations, and other institutional aspects of medicine (Löwy 1987: 597–601). As a result, the discussion is artificially confined to what can be done within an institutional context unconsciously identified with the scientific basis of medicine and thereby sheltered from critique and discussion. But I will argue that what appears most "scientific" about medicine is often better understood as a technical mediation of a social interest. As such, it is penetrated through and through by normative considerations. Bringing out that normative dimension of medicine dispels the illusion of technical necessity that forms the background to individualistic approaches.

Socially considered, ethics appears as a sort of switching post between social demands and technical interventions. For such demands to be taken up by the medical profession they must be translated into the legitimating discourse of medicine; once that happens they tend

---

dilemma in accepting the risks of experimental participation, reduces a moral sacrifice to a mere market relationship, and makes a fool of the patient who dies despite joining a research program.

to be institutionalized. New patient rights become standard protocols as medicine internalizes the social constraints under which it operates. Only a dereifying analysis of medical institutions can reverse the flow and expose the hidden connections between the technical code of medicine and the history of needs it represents.[2]

Until recently the technical code of clinical research recognized no interest of patients in participation. On the contrary, patients' desire to participate was delegitimized by emphasizing such incapacitating factors as ignorance and irrational hopes. The result of this negative judgment was not left to chance but was embodied in a technical code that sharply distinguishes an "experiment" from "treatment" both to protect patients from false claims and to justify procedures that have no therapeutic function, such as the use of placebos. To assert their interests in this situation, patients had to mobilize politically to reclaim hermeneutic authority and to impose changes in the code that governs research.

In the next section I will attempt to establish the existence of such interests *from the standpoint of medicine*, that is to say, in terms of arguments that are internal to the system of medical knowledge. I will rely on the existing medical literature to show that certain classes of patients have a legitimate interest in experimental participation. Although political pressures can manifest new needs, these needs must be rearticulated by such arguments to bring about change in the technical code. Short of some such demonstration, the mere fact that lay people protest is not very interesting; the case does not go beyond politics to effect the self-understanding of the profession. Obviously, under sufficient pressure medicine might make many "unmedical" concessions to popular demands; the point here is to show that some of these concessions sketch the outlines of an institutional alternative.

I hope in this way to provide an example of the close communication between ethics and technique that belies their apparent separateness. If I am successful, this example will confirm the claims made in

2. It is of course commonplace now, on a certain Left at least, to dismiss ethics as an irredeemably individualistic enterprise. This stance finds its relative justification in the often overblown claims for pure, ahistorical rationality in the Habermasian and Rawlsian schools. Nevertheless, a place must be made for ethics in any theory of the professions, medicine in particular. Even where the origins of a medical problem are clearly social, no one wants to visit a doctor more dedicated to social change than to patient welfare. Of course, where commitment to patients is lacking it is usually for less creditable motives, but this is a reason to restructure the profession to ensure that standard procedures embody ethical values, not to reject ethics itself as irrelevant.

the first chapters of this book for the possibility of democratic intervention into technology. Indeed, we are dealing here with a particularly well-guarded technical fiefdom where such intervention seems most implausible. And yet I will show that not only do lay people make innovative claims on medicine, but those claims can be justified medically and incorporated eventually into the practice of medicine.

In what follows, I discuss three bodies of research that are especially helpful for understanding participant interests. These concern (1) the "placebo effect" as an instance of the nonspecific healing power of medical care; (2) the "sick role" in its connection with problems of chronic illness; and (3) the ethical significance of collaboration between researchers and subjects.

Participant interests arise naturally in the experimental context and include not only the hope of cure but also access to physicians, test results, advice, and patient education. The importance of these concerns to volunteers is widely recognized although insufficiently studied. Barrie R. Cassileth found that over half of his respondents gave the desire for the best medical care as their main reason for willingness to participate in research (Cassileth et al. 1982: 968–970). In justifying the parallel track, Dr. Anthony Fauci of the National Institute of Allergy and Infectious Diseases said that "many people join clinical trials for altruistic reasons and also to obtain the medical care that goes with participation—even knowing they may not receive the experimental drug" (Kolata 1989: B5). In the next section, I will offer a fuller account of these surprising explanations for patients' desire to participate in research.

Recognizing participant interests would not tell against moral restraint in recruiting poorly informed or incompetent individuals as subjects, nor would it detract from the principal purpose of experimentation, which must be the acquisition of new knowledge. However, even within these limits, participant interests could be better served by increasing opportunities to participate.

Until recently, the supply of places was regulated entirely by scientific considerations without regard for the number of patients wishing to participate. Many physicians and ethicists considered the scarcity of places to be a blessing in disguise since it protected masses of presumably self-deluding patients. This attitude has now proven untenable; the statistical minimums required to determine safety and effectiveness no longer regulate the number of places, but rather places are multiplied in response to patients' demands.

This point has been made effectively in the political arena, but there remains a subtler implication of the new respect for patients that is not yet sufficiently appreciated. Certain experimental designs further participant interests, while others frustrate them, independent of the scientific validity of the alternatives. Thus one AIDS activist rejects "perspectives [on design] categorically deemphasizing the needs and rights of patients in favor of the primacy of data collection" (Smith 1989: 1547; see also Epstein 1991: 56–57). The *National AIDS Treatment Research Agenda* (1989) prepared by ACT UP (AIDS Coalition to Unleash Power) summarizes a host of detailed suggestions for humanizing experimental treatment. In response to such concerns, some medical commentators have come to believe that "we need to consider alternative study designs that allow the patient maximum hope for cure and the opportunity for some control over his or her destiny" (Goyan 1988: 3053).

In sum, medicine has an *obligation* not simply to obtain informed consent and to avoid harm so far as possible, but to design experiments that serve patients while simultaneously serving science. The case recalls Honneth's discussion of the underdetermination of organizational life, the patterns of which are not unambiguously defined by technical rules but depend also on appeals to norms. Here too we have a scientifically underdetermined range of options among which ethical considerations must finally choose.

The social consequences of this underdetermination are also of interest: the same technical "moves" satisfy multiple social demands. In the right technical context, those demands are no longer mutually exclusive and need not be traded off against each other. The point is not the old idea that technology overcomes social conflict through an ever-expanding supply of consumer goods; rather, technology itself is a potentially pluralistic social mediation. I will return to this idea in chapter 9 in relation to the game of Go. There I will show how tradition and modernity coexist in the apparently value-neutral moves of a game. Here the issue is similar: research and treatment must coexist as double aspects of the practice of medical experimentation.

THE SOCIOTECHNICAL ETHICS OF MEDICAL EXPERIMENTATION

Once participation in research is recognized as a legitimate form of treatment, many more patients are likely to become involved. It is necessary to rethink the whole structure of their care. The fact is that medical institutions rarely accept the heavy responsibility for patient education that could alone give meaning to informed consent. This flaw, which has been tolerated for so long, risks becoming a source of egregious abuse as access to clinical research broadens to include millions of incurably sick individuals. That abuse, in turn, could justify rearguard struggles to reestablish restrictions on opportunities to participate, or it could inspire reforms in the practice of experimental medicine. The choice will depend on the extent to which participant interests are recognized by medical institutions.

EXPERIMENTAL TREATMENT AS A FORM OF CARE

Participant interests can only be legitimated within the professional framework if clinical research can be shown to confer a properly medical benefit on subjects. Then the appropriate means of delivering that benefit can be inscribed in the technical code of research. The hope of cure is not enough because it is usually disappointed. There is simply no way to know if the small chance of success outweighs the risks of participation. Even in the case of dying patients, where risk is of less concern, cure is such an improbable result of research that it is dishonest to hold up tantalizing promises (Glaser and Strauss 1972: 1098–1100). Thus while an argument can be made for the generally beneficial character of hope, from a medical standpoint that argument alone cannot justify the current loosening of regulation.

Where the focus is on hope, there is a serious conflict between patients' desires and their interests as physicians interpret them. This conflict can only be resolved by discovering benefits of participation that are independent of cure. In fact a voluminous literature shows that patients place at least as great store on the "caring" functions of medicine as on actual healing (Powles 1973: 16–24). R. H. Fletcher and his collaborators found, for example, that what patients most valued in their doctor was compassion and availability rather than technical achievements (Fletcher et al. 1983).

Studies of homeopathic and chiropractic medicine indicate that many patients, especially those with chronic illnesses, seek alternative therapy because they miss these caring benefits in the conventional setting (Avina and Schneiderman 1978; Kane et al. 1974). Since medical culture marginalizes the chronically ill, it is not surprising to find widespread dissatisfaction in this group (Kutner 1978). Negative attitudes are sometimes signaled quite crudely to the patients themselves, as in the case of one multiple sclerosis patient whose doctor reportedly said, "You have multiple sclerosis; don't worry; get a book from the library and read about it; if you have any questions, call me" (Hartings et al. 1976: 68).

The emphasis on caring does not necessarily imply a rejection of medical technology. Compassion is often expressed through the administration of drugs or procedures even when they are known to be of little value. John Powles (1973: 20) writes that "the almost exclusive concentration, within modern medical culture, on the technical mastery of disease is more apparent than real. For in addition to countering the challenges to human well-being on the biological level, this technology is serving also to meet the emotional and existential challenges that disease involves."

If participation in research were seen as an effective mode of caring rather than as a defective mode of curing, it could be more easily justified. Participation in clinical trials would then come to possess somewhat the same significance for physicians and patients as the commonplace prescription of symbolically charged but marginally effective drugs. Although the game must be played more honestly in the case of research, clinical trials may be another way in which a highly technologized medical system can offer care to the incurable.

The so-called placebo effect is at work here, and it is clearly the only *predictable* benefit of experimental participation. Now, if the placebo effect were recognized as a normal dimension of medical care, then experimental participation would fall into place as a form of treatment most particularly suited to patients with incurable diseases. Unfortunately, the very term "placebo" connotes deception; we seem to have fallen back into the dilemma of false hopes versus medical responsibilities.

But something very much like the placebo effect occurs constantly in medical practice without the deceptive administration of sugar pills or other fraudulent substitutes for "real" medicine. The simple fact of getting a diagnosis often provides significant relief from pain and other symptoms. Many of medicine's benefits are due not to technical effectiveness but to what anthropologists call "symbolic effectiveness," and this in fact explains most of its value in premodern societies (Lévi-Strauss 1968: 198). The intertwining of mind and body this situation implies has given rise to all sorts of speculations on the neurologic basis of immune response and suchlike. However, for physicians and patients the problem is not scientific but is posed in individual terms, and the solution must lie in respect for patients' needs as an ultimate indicator of as-yet-uncomprehended natural processes.

In view of the widespread role of placebos in ordinary medical practice, Arthur Shapiro and Louis Morris (1978: 371) propose the following rather loose definition: "Any therapy or component of therapy that is deliberately used for its nonspecific, psychological, or psychophysiological effect, or that is used for its presumed specific effect, but is without specific activity for the condition being treated." This definition suits a wide variety of medical interactions that benefit patients through mechanisms that are still unclear (Brody 1980: 8–24).

Howard Brody (1980: 110) argues that since deception is not actually required to achieve the placebo effect, patients should not be deceived to obtain its benefits. Thus even if the placebo effect is all patients are likely to get out of participation in clinical research, that would not justify lying to them about the likelihood of success or enlisting them in incompetent or purely symbolic experiments "for their own good." The demand inscribed in all codes of experimental medicine—that patients be honestly informed and research scientifically sound—stands as before, although this approach recognizes that the research will and indeed ought to have a very different significance for scientists and patients.

Herbert M. Adler and V. B. O. Hammett's account of the placebo effect suggests an approach to the design of more therapeutically effective participation in research. They focus on the therapeutic power of meaning. By this they mean that making sense of one's illness is a condition of well-being and health. Meaning depends in turn on the patient achieving a "systematic" understanding of disease—that is, some sort of rational account of the experience of illness—and on the availability of social support, which they call "group formation." These two factors, according to the authors, are the basis of the placebo effect: "Group formation and system formation . . . are as essential to psychic functioning as nourishment is to physical functioning. . . . [These,] the basic factors composing what is subjectively experienced as a feeling of 'meaning,' are invariably used in all successful interpersonal therapies, and are the necessary and sufficient components of the placebo effect" (Adler and Hammett 1973: 597). If this is true, physicians can maximize the beneficial effects of participation by organizing the medical intervention in a "symbolically effective" way to promote "group formation and system formation." These goals should therefore be coordinated with scientific objectives in experimental design. This requirement holds, incidentally, regardless of whether the trial aims to cure patients or merely to contribute to knowledge.

THE SICK ROLE

The AIDS crisis dramatized two interconnected failures of modern medicine: patients with chronic illnesses are more and more dissatisfied, and medicine delivers experimental treatment poorly. The conflict between the social structure of the institution, the needs of the chronically ill, and the requirements of research accounts for such problems as misinformed subjects, the consequent dubious validity of consent, the interruption of continuity of care on exit from experiments, recruiting difficulties, poor compliance, and so on. These problems can only worsen as the public comes to see the research mission less as a scientific activity than as a treatment system.

These problems suggest the urgent need for reforms in the social organization of medicine. The place to begin consideration of this complex question is the so-called sick role, one of the foundations of the medical institution. The maladaptation of medicine to the needs of human subjects is due in large part to a definition of the sick role which obstructs "group formation and system formation." This in turn explains why few patients understand the reality of the research enterprise, and hence why researchers have such problems recruiting participants for controlled trials once access to unproven drugs is eased.

Contrary to a commonplace usage, the sick role is not a state of pathological psychological withdrawal. The term was originally introduced by Talcott Parsons to define illness in its social aspect as a form of "deviance" involving legitimate temporary release from normal social responsibility in exchange for a sincere effort to recover.[3] "The sick role," he wrote, "channels deviance so that the two most dangerous potentialities, namely, group formation and successful establishment of the claim to legitimacy, are avoided. The sick are tied up, not with other deviants to form a 'sub-culture' of the sick, but each with a

3. Medical "deviants," on Parsons's hypothesis, must demonstrate a will to health, which makes no sense for many chronic patients. Parsons's model therefore requires some modifications. It is obvious that the provision for conditional exemption from responsibilities has no application to individuals who will never recover. Freidson (1970: 238–239) removes this difficulty by offering an "expanded classification" of illness types which recognizes the unconditional legitimacy of withdrawal from social responsibility in the case of serious chronic illness.

group of non-sick, his personal circle and, above all, physicians. The sick . . . are deprived of the possibility of forming a solidary collectivity" (Parsons 1964: 477).

In sum, the sick are condemned to social isolation. While not particularly onerous for individuals suffering from brief acute illnesses, isolation is undoubtedly bad for the chronically ill. There is considerable evidence that they benefit from contact with others who suffer from the same disease. Renée Fox's classic study of clinical research shows the overwhelming importance of the shared experience of mission and risk. Her observations are particularly interesting in the light of the role ascribed to meaning above. "Seen in the broadest possible perspective," she writes, "what we observed in the conference room, laboratory, and on the ward were two groups of men who were faced with common stresses of magnitude: great uncertainty, limitation, hazards, and death. Through a process of interaction with members of their own group and with one another, physicians and patients arrived at comparable ways of dealing with their stresses. . . . Each derived support and guidance from the tight-knit group to which they belonged, and also from their intimate contact and close identification with one another" (Fox 1959: 253).

While the Parsonian isolation is not always maintained, it remains the norm from which departures such as this only occasionally occur, sometimes against considerable medical resistance (Brossat and Pinell 1990). Research on group activity by patients is rare, perhaps because physicians and researchers are not normally present when patients get together, but there are a few studies of the application of group therapy to the chronically ill. I would like to look briefly at three studies that, without intending to, offer excellent reasons to end the social isolation of chronically ill patients.

The studies describe therapy groups designed to reduce anxiety and depression, but in fact discussion was superficial and helped patients in unexpected ways. Despite their original intentions, the researchers actually demonstrated that when patients form a "subculture" through voluntary association, they supply each other with social support, a widely recognized factor in maintaining health (Nuckolls et al. 1972). In addition, other aspects of the experiments reflect Claude Lévi-Strauss's and Adler and Hammett's explanation of the role of symbolic meaning in the placebo effect.

Typically, the researchers described the patients as plunged at first into self-imposed isolation, regardless of the severity of their condition, and sometimes beginning immediately on diagnosis (Chafetz et al. 1955: 961–962). Yet in the groups they quickly opened up to exchange information about symptoms and complaints about the medical profession, particularly its slowness in diagnosing their illness (Chafetz et al. 1955: 962; Hartings et al. 1976: 68). Education, which was not always included in the original protocols, turned out to be one of the patients' chief demands (Chafetz et al. 1955: 963). It helped the "patient . . . resist faddish cures, plan realistically, and feel more in control of his life" (Hartings et al. 1976: 66). In one group medical experts were actually invited to address the patients (Buchanan 1975: 529). In another, "the emphasis on research in the clinic, which carried over as one of the purposes of the group, provided tangible proof of interest in them and in the course of their disease" (Chafetz et al. 1955: 962).

In fact, it is clear from these descriptions that the benefits of the groups had less to do with psychology than with sociology, specifically with the reform of the sick role. In the most successful case, a group of multiple sclerosis patients broke with the expected passivity and isolation and published a newsletter disseminating information on finances, entertainment, treatments, and equipment (Hartings et al. 1976: 73).

Patients requested further meetings long after the experiments were over, but in two of the three cases, the organizers concluded inexplicably that "the advantages of more protracted groups are questionable" (Chafetz et al. 1955: 963; see also Buchanan 1978: 426). These researchers wanted their patients to return to the conventional sick role as soon as possible, despite the latter's interest in creating new relationships.

Only one of the physicians was more accepting of his patients' wishes and allowed his groups to continue meeting beyond the planned end of the experiment. This position seems appropriate given the manifold functions the groups performed for their members. These functions and the new sick role they imply suggest a collaborative model of care for the incurably ill such as has begun to emerge with AIDS. As can be seen from the examples discussed above, this model offers a variety of improvements in the situation of such patients, including, I will argue, a more favorable environment for responsible research and experimental participation.

THE COLLABORATIVE MODEL

Ethicists frequently argue that patients suffering from incurable ailments are "coerced" into experimental participation by their illness.

This position is reasonable if patients are ignorant victims of a process that is likely to yield only knowledge. But it is paternalistic if they are well informed and, perhaps without renouncing the hope of cure, pursue participant interests that can be routinely served by appropriately designed experiments. In other words, as with ordinary treatment, only the informed patient is qualified to weigh risks against benefits. The ethical obligation of medicine is best fulfilled not by prohibitions but by ensuring that patients are well equipped to make such a judgment.

In the absence of a significant effort of this sort, looser regulation may result in vast numbers of uncomprehending patients entering experiments they would never have joined had they known what they were getting into and felt really free to refuse. Studies tend to support F. J. Ingelfinger's (1972: 466) fear that "the process of obtaining informed consent with all its regulations and conditions is no more than an elaborate ritual, a device that, when the subject is uneducated and uncomprehending, confers no more than the semblance of propriety on human experimentation." The sad truth is that most "patients consent to trials simply because they trust their doctors" (Mackillop and Johnston 1986: 187).

There is some evidence that this pessimistic conclusion is less applicable to chronic patients. One study reports "striking differences" in the attitudes of acute and chronic sufferers toward their physicians (Lidz et al. 1983: 542). The former are usually passive, while the latter often participate actively in medical decision making, discussing options and suggesting or rejecting treatment alternatives. The study relates these differences to the different attitudes of acute and chronic patients toward the conventional passive sick role. The authors conclude that "with certain types of chronic patients and in certain types of organizational structures, an active patient role is feasible" (Lidz et al. 1983: 543). These conclusions concur with Thomas S. Szasz and Mark H. Hollander's (1956) theory of "mutual participation" of patient and physician in the search for the best course of action in chronic care.

Such mutual participation can be routinely observed in the symptomatic treatment of chronic illness and in the decisions about treatment during the final weeks or days of life. For example, physicians skilled in managing illnesses such as amyotrophic lateral sclerosis ("Lou Gehrig's disease") or multiple sclerosis learn to listen to patients' discoveries about how to live with their illness and often pass along suggestions from one patient to another. Patients themselves exchange information about symptomatic treatment whenever they meet. Relief of symptoms has implications not only for comfort but also for life extension, and here too patients and physicians often work together to achieve results that could not be achieved in the conventional physician-patient relationship. Finally, patients who depend on such aids as respirators are increasingly involved in the timing of their own death.

This is the context in which it makes sense to talk about experimental medicine as a collaboration between researchers and subjects. This frequently expressed hope, which appears quixotic with regard to the majority of acutely ill patients, may not be so far off the mark in the case of chronic patients who have already learned to participate in their own treatment. In this case, the ethical obligation to the patient is better fulfilled by extraordinary efforts to achieve a higher quality of consent rather than by restricting opportunities to participate. If this obligation is taken seriously, then physicians and patients with chronic incurable illnesses will be able to find relief from some of the tensions surrounding the transformation of modern medicine into a technical enterprise.

Unlike cure, which is essentially an individual matter, experimental treatment involves joining a collective effort to solve a scientific problem (Parsons 1969: 350–351). Admission to that collective should properly be open only to those who share its spirit, whatever personal benefits they may also expect. In a powerful article on this theme, Hans Jonas argues that consent alone does not make the subject something more than the proverbial "guinea pig." "Mere 'consent' (mostly amounting to no more than permission) does not right this reification. The 'wrong' of it can only be made 'right' by such authentic identification with the cause that it is the subject's as well as the researcher's cause—whereby his role in its service is not just permitted by him, but *willed*. That sovereign will of his which embraces the end as his own restores his personhood to the otherwise depersonalizing context" (Jonas 1969: 236). Perhaps a sense of these moral issues motivated the founders of the clinical research center at the National Institutes of Health in 1953 when they laid down the following principle for themselves: "The patient or subject of clinical study is considered a member of the research team" (Curran 1969: 575).

Identification in Jonas's sense is an ideal to which experimental medicine does not always aspire and which it rarely achieves. But despite the difficulties, the collaborative model is not merely a pious wish. It shaped life in the experimental ward Renée Fox studied. Jean Dausset, discoverer of human leukocyte antigen (HLA) typing, designed his experiments around it. He organized an elaborate series of informational meetings and conferences to explain his research to the hundreds of volunteers he required. Dausset's subjects have been called "les heros instruits"—educated heroes—a term which ought someday to apply to all human subjects (Bernard 1978: 197).

The isolation imposed by the conventional sick role is the most important obstacle to this goal. It prevents patients from forming a community within which to receive education and extend social support. How, without such a community, can patients learn enough about research to appreciate the risks of participation, gain a realistic idea of the therapeutic prospects, and understand the usefulness of nontherapeutic experiments and controlled trials? Perhaps the crisis brought on by AIDS will finally result in the institutionalization of an alternative system of care for the chronically ill. Instead of being mere objects of medicine, awaiting cure, patients might then become active partners in a larger research enterprise.

Concretely, this implies two basic changes in traditional practice: (1) *to remove all pressures to participate* by implementing clinical trials in the context of a program of continuing symptomatic care and support for patients that does not require their experimental participation and that is not tied to the duration or success of experiments; and (2) *to ensure adequate understanding* by using patient meetings to educate patients concerning their disease, the role of human subjects in research, and the experimental options.

SCIENCE AND ETHICS

We are now in a position to consider the questions raised at the beginning of this chapter from a different angle. The problem is no longer to decide which is fundamental, body or mind, mechanism or lived experience. Our incomplete understanding of each refers us to the other and our chief concern ought to be coordinating the two in a way that achieves both humane and scientific objectives.

Ethically sound experimental design aims at this goal, in the process breaking down the usual boundary separating patient care from science. But the weakening of that boundary allows movement in both directions, and so far we have discussed only the implications of design for participant interests; on the other side, a cyborg medicine yields a certain epistemological authority to patients. As Steven Epstein (1991: 37) notes, the AIDS movement tries "to stake out some ground on the scientists' own terrain. These activists wrangle with scientists on issues of truth and method. They seek not only to reform science by exerting pressure from the outside, but also to perform science by placing themselves on the inside. They question not just the *uses* of science, not just the *control* over science, but sometimes even the very *contents* of science and the *processes* by which it is produced. Most fundamentally, they claim to speak credibly as experts in their own right—as people who know about things scientific, and who can partake of this special and powerful discourse of truth. Most elusively, they seek to change the ground rules about how the game of science is played."

Clearly, informal self-training may not be worth much in technical fields such as virology. And this is a case where arrogance could be particularly self-destructive. Yet despite the risks, there is something in this new situation for science as well as for patients. Only a well-informed community of patients is likely to bring forward volunteers to aid the research effort despite the ready availability of unproven drugs. Their participation would be known to their community and their generosity perceived by actual beneficiaries instead of remaining an abstract supposition as it is for most human subjects today. And, in a society where respect for medical authority is in sharp decline, participants with such a background are more likely to work responsibly for the success of the research effort, to take medications regularly, keep records and appointments conscientiously, warn clinicians of problems, make useful suggestions, challenge unworkable or inhuman designs from the knowledgeable standpoint of those subjected to them, identify as prejudices pseudoscientific ideas rooted in long practice, and so on.

Although much of what patients can do will be banal, their practices have a more than instrumental status. It is the daily performance of a variety of small tasks, and not simply the passive lending of their bodies, that constitutes a collective research subject. As Haraway (1992: 298) writes, the study of nature "is not about disengaged discovery, but about mutual and usually unequal structuring, about taking risks, about delegating competences." It involves manipulation and control, to be sure, but also challenge, courage, and self-mastery. The research subject is constructed of living human beings linked together through experimental design forged in negotiated ethical bonds.

These bonds are not merely extrinsic constraints placed on free inquiry; they are cognitively significant. They offer a kind of practical insight into aspects of nature (i.e., health) still closed to medical knowledge by the limitations of its mechanistic paradigms and theories. Ethics too gives access to nature, an *other* nature understood neither as a lost utopia nor as a mechanism, but as the essentially unforeseeable that rises up unexpectedly even in the midst of cognitively and technically mastered domains. This is why ignoring patients' attempts to redefine the research process as a form of treatment is a violation of medicine's mission and of the bodies of patients enrolled in clinical trials.

This conclusion has a certain resemblance to Marcuse's notion of an aestheticization of technology. Just as the aesthetic investment of technology promises to bring values to bear on it that reflect scientifically uncomprehended dimensions of nature, so too medical ethics projects a different conception of nature, one that is more fully reconciled to human needs, a liberated and liberating conception that cannot be represented scientifically but which we can hope to live as "human subjects" in a new sense of the term.

PART III

Postmodern Technology

Advertisement for French telematic service. Published in *CRAC: l'echo du clavier,* no. 13, March/April 1987.

CHAPTER SIX

French Theory and Postmodern Technology

From Lyotard to the Minitel

CRACKING THE MODERN FACADE

It is the computer that has put the "post" in postmodernity. No other technology so dominates discussion of the changes our society is undergoing today. No other technology so shapes the image of the future by its promise and its threat. Perhaps the same would have been said of nuclear power or space exploration a generation ago, but these technological marvels promised more and better modernity, growth within the paradigm, not change in the meaning of the modern. This is where the computer is unique: it cancels centuries of certainty about who we are and what we want as members of a modern society. Indeed, some theorists argue that it cancels modernity itself.

Despite the association of postmodernity with computers, it began as an architectural revolt against the International Style, familiar from the tall glass towers that surround us in every major city in the world. "Form follows function," the Bauhaus slogan, gave engineering control of aesthetics. Decorative elements from the past were rejected as artificial and irrational, and the new clean-lined buildings cut loose from history as supposedly rational structures.

Postmodern architecture refuses this distinction between the irrational and the rational, but without it functionalism itself is just another style. Time is no longer an arrow aiming higher; it has been flattened into a menu of styles none of which can claim to be more advanced than the others. Smooth facades are no less ornamented than

123

neoclassical ones, complete with Doric columns; the pathos of rationality, which makes functionalist architecture seem distinctively modern, is lost. Confronted with the smorgasbord of historically inherited possibilities, the postmodern architect constructs an ironic pastiche made up of bits and pieces of styles from different periods.

I have recalled these well-known facts about the origins of postmodernism the better to introduce a discussion of Jean-François Lyotard's *The Postmodern Condition*. This book first introduced the concept to a wide audience outside architecture and it still rewards rereading now that many of its theses have been tested by time.[1] The outcome of that test is also discussed below.

Lyotard repeats at the philosophical level some of the gestures characteristic of contemporary architectural theory. The most important similarity lies in the treatment of modern rationality, which both the architects and the philosopher view as a local phenomenon, not as a set of universal rules valid for all times and places, or, as Lyotard would put it, in all "language games." However, Lyotard has no intention of rejecting modern science. The notion that there are multiple rationalities, that modern science is not alone in understanding the universe, is intended to level the playing field, to allow for difference and variety in a way that the old positivist faith in science would not.

The new element that made Lyotard's interpretation of postmodernity so influential was the link he forged between the computerization of society, scientific advances, and the latest French theory. A look back to the origins of the linguistic turn in French thought will help explain this unusual combination.

During the 1960s a reaction against the existentialism of the postwar period transformed French intellectual life. The principle representative of this trend was the anthropologist Claude Lévi-Strauss, who developed an original analysis of culture under the influence of linguistics, especially the work of Ferdinand de Saussure. Saussure sharply distinguished between the structure of language and the practice of language and abstracted from the latter to concentrate exclusively on the former. He argued that language is built up from contrasts between arbitrary signs and that meaning emerges from a system of differences among inherently meaningless elements. The concept of "structure" referred in the first instance to the underlying logic of such a system.

As Lévi-Strauss adapted this model to anthropology, it revealed dis-

---

1. For his most recent (and rather similar) position on the issues of this paper, see Jean-François Lyotard (1991*a*: chaps. 2 and 4).

turbing implications. The modern idea of the autonomous subject rests on the irreducibility of meaning, disclosed in the immediacy of some primary experience. If structuralism is confined to language, meaning can be located in other domains, for example, perception, life experience, art, or rational insight, and the autonomy of the subject preserved. However, if all of culture is structured like language, everything pertaining to meaning is reducible to a system of differences. As Lévi-Strauss (1963: 641) has commented, "What is meaning according to me? A specific flavor perceived by a consciousness when it tastes a combination of elements none of which taken by itself would offer a comparable flavor."[2]

This theory has deterministic implications, since along with meaning, agency and history are reduced to consequences of structure. Is it a coincidence that such a theory became popular in the midst of France's first flirtation with the notion of a technocratic order? There is room for speculation on the similarity between structuralism and the systems approach to social management that began to gain influence in this same period.[3] Although there are certainly important differences, both eliminate the traditional notion of history in favor of a deterministic model of rational order.

Naturally, howls of protest went up from Jean-Paul Sartre, from phenomenologists like Paul Ricoeur, and from orthodox Marxists as structuralism invaded intellectual territory each claimed as its own. But none of these reactions was able to stem the structuralist tide. At most they contributed to an antitechnocratic social consciousness that finally emerged in the events of May 1968 as the basis of a new form of radicalism.

But in the intellectual world, the really effective reaction against structuralism came not from the old theories it challenged but from within the linguistic camp itself. In the late sixties and seventies so-called poststructuralist thinkers proposed new theories of agency.[4] These were younger intellectuals who had renounced the old concept of the autonomous subject but who also rejected a determinism that reduced

2. See also Paul Ricoeur's remarkable critique of Lévi-Strauss in the same issue of *Esprit*.

3. Needless to say, this comparison is irrelevant to the specifically anthropological contribution of Lévi-Strauss.

4. Apart from the well-known works of Foucault and Deleuze, which represent unusually radical formulations of the position, its influence can be seen throughout the French literary theory and philosophy of this period. For examples, the reader is referred to Michel de Certeau (1980), Marcel Détienne and Jean-Pierre Vernant (1974), and Louis Marin (1978). For a broad interpretation of the relation of poststructuralism to technology, see Mark Poster (1990).

participation in history to an empty illusion. They created a new concept of agency by reevaluating the pragmatics of usage and argued that the practice of a structure can alter its form. Today, Foucault's analysis of strategies of power is the most influential survival of this attempt in France to reconstruct agency in the framework of a theory of cultural coding.

Like Foucault's theory of strategies, Lyotard's pragmatics of language games attempts to reestablish the claims of agency in a structural universe. And both Foucault and Lyotard arrive at a similar conclusion, the rejection of a single model of rationality, and hence also of any form of technocratic determinism. In Lyotard this position takes the form of a "paralogic" of multiple rationalities, which may be conceived as islands of order in a radically contingent world. Scientific rationality is just one of these islands, the hegemonic one, to be sure, but by no means the only one. Here we are at the opposite extreme from Lévi-Strauss's attempt to find an underlying rational structure to all of language and culture.

This, then, is the background that shaped the special sensibility Lyotard brought to the notion of postmodernity. He offers a sober evaluation of the hegemony of scientific rationality in contemporary society and eschews humanist regrets. The order of the day is not romantic protest against dystopian rationality, but exploration of the margin of maneuver opened unintentionally by the new system.[5]

THE CRISIS OF NARRATION

The Postmodern Condition is above all an attack on what Lyotard calls "grand narratives" or "metanarratives." These are the stories we tell ourselves about our destiny as members of a nation, race, class, or species. Grand narratives define the community and legitimate its enterprises. They are most obviously associated with traditional societies and religious myths, but despite secularization modernity continues to depend on narrative legitimation. Postmodernity arises from a general crisis of modern narration under the impact of its own self-contradictions and changes in science and technology.

Lyotard's social theory is based on a contrast between narrative and denotative knowledge. Narrative knowledge is the cultural repository of societies in which tradition is transmitted through storytelling. Lyo-

5. See Feenberg (1991: chap. 4) for a discussion of de Certeau's theory of tactics as margin of maneuver.

tard explains it in terms of the three positions in discourse: the narrator who tells the story, the narratee who listens to the story, and the hero, the object of the narration, whose name is taken by members of the community who are themselves therefore represented in the story. The narrator draws his authority from his own past experience as narratee, ultimately from the community itself.

Here knowledge consists in illustrative examples rather than factual propositions, and it is presented through social interactions, such as performances, against the background of a solidary community. This type of knowledge mixes the denotative, the prescriptive, and the aesthetic in indissoluble combinations that are as important for establishing the identity of interlocutors as for their positive content.

In traditional communities, denotative knowledge has not yet separated out as a specific domain. When it does so, it transforms the pragmatics of cognitive discourse, establishing the rule of proof for distinct factual claims. However, narration merely changes functions in response to this autonomization of the denotative. It ceases to bear the whole content of the culture and instead legitimates denotative knowledge, which now contains the chief stock of things known.

Plato is the model of this notion of narrative legitimation. In *The Republic*, when it comes to justifying philosophy, he has nothing better to offer than a story about escape from the cave. That story itself illustrates why people listen to stories rather than engage in rational discourse. Plato was surely aware of the ironic paradox of pursuing a narrative legitimation of denotative knowledge. It is a paradox that characterizes the whole philosophical tradition.

In the modern world, there are two principal grand narratives, one based on the notion of enlightenment, and the other the story of political liberation. These metanarratives about knowledge and freedom require metasubjects, such as the People, the Human Race, the World Spirit, whose adventures provide the content of the story. Lyotard discusses two of these stories at length: the adventure of knowledge in Hegel, who describes the long struggle in which the special sciences are drawn together in the life process of an absolute knower, and the adventure of freedom in Kant, who conceives the human race as a moral agent in pursuit of autonomy and freedom.

But Lyotard shows that these narratives undermine themselves. For example, to motivate the legitimating metanarrative, Hegel must begin by placing all specific knowledges in question. Although his skepticism about the immediate claims of knowledge is finally overcome in absolute enlightenment, it could also be prolonged in a crisis of knowledge in general. This is exactly what happens in Nietzsche, where reason turns on itself and questions its own claims most radically.[6]

Lyotard believes that grand narratives have broken down in recent years; no metasubject can have an adventure of which our present would be the legitimate outcome. At this point, his story begins to involve technology significantly, for technical change—essentially the emergence of information technology—underlies the social generalization of the crisis of narration. The computer serves here as a symbol of all these new technologies, whether they be electronic, biological, or managerial.

For Lyotard computers depersonalize and mechanize knowing, which becomes a functioning element in society, a kind of technique and a market good, rather than a "true" representation of reality. This is also the end of the humanistic ideal of knowledge as the self-construction of the subject.

> Along with the hegemony of computers comes a certain logic, and therefore a certain set of prescriptions determining which statements are accepted as "knowledge" statements.
>
> We may thus expect a thorough exteriorization of knowledge with respect to the "knower," at whatever point he or she may occupy in the knowledge process. The old principle that the acquisition of knowledge is indissociable from the training (*Bildung*) of minds, or even of individuals, is becoming obsolete and will become ever more so. . . . Knowledge is and will be produced in order to be sold, it is and will be consumed in order to be valorized in a new production: in both cases, the goal is exchange. Knowledge ceases to be an end in itself, it loses its "use-value." (Lyotard 1991*b*: 4)

The computer is thus both a device and a cultural transformer. In its double role, it resembles the Panopticon in Foucault's theory of the rise of social discipline. Both the computer and the Panopticon do a technical job of work while at the same time encoding social reality in new forms. In Lyotard's terminology, the language system that corresponds to the computer is the "cognitive regime of phrases," similar to the Foucauldian "regime of truth" that emerges from modern disciplinary techniques. But there is also an important distinction between the two approaches. Lyotard's sense of systematic construction is es-

---

6. This is the typical move of the dialectic of enlightenment, in which reason challenges its own legitimacy.

sentially Kantian. In Foucault all language systems are historical in character, whereas in Lyotard they are based on faculties—the faculty of knowing, the moral faculty, and so on.

Lyotard concludes that computer technology shatters the modern constellation formed by cognitive discourse and its narrative legitimation. Denotative knowledge alone can now claim cognitive validity, but it cannot establish its own ultimate legitimacy. It is cut adrift like other language games, and it is this situation that creates the space within which the illusions of modernity, its faith in progress in particular, can be demystified. The structuralist critique of history is an obvious consequence of this situation. Indeed, it articulates that situation so clearly that it no longer seems meaningful to seek a route back to an integral community with its self-evident meanings and immediate certainties. "Most people have lost the nostalgia for the lost narrative" (Lyotard 1991b: 41).

This is where Lyotard parts company with the Frankfurt School. Its critical ideal is an outmoded utopianism, the myth of a unified self and society. That myth may be projected back into the past as an organic origin or into the future as a Habermasian rational consensus. In either case, with the failure of class struggle, the agent corresponding to utopian ends in Marx, the Frankfurt School's opposition becomes a humanistic point of honor without practical consequences. At the same time, it overestimates the efficiency of modern societies, their ability to reduce the social bond to an effect of technical mastery. Instead of atomized masses whose truth is conserved in high art or philosophical critique, Lyotard sees an unstable and pluralistic social ferment that continuously generates new ideas and values. The task of the thinker today is neither to restore a lost unity of man and nature (Marcuse, Adorno) nor to rekindle the dying embers of the Enlightenment (Habermas), but rather to reflect on the the emerging language games of a postmodern society.

POSTMODERN PRAGMATICS

As narrative strategies of legitimation break down, postmodern societies develop two alternative ways of attempting to recover their legitimacy: "performativity," or efficiency, and "paralogy," or the pursuit of originality.

The technocratic notion that knowledge and the social order can be legitimated simply by the continuous perfecting of means, without

appeal to either traditional symbols or modern ideals, has enjoyed increasingly widespread currency since World War II. It responds to dis-
illusionment with "ideology," that is, with the narrative myths of both
capitalism and communism. But the idea of technocracy depends on
two self-contradictory premises: confidence in the validity of science,
which technocracy undermines by subordinating research to the market, and belief in the possibility of constructing deterministic systems,
which science itself has now discredited.

Modern science needs ever more technology for the production and
verification of facts. This leaves it increasingly dependendent on corporations and the state, which supply the technical means of knowing.
But what these institutions want from science and technology is not
their truth but merely the efficiency they make possible. Such different
expectations create potential for conflict and raise questions about the
possibility of incorporating science into the social system as just another more or less operational component. Can technocratic administration digest this peculiar morsel which it desperately needs but which
appeals for its legitimacy to an ideal of truth that transcends the system?

Meanwhile, science itself is gradually penetrated by the ethos of the
institutions on which it depends. As the pursuit of truth becomes just
another business, a new concept of truth as "performativity" replaces
traditional realism. But can mere command of the techniques of proof
substitute for any larger notion of cognitive legitimation; in other words,
can knowledge be nothing more than the product of an agonistic in
which alliance with funding souces is the key to victory?[7]

These questions raise a doubt, but for Lyotard the decisive argument
against legitimation by performativity lies elsewhere, in the content of
science itself. He is skeptical of the entire technocratic project because
the ideal of total control simply has no place in the messy world we inhabit. Modern science has betrayed its technocratic offspring by deciding not to purge disorder from theory but to make sense of a fragmented universe. Quantum mechanics, Gödel's theorem, chaos theory,
the theory of fractals, and other new approaches signal such a fundamental epistemological shift.

The evolution of scientific knowledge discredits legitimation by mere
performativity while suggesting a postmodern alternative. Lyotard calls
this alternative "paralogic legitimation"—that is, legitimation through

7. It would be interesting to study the emergence of the social constructivist school
of sociology of science in the light of Lyotard's analysis.

originality, innovation, and difference which, he claims, prevails at least in scientific institutions. The goal of science is not efficiency but invention; the successful scientist does not streamline the system but modifies it. Given the fact that science has provided models for social legitimation in the past (for example, by objective knowledge), might not paralogy have a similar destiny? Perhaps we can reconceptualize freedom in postmodern society in terms of a new understanding of science.

This is Lyotard's gamble. In his view contemporary society is torn between two possible futures, the terroristic pursuit of a total system, dedicated to maximizing efficiency at the price of uniformity and unfreedom, and an emerging model of temporary contracts between individuals and groups who recognize the local character of all agreements and claims. This latter model is paralogical in its respect for difference, for the multiplicity of language games. This respect for difference distinguishes it from dialectical opposition, which is merely an antisystem awaiting its chance at power. Paralogy is a micropolitics that rejects totalization and favors the specific and the local. It represents a new type of resistance.

The computer once again plays a decisive role in the argument. According to Lyotard (1991b: 67), "We are finally in a position to understand how the computerization of society affects this problematic. It could become the 'dream' instrument for controlling and regulating the market system, extended to include knowledge itself and governed exclusively by the performativity principle. . . . But it could also aid groups discussing metaprescriptives by supplying them with the information they usually lack for making knowledgeable decisions. The line to follow for computerization to take the second of these two paths is, in principle, quite simple: give the public free access to the memory and data banks."

POSTMODERN TECHNOLOGY

The Postmodern Condition was published in 1979. Its analysis of the computer was necessarily speculative at that early date. At times Lyotard's speculations prove no more prescient than those of earlier prophets of postindustrialism. Like them, he overestimates such initially promising losers as public access to data banks and computer-aided instruction. Indeed, his understanding of computers seems rather limited. He worries, for example, that in the future knowledge will be restricted to what can be expressed in "machine language" (Lyotard 1991*b*: 4).[8] Machine language is a technical term referring to the most basic level at which instructions are encoded in computer hardware. While the structure of the computer at this level may indeed restrict what can be *calculated*, there is no reason to worry that machine language will restrict the *representation* of knowledge in computer readable formats, and this would seem to be the important question for the humanities. One might just as well worry about the poverty of a twenty-six-letter alphabet, yet Shakespeare comes through alright!

Despite these limitations, Lyotard grasps what I have called the "ambivalence" of the computer. By this I mean that the computer can serve both as a control system and as a medium for disseminating knowledge and communication opportunities throughout a fluid network (Feenberg 1991: chap. 5). If postmodernity, as a world of multiple rationalities, is to have a technical base, the computer must possess both these contradictory potentialities. Were the archetype of technical advance merely an instrument of control, the theory would end in dystopian pathos and lack the hint of an alternative path. But is there any evidence that the computer can play such an emancipatory role?

To answer this question I want to turn briefly to French telematics, which emerged in the early 1980s just as the theme of postmodernity came under discussion. (The next chapter offers a more detailed account.) The Minitel system was introduced quite deliberately by the French state as a means of accelerating the postindustrialization of French society. The system was originally conceived as a domestic information utility, a first step toward that universal dissemination of data Lyotard, among others, was demanding at the time.

Videotex was chosen as the system software. Videotex transmits information over networks from large computers, which store data, to terminals that can be located anywhere, including in homes. The network can carry train schedules, legal information, and so on, and also mediate certain kinds of transactions, for example, banking and telemarketing. In the late 1970s and early 1980s it was widely believed that videotex would usher in the postindustrial age. But despite the plausibility of the sales pitch, the results were disappointing everywhere it was introduced except, strangely enough, in France. There the system not only worked, it was a huge success with, at this time, over six

8. The translators render "langage de machine" (p. 13 in the French edition) inaccurately as "computer language."

million terminals distributed and thousands of services running. There is nothing like it yet in the United States.

The unique evolution of the French system partially confirms, partially disconfirms, postmodern expectations. This is not surprising, since Lyotard shared the illusions of the early prophets of telematics on whom he relied for information about computers. Roughly speaking, they believed that the computer age would, if pursued in the right spirit, finish the work of Enlightenment by raising the educational level of the population and expanding its opportunities to participate in responsible self-government. Scientific-technical rationality would transcend its professional origins and become the foundation of a general culture. These rationalistic expectations led them to believe that the public would respond positively to the offer of enhanced access to information, which it would need to participate in an advanced society as they imagined it.

Telematic rationalism reflected the hegemony of science and technology in modern bureaucratic and academic culture. That hegemony was applauded by the designers of the system and accepted with resignation but—significantly—without nostalgia by the postmodern theorist. But this was not at all what the most active users had in mind, and it was they who determined the evolution of the system. In fact, they transformed it in the application.

In 1979 the standard view of the computer limited it to information storage and calculating. Few foresaw its current success as a communications medium. It was in France that this redefinition of the computer first occurred on a massive scale. Here, briefly, is how it happened. Among the many host computers on the new telematic network were some on which it was possible to send messages to the system operators or to place classified ads. Skillful users hacked the primitive communication utility on one of these hosts and turned it into a messaging system accessible to all. Soon messaging became one of the most popular activities on the network, which was transformed from an information supplier to a new communication medium.

And a strange new kind of communication it is. In this bizarre social universe, anonymity calls forth an original language game that demands new types of moves. Everyone is a performer using language as the sole medium of self-presentation and seduction. Here identity is an outcome rather than a presupposition of the communication. Success might consist in obtaining the other's phone number and arranging a date, perhaps for a sexual adventure, or just as evidence of the power of one's discourse.[9] This type of communication practice represents the epitome of a world of temporary contracts based on verbal inventiveness suggested in Lyotard's paralogic of postmodernity. Here we have a surprising prefiguration of an antitechnocratic society that invests high technology with new forms of self-expression.

Yet it is difficult to find evidence here of the pursuit of the sort of "local" rationality in which postmodernity is supposed to consist. Instead, telematics reveals the role of the computer in constructing new forms of sexual and personal identity, and it is unclear just how identity, which Lyotard associates primarily with narrative, is supposed to relate to local rationality. Like most of us at the time he wrote this book, Lyotard did not feel the need to broach this problem since the primary supports of identity, such as states and parties, seemed to be losing credibility in the general crisis of narrative (Lyotard 1991b: 14). Today, of course, the situation has changed radically and this problem is of central concern.

SOCIAL MEMORY

The French experience with videotex indicates that we are heading toward a "communication" rather than an "information" age. This trend is evident in the rapid growth of communication applications on many different types of computer networks. For example, the academic Internet was originally created with the idea that researchers needed to exchange files and data, but today its millions of subscribers use it mainly to exchange personal messages. Meanwhile, local bulletin boards and corporate networks link millions of other users around the world. It is only a matter of time before computer-mediated communication (CMC) becomes a standard feature of daily life. That evolution promises social changes quite different from the generalization of access to information which Lyotard identified with the promise of the computer. These changes will affect not just the distribution of knowledge but the very structure within which the distinction between its narrative and denotative modes has so far been defined.

The French system employs a very primitive terminal; as a result, it has been largely confined to exploring anonymity in synchronous com-

---

9. There is an interesting literature on anonymity in electronic communications in France. See, for example, Alain Briole and Adam-Franck Tyar (1987) and J. Jouet and P. Flichy (1991).

munication. Its social impact is limited by the fact that the messages exchanged by users are generally unrehearsed and ephemeral. Systems that make a more extensive use of asynchronous electronic mail promise wider impacts.

The computer offers the first effective electronic mediation of the small group activities in which most office work goes on. In fact, mediated group activity has become commonplace among researchers and in many large corporations. What happens in these new groups? How do they differ from their face-to-face counterparts? In the remaining pages of this chapter, I want to introduce a theoretical framework for discussing these questions different from both the postindustrial and postmodern models.

Lyotard's distinction between narrative and denotative knowledge systems is rooted in a theoretical tradition that contrasts oral and literate cultures. One powerful hypothesis about modern individualism holds that it grew out of printing and literacy (McLuhan 1964; Ong 1977). The autonomization of the denotative language game, which characterizes literate culture, is associated with a technology, writing, through which knowledge can be recorded and transmitted separate from the social interactions of narrator and narratee.

With the invention of printing, this new relation to discourse became general. The community-centered mode of cultural transmission by storytelling declined, and a new cognitive space opened within which modern individualism developed. The spread of written discourse fostered the corresponding spread of a new subjectivity: the eye (I) of the reader is an individual. The organic community of speech, based on repetition and performance, gave way to the privacy of the modern individual, suddenly distanced from the language of the community. In this new position the individual gains control of a personal language, which is "doubled" because the speaker-writer is no longer identified with his or her own words but uses them for "effect." This distance is the essence of modern individuality. As distance is lost in the pseudo-synchronous broadcasting of performance, individuality declines in its turn and a mass society emerges (Ong 1971: 284–303; Katz 1980: 84–89).

Marshall McLuhan, for one, welcomed these developments and announced the end of literate culture and the rise of a new "oral" culture based on broadcasting. He predicted the rise of a new form of collectivism based on the replacement of "literate, fragmented Western man" by "a complex and depth-structured person emotionally aware of his total interdependence with the rest of human society" (McLuhan 1964: 50–51).

McLuhan's vision of electronic solidarity puts a pretty face on the corresponding nightmare of a one-dimensional society. And insofar as Lyotard rejects the one-dimensionality thesis as a vestige of a now-transcended deterministic science, he would also reject McLuhan's psychological projection. His own vision of happy fragmentation modifies rather than cancels the traditional notion of individualism. However, Lyotard does not give us much in the way of an argument for the developments he foresees. Unaware as he was of the role computer-mediated communication was soon to play, he could not adapt the contrast between oral and literate cultures to the new situation it created.

In this situation, the basic concepts of that tradition require radical generalization. I therefore propose to substitute for them the distinction between *repeatable* and *retrievable* discourse. Texts "stored" in human memory are "accessed" through "repetition" or performance. In cultures which rely heavily on repetition, cultural transmission is frequently assigned to special individuals, and access to the text is not under individual control but regulated socially through participation in public functions and audiences. The very existence of the community depends on a performance ethos that organizes its social memory. This is the original paradise of narration Lyotard describes.

Retrieval, on the contrary, involves accessing a permanent text, such as a book or diskette. In principle there is no reason why such access should not be entirely under individual control since the technologies of retrieval do not require the presence of other human beings. With computer networking, we see whole communities organized around retrievability instead of around face-to-face oral interaction. Such communities, existing in significant measure through an exchange of written texts, have the peculiar ability to recall and inspect their entire past. Nothing quite like this is available to a community based on the spoken word. Here we have the invention of a new form of social memory comparable to storytelling, books, and mass communications, each of which supports recall of the past through different types of "iteration" (Derrida 1972).

Today the difference between retrieval and repetition no longer correlates neatly with the distinction between writing and speech: answering machines routinely present us with speech as a retrievable text, computer dialogue systems allow synchronous written conversation, and sophisticated teleconferencing and phonemail systems and computerized voice management technology will soon shift the balance toward retrievability in business communications. Thus we can agree with Derrida (1972: 392) that "we are not witnessing an end to writing which would restore transparency or immediacy to social relations according to McLuhan's ideological representation."

This shift has remarkable social implications. What if the dominant medium of the next century is not structured like broadcast television but like computer networking? CMC seems to promise that writing will once again become a universal form of expression. Such a shift toward generalized retrievability suggests a different future of "postmodern" individualism, not as a retrograde reminder of the dying past, but in response to the most advanced methods of mediating experience. Perhaps something like Lyotard's notion of a paralogic society would emerge. As Mark Poster (1990: 128) argues, "Computer writing is the quintessential postmodern linguistic activity. With its dispersal of the subject in nonlinear spatio-temporality, its immateriality, its disruption of stable identity, computer writing institutes a factory of postmodern subjectivity, a machine for constituting non-identical subjects, an inscription of an other of Western culture into its most cherished manifestation."

THE LOSS OF THE CODE

It is commonplace to point out that such an evolution will be a mixed blessing. The computerization of society may sharpen class differences by disqualifying all those who do not master the new technology. Certainly something very much like this happens in sectors of the job market that require constant upgrading of computer skills. But in fact the problem is not so much that the masses will be left out of the computer revolution as that the terms of their inclusion will be radically unfavorable.

Lionel Gossman argues that the distinction between oral cultures and literate cultures hinges on the relation between the code of interpretation and the discourse to which it applies. In oral cultures, in which the community is organized around synchronic speech, the code is known immediately by all. The tradition is not an object of study, and interpretation follows no explicit canon. Rather, individuals are members of the community precisely insofar as the tradition lives in them and they need therefore make no conscious interpretive effort to understand any well-formed utterance. "Almost all the elements in the tradition are thus fully intelligible in the light of present experience. There can be few problems of interpretation, since the process of pres-ervation is at the same time a process of interpretation" (Gossman 1971: 779).

A culture based on writing has a radically different structure: "Written literature, on the other hand, is asynchronic, since texts from various periods, crystallizations of various moments in the literary tradition, are preserved graphically and are available to subsequent generations of readers and writers as well as to totally non-indigenous groups" (Gossman 1971: 779). The meaning of these texts is not self-evident because they have been detached from the author and from all specific social contexts and purposes. "Codes and performance are separated, and interpretation becomes a central concern" (Gossman 1971: 779). Where the codes of interpretation are not universally available to members of the community, those who do not have access must follow the leadership of those who do.

In the (still continuing) era of broadcasting an attempt has been made to retain some of the immediacy of an oral culture in the midst of a complex society more and more dependent on writing. To the extent that common codes and ritual events persist, it has been through television (Katz 1980). The full force of the passage to a world based on literacy may have been blunted by this fact, even as television itself contributed to delaying the incorporation of the lower classes into the world of literary culture. The coding of experience remains relatively unproblematical as a result, despite the weakening of traditional community since World War II.

It is this constellation that is beginning to break down. The new communications technologies promise a transition to a world in which structures of experience and interpretation we associate with literate culture will become universal, replacing the pseudo-oral community of broadcasting. Optimistic assessments of the prospects of this new form of social communication, such as Lyotard's, presuppose an underlying base of literary competences, a universalization of fairly sophisticated interpretive skills, the general availability of the codes of meaning in terms of which an increasingly diverse and complex social reality can be organized in sensible patterns.

If we do not share these optimistic assumptions, we face disturbing possibilities. How will the fractured and disqualified population of the new society use the technologies that give its work value and mediate its social interactions? We have reached the point where what computer specialists call the problem of "interface design" has become a social problem, and we do not yet know the solution.

Perhaps we are already drifting toward chaos in a radically disorganized communicative environment increasingly inhabited by individuals who have lost the survival code of social meaning required in the technological core of the society. Or will they be managed by subordinating them strictly to the orders of ever smarter machines? Anarchy, or artificial intelligence, chaos or a system of totally ritualized mass participation in an incomprehensible set of mechanical routines?

There is a third possibility: perhaps humanized technological designs will succeed in mimicking familiar objects so successfully that ordinary people will be at home in the world the computer makes and able to exercise some control there. This is the promise of virtual reality, which is less an attempt to realize fantasies in an imaginary world, as journalistic cliché would have it, than to provide new and more "intuitive" ways of operating machines. If that promise is fulfilled, the pseudo-orality of broadcasting will be gradually replaced by a corresponding form of interactivity. Some of the barriers to full participation in a technological society would be overcome by technology itself.

But ease of use has its price. In a user-friendly world, there would be no clear boundary between reality and the fantastic constructions of the computer. New forms of oppression might well arise in a society that was so epistemologically impaired. Might that society also give rise to new resistances? This is the theme of cyberpunk science fiction, which explores the dystopian threat of the deep penetration of the psyche by machines and the new forms of struggle that arise when the definition of reality has been turned over to technology.

EPILOGUE: ANTICIPATIONS OF INTERACTION

Lyotard's paralogical alternative to both technocracy and dystopianism anticipates current attitudes toward technology as they have been shaped by the computerization of society. As I argued in chapter 2, technology increasingly appears as a contested zone we are *within* rather than an enemy oppressing us from *without*. Paralogical action bears precisely this sort of *interactive* relation to the technical field.

Cyberpunk science fiction is a familiar symbol of this change. William Gibson's novel *Neuromancer* (1984) opened the era of virtual reality by supplying a language and an imaginative system with which to assemble existing simulation technologies into a new vision of the future. In Gibson's totally computerized world the interface is a "consensual hallucination" of solid objects and trajectories amidst which users navigate with familiar gestures and bodily movements—also hallucinated of course. The code of interpretation is no longer literate. On-line activity does not consist in arcane strokes at the keyboard, but now takes on the pathos of action: attack, defense, flight, struggle, and so on. It becomes, in sum, narratable, confounding the strict demarcation of science and story that seems to condemn an advanced society to bland white-coated inhumanity.

The world Gibson describes is grim but not strictly speaking dystopian. It is true that elites rule it with immensely powerful means, but those means are so complex that they give rise to all sorts of phenomena over which no one really has control. There are many small openings through which a clever hacker can enter the system and commit a variety of unprogrammed deeds. The future is not clear but may yet be altered by human action on the network.

Gibson's work is a continuation of the new directions in science fiction explored by authors such as J. G. Ballard, Samuel Delany, Philip Dick, and Ursula Le Guin in the late 1960s and the 1970s. Looking back, it is now clear that their break with the conventions of the "hard science fiction" tradition of Jules Verne, H. G. Wells, Hugo Gernsback, and John Campbell was not simply a personal inspiration but reflected deeper social changes.

This final section examines three novels that prepare the theme of postmodernity. They are Ursula Le Guin's *The Lathe of Heaven*, Philip K. Dick's *Ubik,* and *The Futurological Congress* by Stanislaw Lem. Like Lyotard's work, these novels anticipated the contemporary interactivist sensibility. They are tales of what I will call "absolute technologies" that, long before head-mounted displays and data gloves, already threatened the ontological core of reality itself.

The novels I have selected are all based on a sense of the fragility of the real, which Lem (1974: 122) calls "actualysis," or the "breaking down, the eroding of reality" in the face of modern technology. There is no longer any private retreat in which to constitute independent individuality, or an immediate public space of reality testing through direct social interaction and conflict. These stories exhibit a disturbing undercurrent of worry about the unity and reality of the subject caught in a hyperbolic doubt that now embraces the *cogito* itself. Total technical mediation has destabilized both personal identities and objective reality.

The fanciful premise of Le Guin's *The Lathe of Heaven* (1971) is the existence of a man whose dreams come true. George Orr alone recalls the world as it was before each change, so it seems no harm is done. But responsibility for altering the fabric of the universe is too much for him, and he sleeps as little as possible to avoid it. Eventually his sleeplessness brings him to the attention of the authorities and he falls into the hands of an unscrupulous psychiatrist who transforms his native ability to have "effective dreams" into a tool for changing the world.

The psychiatrist's posthypnotic suggestions have an oracular quality. Diffracted by Orr's unconscious, they never quite bring about the intended effect. For example, the psychiatrist's call for world peace produces an extraterrestrial invasion which does finally bring the nations of the earth together on the same side. The good doctor possesses an absolute technology, capable of dissolving the solid stuff of reality in fantasy, but its unpredictability is in proportion to its power. Effective dreaming as it is used and abused in the novel can stand for the inner flaw of modern technological Prometheanism.

But Le Guin does not quite recommend passivity. Effective dreaming is an ontological revelation which, in the right hands, belongs to the inherent process of the universe. "Everything dreams. The play of form, of being, is the dreaming of substance" (Le Guin 1971: 161). The trick is to learn how to do it, not arbitrarily, but in harmony with the infinite complexity of the whole.

Philip Dick's *Ubik* (1969) is even stranger than Le Guin's tale. In Dick's story psychic skills such as telepathy are marketed as an advanced form of industrial espionage. In response, "prudence organizations" have emerged to restore threatened privacy once again by blocking psychic transmissions. Not only have the boundaries between egos collapsed, but biological limits are blurred by the discovery of "half-life," the maintenance of psychic activity after death. The dead, frozen in "cold pack" in "moratoria"—the best are in Switzerland, of course—are electronically networked with each other and the living.

As far as one can tell, the main characters in the novel, members of an ill-fated prudence team, are all dead throughout most of the story. They continue to function as persons in a collectively hallucinated world over several hundred astonishing pages. Their hallucination thins out occasionally, and only judicious applications of the Absolute in the form of an aerosol spray called "Ubik" can reconstitute the crumbling fabric of their reality.

Their condition represents an extreme case of the weakening of the separate identities of persons and the independence and objectivity of the real in a totally mediated society. But Dick's universe is not the deterministic technocracy of earlier science fiction; rather, it is a place of such confusing complexity that no one is really in charge. Even in their catastrophic situation the characters explore moral possibilities and struggle against evil. *Ubik* is a black comic fantasy, to be sure, but one that may reveal something important about a future in which (to paraphrase a line from the story) the "definition of [the] self-system lacks authentic boundaries" (Dick 1973: 45).

Lem's *Futurological Congress* (1974) also explores the breakdown of traditional notions of individuality under conditions of total mediation. His hero is caught in a cloud of hallucinogenic tear gas used for crowd control in riot-torn Costa Rica, where he is attending a "futurological congress." The novel drifts in and out of the "real" world as the hero hallucinates future societies, each stranger than the last. The final and most consistent of these imaginary worlds is entirely organized around drugs. "Pharmacocracy" has replaced broadcasting as a means of social control, and the world depicted in most of the novel is a pure "virtual reality."

This element of the story—deception of the masses—is more or less familiar; however, Lem's fantasy also includes an original component. In his society of the future it is considered "civilized" to suppress all personal spontaneity and to take the appropriate drugs, not so much to control as to legitimate socially one's own emotions and behavior. The angry individual does not suppress his anger with a calmant but establishes its reality by taking "furiol," and similarly the happy individual must quickly consume a dose of "euphorium" to justify his blissful smile. "The distinction between manipulated and natural feelings has ceased to exist" (Lem 1974: 116).

Personal identity loses its natural immediacy, a point more crudely made when Lem's hero finds his brain transplanted into several different bodies. At the same time, the individuals appear to have gained a kind of technical self-mastery which exactly parallels the new mechanisms of social control. Here deterritorialization has reached so far into the self that individuals identify with the technical subject of their own lives. They are engaged in the constant "programming" of their inner states through drugs, against the background of the larger programming of social consciousness by the state. The inner world has dissolved under the control of these technologies.

The next chapter will return to some of the questions raised by these novels. They contain remarkable anticipations of the structure of the contemporary interactive relation to a computer-mediated society. Today the individual is constantly solicited by machines to participate in their operations. At the same time, where human communication is mediated by computers, subjects' power over their own self-presentation and language is greatly enlarged. Shared virtual reality represents the final realization of the astonishing fantasies depicted in these novels (Lem 1984: 102). For those able to master the system, new possibilities will surely open up, perhaps some version of the hopeful ones implied in Lyotard's paralogics, Le Guin's effective dreaming, or at least the moral universe of Dick's half-life. For those who cannot grasp the new codes, Lem's dystopian fantasy beckons.

These visions of the future suggest an ominous conclusion: perhaps the disagreement between optimists and pessimists is not really about alternative futures but about a single future that contains different destinies. These destinies would correspond roughly with the class divisions that cut across our society today, divisions that may succeed in reproducing themselves in new ways in a new technological setting. The very same technological advances that enhance participation for those able to master a postmodern society of fluid social and semiological relations based on elaborate forms of written expression may spread dystopian anguish among the excluded.

This divided condition recalls one of the strange features of the nightmare world of *Ubik*. In Dick's fantasy of "half-life" the inhabitants' remaining vital energies are expended in the effort to keep up to date with current fashions. Dying consists in falling back through the stages of form and mode, back through years and decades of evolving style, toward ultimate nonexistence. This process affects the structure of the individual's world, which must be maintained in the present through constant infusions of life force.

This bizarre image of death as "world deterioration" may serve as a metaphor for the new hazards of postmodern society. Perhaps we are beginning to see the first real signs of a threat promised from the beginning of the industrial age: a society in which the rate of technological advance has finally accelerated to the point where social position will be determined by position in the continuum of change.

CHAPTER SEVEN

From Information
to Communication

The French Experience with Videotex

INFORMATION OR COMMUNICATION?

Notions like "postindustrial society" and the "information age" are forecasts—social science fictions—of a social order based on knowledge (Bell 1973). The old world of coal, steel, and railroads will evaporate in a cloud of industrial smoke as a new one based on communications and computers is born. The popularizers of this vision put a cheerful spin on many of the same trends deplored by dystopian critique, such as higher levels of organization and integration of the economy and the growing importance of expertise.

Computers play a special role in these forecasts because the management of social institutions and individual lives depends more and more on swift access to data. Not only can computers store and process data, they can be networked to distribute it as well. In the postindustrial future, computer-mediated communication (CMC) will penetrate every aspect of daily life and work to serve the rising demand for information.

In the past decade, these predictions have been taken up by political and business leaders with the power to change the world. One learns a great deal about a vision from attempts to realize it. When, as in this case, the results stray far from expectations, the theories that inspired the original forecast are called into question. This chapter explores the gap between theory and practice in a particularly important case of mass computerization, the introduction of videotex in France.

Videotex is the CMC technology best adapted to the rapid delivery of data. Videotex is an on-line library that stores "pages" of information in the memory of a host computer accessible to users equipped with a terminal and modem. Although primarily designed for consultation of material stored on the host, some systems also give users access to each other through electronic mail, "chatting," or classified advertisements. This, then, is one major technological concretization of the notion of a postindustrial society.

The theory of the information age promised an emerging videotex marketplace. Experience with videotex, in turn, tested some of that theory's major assumptions in practice. Early predictions had most of us linked to videotex services long ago (Dordick et al. 1979). By the end of the 1970s, telecommunications ministries and corporations were prepared to meet this confidently predicted future with new interactive systems. But today most of these experiments are regarded as dismal failures.

This outcome may be due in part to antitrust rulings that prevented giant telephone and computer companies from merging their complementary technologies in large-scale public CMC systems. The Federal Communications Commission's failure to set a standard for terminals aggravated the situation. Lacking the resources and know-how of the big companies, their efforts uncoordinated by government, it is not surprising that smaller entertainment and publishing firms were unable to make a success of commercial videotex (Branscomb 1988).

Disappointing results in the United States have been confirmed by all foreign experiments with videotex, with the exception of the French Teletel system. The British, for example, pioneered videotex with Prestel, introduced three years before the French came on the scene. Ironically, the French plunged into videotex on a grand scale in part out of fear of lagging behind Britain!

Prestel had the advantage of state support, which no American system could boast. But it also had a corresponding disadvantage: overcentralization. At first information suppliers could not connect remote hosts to the system, which severely limited growth in services. What is more, Prestel relied on users to buy a decoder for their television sets, an expensive piece of hardware that placed videotex in competition with television programming. The subscriber base grew with pathetic slowness, rising to only seventy-six thousand in the first five years (Charon 1987: 103–106; Mayntz and Schneider 1988: 278).

Meanwhile, the successful applications of CMC were all organized by and for private businesses, universities, or computer hobbyists. The general public still has little or no access to the networks aimed at these markets and no need to use such specialized on-line services as bibliographic searches and software banks. Thus after a brief spurt of postindustrial enthusiasm for videotex, CMC is now regarded as suitable primarily for work, not for pleasure; it serves professional needs rather than leisure or consumption (Ettema 1989).

As I will explain below, the Teletel story is quite different. Between 1981, the date of the first tests of the French system, and the end of the decade, Teletel became by far the largest public videotex system in the world with thousands of services, millions of users, and hundreds of millions of dollars in revenues. Today Teletel is the brightest spot in the otherwise unimpressive commercial videotex picture.

This outcome is puzzling. Could it be that the French are different from everyone else? That rather silly explanation became less plausible as Compuserve and the Sears/IBM Prodigy system grew to a million subscribers. While the final evaluation of these systems is not yet in, their sheer size tends to confirm the existence of a home videotex market. How, then, can we account for the astonishing success of Teletel, and what are its implications for the information-age theory that inspired its creation?

Teletel is particularly interesting because it employs no technology not readily available in all those other countries where videotex was tried and failed. Its success can only be explained by identifying the *social inventions* that aroused widespread public interest in CMC. A close look at those inventions shows the limitations not only of prior experiments with videotex but also of the theory of the information age (Feenberg 1991: chap. 5).

THE EMERGENCE OF A NEW MEDIUM

While Teletel embodies generally valid discoveries about how to organize public videotex systems, it is also peculiarly French. Much that is unique about it stems from the confluence of three factors: (1) a specifically French politics of modernization; (2) the bureaucracy's voluntaristic ideology of national public service; and (3) a strong oppositional political culture. Each of these factors contributed to a result no single group in French society would willingly have served in the beginning. Together they opened the space of social experimentation that Teletel made technically possible.

MODERNIZATION

The concept of modernity is a live issue in France in a way that is difficult to imagine in the United States. Americans experience modernity as a birthright; America does not *strive* for modernity, it *defines* modernity. For that reason, the United States does not treat its own modernization as a political issue but relies on the creative chaos of the market.

France, on the other hand, has a long tradition of theoretical and political concern with modernity as such. In the shadow of England at first and later of Germany and the United States, France has struggled to adapt itself to a modern world it has always experienced at least to some extent as an external challenge. This is the spirit of the famous Nora-Minc Report that President Giscard d'Estaing commissioned from two top civil servants to define the means and goals of a concerted policy of modernization for French society in the last years of the century (Nora and Minc 1978).

Simon Nora and Alain Minc called for a technological offensive in "telematics," the term they coined to describe the marriage of computers and communications. The telematic revolution, they argued, would change the nature of modern societies as radically as the industrial revolution. But, they added, "'Telematics,' unlike electricity, does not carry an inert current, but rather information, that is to say, power" (Nora and Minc 1978: 11). "Mastering the network is therefore an essential goal. Its framework must therefore be conceived in the spirit of public service" (Nora and Minc 1978: 67). In sum, just as war is too important to be left to the generals, so postindustrial development is too important to be left to businessmen and must become a political affair.

Nora and Minc (1978: 41–42) paid particular attention to the need to win public acceptance of the telematic revolution and to achieve success in the new international division of labor through targeting emerging telematic markets. They argued that a national videotex service could play a central role in achieving these objectives. This service would sensitize the still backward French public to the wonders of the computer age while creating a huge protected market for computer terminals. Leveraging the internal market, France would eventually become a leading exporter of terminals and so benefit from the expected restructuring of the international economy instead of falling further behind (Nora and Minc 1978: 94–95). These ideas lay at the origin of the Teletel project, which, as a peculiar mix of propaganda and industrial policy, had a distinctly statist flavor from the very beginning.

VOLUNTARISM

So conceived, the project fell naturally into the hands of the civil service. This choice, which seems strange to Americans contemptuous of bureaucratic ineptness, makes perfect sense in France, where business has an even more negative image than government.

When it is the bureaucracy rather than the corporation that spearheads modernization, the esprit de corps of the civil service leaves its mark on the outcome. In France this is not such a bad thing. French bureaucrats define the nation in terms of the uniform provision of services such as mail, phone, roads, schools, and so on. Delivering these services is a moral mission predicated on "republican" ideals such as egalitarianism. The French call this bureaucratic approach "voluntaristic" because, for better or worse, it ignores local situations and economic constraints to serve a universal public interest.

One must keep this voluntaristic sense of mission in mind to understand how the French telephone company, charged with developing Teletel, could have conceived and implemented a national videotex service without any guarantee of profitable operation. In fact, Teletel was less a moneymaking scheme than a link in the chain of national identity. As such, it was intended to reach every French household as part of the infrastructure of national unity, just like the telephone and the mails (Nora and Minc 1978: 82).

To achieve this result, the telephone company proceeded to distribute millions of free terminals, called "Minitels." Although early advertising was mainly directed at prosperous neighborhoods, anyone could request a Minitel. Eventually all phone subscribers were to be equipped. France would leapfrog out of its position as the industrial country with the most backward telephone system right into the technology of the next century.

An American telephone company would certainly have charged for such an elaborate upgrade of the users' equipment. Even the French Telecom was a bit worried about justifying this unprecedented bounty. The excuse it came up with was the creation of a national electronic phone directory, accessible only by Minitel, but in fact the main point of the exercise was simply to get a huge number of terminals out the door as quickly as possible (Marchand 1987: 32–34). Free distribution of terminals preceded the development of a market in services, which it was supposed to bring about. Just as roadside businesses follow highways, so telematic businesses were expected to follow the distribution of Minitels.

The first four thousand Minitels were delivered in 1981 (Marchand 1987: 37); ten years later over five million have been distributed. The speed and scale of this process are clues to the economics of the great telematic adventure. The telephone company's ambitious modernization program had made it the largest single customer for French industry in the 1970s. The daring telematic plan was designed to take up the slack in telephone production that was sure to follow the rapid saturation of that market, thereby avoiding the collapse of a major industrial sector.

OPPOSITION

As originally conceived, Teletel was designed to bring France into the information age by providing a wide variety of services. But is more information what every household needs (Iwaasa 1985: 49)? And who is qualified to offer information services in a democracy (Marchand 1987: 40ff.)? These questions received a variety of conflicting answers in the early years of French videotex.

Modernization through national service defines the program of a highly centralized and controlling state. To make matters worse, the Teletel project was initiated by a conservative government. This combination at first inspired widespread distrust of videotex and awakened the well-known fractiousness of important sectors of opinion. The familiar pattern of central control and popular "resistance" was repeated once again with Teletel, a program that was "parachuted" on an unsuspecting public and soon transformed by it in ways its makers had never imagined.

The press led the struggle against government control of videotex. When the head of the telephone company announced the advent of the paperless society (in Dallas of all places), publishers reacted negatively out of fear of losing advertising revenues and independence. The dystopian implications of a computer-ruled society did not pass unnoticed. One irate publisher wrote, "He who grasps the wire is powerful. He who grasps the wire and the screen is very powerful. He who will someday grasp the wire, the screen, and the computer will possess the power of God the Father Himself" (Marchand 1987: 42).

The press triumphed with the arrival of the socialist government in 1981. To prevent political interference with on-line "content," the telephone company was allowed to offer only its electronic version of the telephone directory. The doors to Teletel were opened wide by the standards of the day: anyone with a government-issued publishers' license could connect a host to the system. In 1986 even this restriction was abandoned; today anyone with a computer can hook up to the system, list a phone number in the directory, and receive a share of the revenues the service generates for the phone company.

Because small host computers are fairly inexpensive and knowledge of videotex as rare in large as in small companies, these decisions had at first a highly decentralizing effect. Teletel became a vast space of disorganized experimentation, a "free market" in on-line services more nearly approximating the liberal ideal than most communication markets in contemporary capitalist societies.

This example of the success of the market has broad implications, but not quite so broad as the advocates of deregulation imagine. The fact that markets sometimes mediate popular demands for technical change does not make them a universal panacea. The conditions that make such a use of markets possible are quite specific. Frequently, for example, where large corporations sell well-established technologies, they use markets to stifle the demands existing products cannot meet or rechannel them into domains where basic technical change need not occur. Nevertheless, consumers do occasionally reopen the design process through the market. This is certainly a reason to view markets as ambivalent institutions with a potentially dynamic role to play in the development of new technology.

COMMUNICATION

Surprisingly, although phone subscribers were now equipped for the information age, they made relatively little use of the wealth of data available on Teletel. They consulted the electronic directory regularly, but not much else. Then, in 1982, hackers transformed the technical support facility of an information service called Gretel into a messaging system (Bruhat 1984: 54–55). After putting up a feeble (perhaps feigned) resistance, the operators of this service institutionalized the hackers' invention and made a fortune. Other services quickly followed with names like "Désiropolis," "La Voix du Parano," "SM," "Sextel." "Pink" messaging became famous for spicy pseudononymous conversations in which users sought like-minded acquaintances for conversation or encounters.

Once messaging took off on a national scale, small telematic firms reworked Teletel into a communication medium. They designed programs to manage large numbers of simultaneous users emitting rather than receiving information, and they invented a new type of interface. On entering these systems, users are immediately asked to choose a pseudonym and to fill out a brief "C.V." (curriculum vitae, or *carte de visite*). They are then invited to survey the C.V.'s of those currently on-line to identify like-minded conversational partners. The new programs employ the Minitel's graphic capabilities to split the screen, assigning each of as many as a half-dozen communicators a separate space for their messages. This is where the creative energies awakened by telematics went in France, and not into meeting obscure technical challenges dear to the hearts of government bureaucrats such as ensuring French influence on the shape of the emerging international market in data bases (Nora and Minc 1978: 72).

The original plans for Teletel had not quite excluded human communication, but they certainly underestimated its importance relative to the dissemination of data, on-line transactions, and even video games (Marchand 1987: 136). Messaging is hardly mentioned in early official documents on telematics (e.g., Pigeat et al. 1979.) The first experiment with Teletel, at Vélizy, revealed an unexpected enthusiasm for communication. Originally conceived as a feedback mechanism linking users to the Vélizy project team, the messaging system was soon transformed into a general space for free discussion (Charon and Cherky 1983: 81–92; Marchand 1987: 72). Even after this experience no one imagined that human communication would play a major role in a mature system. But that is precisely what happened.

In the summer of 1985 the volume of traffic on Transpac, the French packet switching network, exceeded its capacities and the system crashed. The champion of French high tech was brought to its knees as banks and government agencies were bumped off-line by hundreds of thousands of users skipping from one messaging service to another in search of amusement. This was the ultimate demonstration of the new telematic dispensation (Marchand 1987: 132–134). Although only a minority of users were involved, by 1987 40 percent of the hours of domestic traffic were spent on messaging (Chabrol and Perin 1989: 7).

Pink messaging may seem a trivial result of a generation of speculation on the information age, but the case can be made for a more positive evaluation. Most important, the success of messaging changed the generally received connotations of telematics, away from information toward communication. This in turn encouraged—and paid for—a wide variety of experiments in domains such as education, health, and news (Marchand 1987; Bidou et al. 1988). Television programs, for example, now advertise services on Teletel where viewers can obtain supplementary information or exchange opinions, adding an interactive element to the one-way broadcast. Politicians engage in dialogue with constituents on Teletel, and political movements open messaging services to communicate with their members. Educational experiments have brought students and teachers together for electronic classes and tutoring, for example at a Paris medical school. And a psychological service offers an opportunity to discuss personal problems and seek advice.

Perhaps the most interesting experiment occurred in 1986 when a national student strike was coordinated on the messaging service of the newspaper *Libération*. The service offered information about issues and actions, on-line discussion groups, hourly news updates, and a game mocking the minister of education. It quickly received three thousand messages from all over the country (Marchand 1987: 155–158).

These applications reveal the unsuspected potential of the medium for creating surprising new forms of sociability. Rather than imitating the telephone or writing, they play on the unique capacity of telematics to mediate highly personal, anonymous communication. These experiments prefigure a very different organization of public and private life in advanced societies (Feenberg 1989a: 271–275; Jouet and Flichy 1991).

THE SYSTEM

Although no one planned all its elements in advance, eventually a coherent system emerged from the play of these various forces. Composed of rather ordinary elements, it formed a unique whole that finally broke the barriers to general public acceptance of CMC technology. The system is characterized by five basic principles:

1. *Scale.* Only a government or a giant corporation has the means to initiate an experiment such as Teletel on a large enough scale to en-

sure a fair test of the system. Smaller pilot projects all founder on a chicken-and-egg dilemma: to build a market in services one needs users, but users cannot be attracted without a market in services. The solution, demonstrated in France, is to make a huge initial investment in transmission facilities and terminals in order to attract enough new and occasional users at an early stage to justify the existence of a critical mass of services.

2. *Gratuity.* Perhaps the single most revolutionary feature of the system was the free distribution of terminals. The packet switching network and the terminals were treated as a single whole, in contradistinction to every other national computer network. Gratuity dictated wise decisions about terminal quality: durability and simple graphics. It also ensured service providers a large base to work from very early on, long before the public would have perceived the interest of the unfamiliar system and invested in a costly terminal or subscription.

3. *Standardization.* The monopoly position of the French telephone company and the free distribution of Minitel terminals ensures uniformity in several vital areas. Equipment and sign-on procedures are standardized, and service is offered from a single national phone number at a single price, independent of location. (There is now a slightly more complex price structure.) The phone company employs its billing system to collect all charges, sharing the income with service providers.

4. *Liberalism.* The decision to make it easy to hook up host computers to the packet switching network must have gone against the telephone company's ingrained habit of controlling every aspect of its technical system. However, once this decision was made, it opened the doors to a remarkable flowering of social creativity. Although the Minitel was designed primarily for information retrieval, it can be used for many other purposes. The success of the system owes a great deal to the mating of a free market in services with the flexible terminal.

5. *Identity.* The system acquired a public image through its identification with a project of modernization and through the massive distribution of distinctive terminals. A unique telematic image was also shaped by the special phone directory, the graphic style associated with Teletel's alphamosaic standard, the adoption of videotex screen management instead of scrolling displays, and the social phenomenon of the pink messaging.

THE CONFLICT OF CODES

This interpretation of Teletel contradicts the deterministic assumptions about the social impact of computers that inspired Nora, Minc, and many other theorists of postindustrialism. The logic of technology simply did not dictate a neat solution to the problem of modernization in this case; instead, a very messy process of conflict, negotiation, and innovation produced a socially contingent result. What are these social factors and how did they influence the development of CMC in France?

SOCIAL CONSTRUCTIVISM

Teletel's evolution confirms the social constructivist approach introduced in chapter 1. Unlike determinism, social constructivism does not rely exclusively on the technical characteristics of an artifact to explain its success. According to the "principle of symmetry," there are always alternatives that might have been developed in the place of the successful one. What singles out an artifact is not some intrinsic property such as "efficiency" or "effectiveness" but its relationship to the social environment.

As we have seen in the case of videotex, that relationship is negotiated among inventors, civil servants, businessmen, consumers, and many other social groups in a process that ultimately defines a specific product adapted to a specific mix of social demands. This process is called "closure"; it produces a stable "black box," an artifact that can be treated as a finished whole. Before a new technology achieves closure, its social character is evident, but once it is well established, its development appears purely technical, even inevitable to a naive backward glance. Typically, later observers forget the original ambiguity of the situation in which the black box was first closed (Latour 1987: 2–15).

Pinch and Bijker illustrate their method with the example of the bicycle. In the late nineteenth century, before the present form of the bicycle was fixed, design was pulled in several different directions. Some customers perceived bicycling as a competitive sport, while others had an essentially utilitarian interest in transportation. Designs corresponding to the first definition had high front wheels that were rejected as unsafe by the second type of rider, who preferred designs with two equal-sized low wheels. Eventually, the low wheelers won out and the entire later history of the bicycle down to the present day stems from that line of technical development. Technology is not determining in this example; on the contrary, the "different interpretations by social groups of the content of artefacts lead via different chains of problems and solutions to different further developments" (Pinch and Bijker 1984: 423).

This approach has several implications for videotex. First, the design of a system like Teletel is not determined by a universal criterion of efficiency but by a social process that differentiates technical alternatives according to a variety of criteria. Second, that social process is not about the application of a predefined videotex technology, but concerns the very definition of videotex and the nature of the problems to which it is addressed. Third, competing definitions reflect conflicting social visions of modern society concretized in different technical choices. These three points indicate the need for a revolution in the study of technology. The first point widens the range of social conflict to include technical issues which, typically, have been treated as the object of a purely "rational" consensus. The other two points imply that meanings enter history as effective forces not only through cultural production and political action but also in the technical sphere. To understand the social perception or definition of a technology one needs a hermeneutic of technical objects.

Technologies are meaningful objects. From our everyday commonsense standpoint, two types of meanings attach to them. In the first place, they have a function, and for most purposes their meaning is identical with that function. However, we also recognize a penumbra of "connotations" that associate technical objects with other aspects of social life independent of function (Baudrillard 1968: 16–17). Thus automobiles are means of transportation, but they also signify the owner as more or less respectable, wealthy, and sexy.

In the case of well-established technologies, the distinction between function and connotation is usually clear. There is a tendency to project this clarity back into the past and to imagine that the technical function preceded the object and called it into being. The social constructivist program argues, on the contrary, that technical functions are not pregiven but are discovered in the course of the development and use of the object. Gradually certain functions are locked in by the evolution of the social and technical environment, as for example the transportation functions of the automobile have been institutionalized in low-density urban designs that create the demand automobiles satisfy. Closure thus depends in part on building tight connections in a larger technical network.

In the case of new technologies, there is often no clear definition of function at first. As a result, there is no clear distinction between different types of meanings associated with the technology: a bicycle built for speed and a bicycle built for safety are both functionally and connotatively different. In fact, connotations of one design may be functions viewed from the angle of the other. These ambiguities are not merely conceptual, since the device is not yet "closed" and no institutional lock-in ties it decisively to one of its several uses. Thus ambiguities in the definition of a new technology must be resolved through technical development itself. Designers, purchasers, and users all play a role in the process by which the meaning of a new technology is finally fixed.

Technological closure is eventually consolidated in a technical code. Technical codes define the object in strictly technical terms in accordance with the most general social meanings it has acquired. For bicycles, this was achieved in the 1890s. A bicycle safe for transportation could only be produced by conforming to a code which dictated a seat positioned well behind a small front wheel. When consumers encountered a bicycle produced according to this code, they immediately recognized it for what it was: a "safety" in the terminology of the day. That definition in turn connoted women and older riders, trips to the grocery store, and so on, and negated associations with the young sportsman out for a thrill.

Technical codes are interpreted with the same hermeneutic procedures used to interpret texts, works of art, and social actions (Ricoeur 1979). But the task gets complicated when codes become the stakes in significant social disputes. Then ideological visions are sedimented in technical design. This is what explains the "isomorphism, the formal congruence between the technical logics of the apparatus and the social logics within which it is diffused" (Bidou et al. 1988: 18). These patterns of congruence explain the impact of the larger sociocultural environment on the mechanisms of closure (Pinch and Bijker 1984: 409). Videotex is a striking case in point. In what follows I will trace the pattern from the highest level of worldviews down to the lowest level of technical design.

The issue in this case is the very nature of a postindustrial society. The "information" age was originally conceived as a scientized society, a vision that legitimated the technocratic ambitions of states and corporations. The rationalistic assumptions about human nature and society that underlie this fantasy have been familiar for a century or more as a kind of positivist utopia.

Its principal traits are familiar. Scientific-technical thinking becomes the logic of the whole social system. Politics is merely a generalization of the consensual mechanisms of research and development. Individuals are integrated to the social order not through repression but through rational agreement. Their happiness is achieved through technical mastery of the personal and natural environment. Power, freedom, and happiness are thus all based on knowledge.

This global vision supports the generalization of the codes and practices associated with engineering and management. One need not share an explicit utopian faith to believe that the professional approaches of these disciplines are useful even outside the organizational contexts in which they are customarily applied. The spread of ideas of social engineering based on systems analysis, rational choice theory, risk-benefit analysis, and so on, testifies to this new advance in the rationalization of society. Similar assumptions influenced the sponsors of Teletel, not surprisingly given the cult of engineering in the French bureaucracy.

At the microlevel these assumptions are at work in the traditional computer interface, with its neat hierarchies of menus consisting of one-word descriptors of "options." A logical space consisting of such alternatives correlates with an individual "user" engaged in a personal strategy of optimization. Projected onto society as a whole in the form of a public information service, this approach implies a world in which "freedom" is the more or less informed choice among preselected options defined by a universal instance such as a technocratic authority. That instance claims to be a neutral medium, and its power is legitimated precisely by its transparency: the data is accurate and logically classified. But it does not cease to be a power for that matter.

Individuals are caught up in just such a system as this in their interactions with corporate, government, medical, and scholastic institutions. Videotex streamlines this technocratic universe. In fact, some of the most successful utilitarian services on Teletel offer information on bureaucratic rules, career planning, and examination results. These services play on the "anxiety effect" of life in a rational society: individuality as a problem in personal self-management (Bidou et al. 1988: 71). But the role of anxiety reveals the darker side of this utopia. The system appears to embody a higher level of social rationality, but it is a nightmare of confusing complexity and arbitrariness to those whose lives it shapes. This is the "Crystal Palace" so feared and hated in Dostoevsky's "underground," or an Alphaville where the computer's benign rule is the ultimate dehumanizing oppression.

THE SPECTRAL SUBJECT

Teletel was caught up in a dispute over which sort of postindustrial experience would be projected technologically through domestic computing. As we have seen, the definition of interactivity in terms of a rationalistic technical code encountered immediate resistance from "users" who ignored the informational potential of the system and instead employed it for anonymous human communication and fantastic encounters.

These unexpected applications revealed another whole dimension to everyday experience in postindustrial societies masked by the positivist utopia. As the gap between individual person and social role widens, and individuals are caught up in the "mass," social life is increasingly reorganized around impersonal interactions. The individual slips easily between roles, and identifies fully with none of them, falls in and out of various masses daily, and belongs wholly to no community. The solitude of the "lonely crowd" consists in a multitude of trivial and ambiguous encounters. Anonymity plays a central role in this new social experience and gives rise to fantasies of sex and violence that are represented in mass culture and, to a lesser extent, realized in individuals' lives.

Just as videotex permits the individual to personalize an anonymous query to a career planning agency or a government bureaucracy, so the hitherto inarticulate relationship to erotic texts can now achieve personality, even reciprocity, thanks to the telephonic link supplied by the Minitel. The privacy of the home takes on functions previously assigned public spaces like bars and clubs, but with an important twist: the blank screen serves not only to link the interlocutors but also to shield their identities.

As with newspaper "personals," individuals have the impression that the Minitel gives them full command of all the signals they emit, unlike risky face-to-face encounters where control is uncertain at best. Enhanced control through written self-presentation makes elaborate identity games possible. "Instead of identity having the status of an initial given (with which the communication usually begins), it becomes a stake, a product of the communication" (Baltz 1984: 185).

The experience of pseudononymous communication calls to mind Erving Goffman's (1982: 31) double definition of the self as an "image" or identity and as a "sacred object" to which consideration is due: "the self as an image pieced together from the expressive implications of the full flow of events in an undertaking; and the self as a kind of player in a ritual game who copes honorably or dishonorably, diplomatically or undiplomatically, with the judgemental contingencies of the situation." By increasing control of image while diminishing the risk of embarrassment, messaging alters the sociological ratio of the two dimensions of selfhood and opens up a new social space.

The relative desacralization of the subject weakens social control. It is difficult to bring group pressure to bear on someone who cannot see frowns of disapproval. CMC thus enhances the sense of personal freedom and individualism by reducing the "existential" engagement of the self in its communications. "Flaming"—the expression of uncensored emotions on-line—is viewed as a negative consequence of this feeling of liberation. But the altered sense of the reality of the other may also enhance the erotic charge of the communication (Bidou et al. 1988: 33).

Marc Guillaume has introduced the concept of "spectrality" to describe these new forms of interaction between individuals who are reduced to anonymity in modern social life and yet succeed in using that anonymity to shelter and assert their identities. "Teletechnologies, considered as a cultural sphere," he has written, "respond to a massive and unconfessed desire to escape partially and momentarily both from the symbolic constraints which persist in modern society and from totalitarian functionality. To escape not in the still ritualized form of those brief periods of celebration or disorder permitted by traditional societies, but at the convenience of the subject, who pays for this freedom by a loss. He becomes a *spectre* . . . in the triple sense of the term: he fades away in order to wander freely like a phantom in a symbolic order which has become transparent to him" (Guillaume 1982: 23).

Social advance appears here not as the spread of technocratic elements throughout daily life, but as the generalization of the commutative logic of the telephone system. To fully understand this alternative, it is once again useful to look at the technical metaphors that invade social discourse. National computer networks are based on the X.25 standard, which enables host computers to serve distant "clients" through the telephone lines. Although the network can link all its hosts much as the telephone system links all subscribers, that is not what it was originally designed to do. Rather, it was supposed to enable clusters of users to share time on particular hosts. In the usual case, neither the users nor the hosts are in communication with each other.

Teletel was designed as an ordinary X.25 network in which the user is a point in a star-shaped interaction, hierarchically structured from a center, the host computer. But in the practice of the system the user became an agent of general horizontal interconnection (Guillaume 1989: 177ff.). This shift symbolizes the emergence of "networking" as an alternative to both formal organization and traditional community. The computer system provides a particularly favorable environment in which to experiment with this new social form.

In CMC the pragmatics of personal encounter are radically simplified, reduced, in fact, to the protocols of technical connection. Correspondingly, the ease of passage from one social contact to another is greatly increased, again following the logic of commutation. Pink messaging is merely a symptom of this transformation, punctuating a gradual process of change in society at large.

A whole rhetoric of liberation accompanies the generalized breakdown of the last rituals blocking the individuals in the redoubt of the traditional self. Personal life becomes an affair of network management as family and other stable structures collapse. The new postmodern individuals are described as supple, adaptable, capable of staging their personal performances on many and changing scenes from one day to the next. The network multiplies the power of its members by joining them in temporary social contracts along coaxial pathways of mutual confidence. The result is a postmodern "atomisation of society into flexible networks of language games" (Lyotard 1979: 34).

CMC profoundly alters the spatiotemporal coordinates of daily life, accelerating the individual beyond the speed of paper which is still the maximum velocity achieved by shuffling corporate and political dinosaurs. One achieves thereby a relative liberation: if you cannot escape the postindustrial nightmare of total administration, at least multiply the number of connections and contacts so that their point of intersection becomes a rich and juicy locus of choice. To be is to connect.

The struggle over the definition of the postindustrial age has only just begun.

THE SOCIAL CONSTRUCTION
OF THE MINITEL

As we have seen, the peculiar compromise that made Teletel a success was the resultant of these forces in tension. I have traced the terms of that compromise at the macrolevel of the social definition of videotex in France, but its imprint can also be identified in the technical code of the system interface.

WIRING THE BOURGEOIS INTERIOR

The Minitel is a sensitive index of these tensions. Those charged with designing it feared public rejection of anything resembling a computer, typewriter, or other professional apparatus and worked to fit it into the social context of the domestic environment. They carefully considered the "social factors" as well as the human factors involved in persuading millions of ordinary people to admit a terminal into their home (Feenberg 1989b: 29).

This is a design problem with a long and interesting history. Its presupposition is the separation of public and private, work and home, which begins, according to Walter Benjamin (1978: 154), under the July Monarchy: "For the private person, living space becomes, for the first time, antithetical to the place of work. The former is constituted by the interior; the office is its complement. The private person who squares his accounts with reality in his office demands that the interior be maintained in his illusions."

The history of design shows these intimate illusions gradually shaped by images drawn from the public sphere through the steady invasion of private space by public activities and artifacts. Everything from gas lighting to the use of chrome in furniture begins life in the public domain and gradually penetrates the home (Schivelbusch 1988; Forty 1986: chap. 5). The telephone and the electronic media intensify the penetration by decisively shifting the boundaries between the public and the private sphere.

The final disappearance of what Benjamin calls the "bourgeois

interior" awaits the generalization of interactivity. The new communications technologies promise to attenuate and perhaps even to dissolve
the distinction between the domestic and the public sphere. Telework
and telemarketing are expected to collapse the two worlds into one.
"The home can no longer pretend to remain the place of private life,
privileging noneconomic relations, autonomous with respect to the commercial world" (Marchand 1984: 184).

The Minitel is a tool for accomplishing this ultimate deterritorialization. Its modest design is a compromise on the way toward a radically different type of interior. Earlier videotex systems had employed
very elaborate and expensive dedicated terminals, television adapters,
or computers equipped with modems. So far, outside France, domestic
CMC has only succeeded where it is computer based, but its spread
has been largely confined to a hobbyist subculture. No design principles for general distribution can be learned from these hobbyists, who
are not bothered by the incongruous appearance of a large piece of
electronic equipment on the bedroom dresser or the dining room table.
Functionally, the Minitel is not even a computer in any case. It is just a
"dumb terminal," that is, a video screen and keyboard with minimal
memory and processing capabilities and a built-in modem. Such devices have been around for decades, primarily for use by engineers to
operate mainframe computers. Obviously designs suitable for that purpose would not qualify as attractive interior decoration.

The Minitel's designers broke with all these precedents and connoted it as an enhancement of the telephone rather than as a computer
or a new kind of television, the two existing models (Giraud 1984: 9).
Disguised as a "cute" telephonic device, the Minitel is a kind of Trojan
horse for rationalistic technical codes.

It is small, smaller even than a Macintosh, with a keyboard that can
be tilted up and locked to cover the screen. At first it was equipped
with an alphabetical keypad to distinguish it from a typewriter. That
keypad pleased neither nontypists nor typists and was eventually replaced with a standard one; however, the overall look of the Minitel
remained unbusinesslike (Marchand 1987: 64; Norman 1988: 147).
Most important, it has no disks and disk drives, the on-off switch on
its front is easy to find, and no intimidating and unsightly cables pro-
trude from its back, just an ordinary telephone cord.

The domesticated Minitel terminal adopts a telephonic rather than
a computing approach to its users' presumed technical capabilities.

Computer programs typically offer an immense array of options, trading off ease of use for power. Furthermore, until the success of Windows, most programs had such different interfaces that each one required a special apprenticeship. Anyone who has ever used early DOS communications software, with its opening screens for setting a dozen obscure parameters, can understand just how inappropriate it would be for general domestic use. The Minitel designers knew their customers well and offered an extremely simple connection procedure: dial up the number on the telephone, listen for the connection, press a single key.

The design of the function keys also contributed to ease of use. These were intended to operate the electronic telephone directory. At first there was some discussion of giving the keys highly specific names suited to that purpose, for example, "City," "Street," and so on. It was wisely decided instead to assign the function keys general names such as "Guide," "Next Screen," "Back," rather than tying them to any one service (Marchand 1987: 65). As a result, the keyboard imposes a standard and very simple user interface on all service providers, something achieved in the computing world by Windows, but only with much more elaborate equipment.

The Minitel testifies to the designers original skepticism with regard to communication applications of the system: the function keys are defined for screen-oriented interrogation of data banks, and the keypad, with its unsculptured chiclet keys, is so clumsy it defies attempts at touch typing. Here the French paid the price of relying on a telephonic model: captive telephone company suppliers ignorant of consumer electronics markets delivered a telephone-quality keypad below current international standards for even the cheapest portable typewriter. Needless to say, export of such a terminal has been difficult.

AMBIVALENT NETWORKS

So designed, the Minitel is a paradoxical object. Its telephonic disguise, thought necessary to its success in the home, introduces ambiguities into the definition of telematics and invites communications applications not anticipated by the designers (Weckerlé 1987: I, 14–15). For them the Minitel would always remain a computer terminal for gathering data, but the domestic telephone, to which the Minitel is attached, is a social, not an informational medium. The official technical definition of the system thus enters into contradiction with the telephonic practices that immediately colonize it once it is installed in the home (Weckerlé 1987: I, 26).

To the extent that the Minitel did not rule out human communication altogether, as have many videotex systems, it could be subverted from its intended purpose despite its limitations. For example, although the original function keys were not really designed for messaging applications, they could be incorporated into messaging programs, and users adapted to the poor keyboard by typing in a kind of on-line shorthand rich in new slang and inventive abbreviations. The Minitel thus became a communication device.

The walls of Paris were soon covered with posters advertising messaging services. A whole new iconography of the reinvented Minitel replaced the sober modernism of official Telecom propaganda. In these posters, the device is no longer a banal computer terminal, but is associated with blatant sexual provocation. In some ads, the Minitel walks, it talks, it beckons; its keyboard, which can flap up and down, becomes a mouth, the screen becomes a face. The silence of utilitarian telematics is broken in a bizarre cacophony.

In weakening the boundaries of private and public, the Minitel opens a two-way street. In one direction, households become the scene of hitherto public activities, such as consulting train schedules or bank accounts. But in the other direction, telematics unleashes a veritable storm of private fantasy on the unsuspecting public world. The individual still demands, in Benjamin's phrase, that the "interior be maintained in his illusions." But now those illusions take on an aggressively erotic form and are broadcast over the network.

The technical change in the Minitel implied by this social change is invisible but essential. It was designed as a client node, linked to host computers, and was not intended for use in a universally switched system which, like the telephone network, allows direct connection of any subscriber with any other. Yet as its image changed, the Telecom responded by creating a universal electronic mail service, called Minicom, which offers an electronic mailbox to everyone with a Minitel. The Minitel was finally to be fully integrated to the telephone network.

Despite the revenues earned from these communications applications, the Telecom grumbles that its system is being misused. Curiously, those who introduced the telephone a century ago fought a similar battle with users over its definition. The parallel is instructive. At first the telephone was compared to the telegraph and advertised primarily as an aid to commerce. There was widespread resistance to social uses of the telephone, and an attempt was made to define it as a serious instrument of business (Fischer 1988*a*; Attali and Stourdze 1977). In opposition to this "masculine" identification of the telephone, women gradually incorporated it into their daily lives as a social instrument (Fischer 1988*b*). As one telephone company official complained in 1909, "The telephone is going beyond its original design, and it is a positive fact that a large percentage of telephones in use today on a flat rental basis are used more in entertainment, diversion, social intercourse and accommodation to others than in actual cases of business or household neccesity" (quoted in Fischer 1988*a*: 48).

In France erotic connotations clustered around these early social uses of the telephone. It was worrisome that outsiders could intrude in the home while the husband and father were away at work. "In the imagination of the French of the Belle Epoque, the telephone was an instrument of seduction" (Bertho 1981: 243). So concerned was the phone company for the virtue of its female operators that it replaced them at night with males, presumably proof against temptation (Bertho 1981: 242–243).

Despite these difficult beginnings, by the 1930s sociability had become an undeniable referent of the telephone in the United States. (In France the change took longer.) Thus the telephone is a technology which, like videotex, was introduced with an official definition rejected by many users. And like the telephone, the Minitel too acquired new and unexpected connotations as it became a privileged instrument of personal encounter. In both cases, the magic play of presence and absence, of disembodied voice or text, generates unexpected social possibilities inherent in the very nature of mediated communication.

CONCLUSION: THE FUTURE OF THE COMMUNICATION SOCIETY

In its final configuration, Teletel was largely shaped by the users' preferences (Charon 1987: 100). The picture that emerges is quite different from initial expectations. What are the lessons of this outcome? The rationalistic image of the information age did not survive the test of experience unchanged. Teletel today is not just an information marketplace. Alongside the expected applications, users invented a new form of human communication to suit the need for social play and encounter in an impersonal, bureaucratic society. In so doing, ordinary people overrode the intentions of planners and designers and converted a postindustrial informational resource into a postmodern social environment.

The meaning of videotex technology has been irreversibly changed by this experience. But beyond the particulars of this example, a larger picture looms. In every case, the human dimension of communication technology emerges only gradually from behind the cultural assumptions of those who originate it and first signify it publicly through rationalistic codes. This process reveals the limits of the technocratic project of postindustrialism.

PART IV

Multicultural Modernity

Telephone cards issued by NTT. The card at center right shows
Kitarō Nishida.

CHAPTER EIGHT

The Problem of Modernity in Nishida's Philosophy

What we call the study of the Orient today has meant only taking the Orient as an object of study. As yet a profound reflection about the oriental way of thinking, in order to evolve a new method of thinking, has not been undertaken.

—*Kitarō Nishida 1958a: 356*

THE PROBLEM OF MODERNITY

In the 1930s and early 1940s, Japanese philosophy reflected the political climate by becoming increasingly nationalistic and authoritarian. With a few honorable exceptions, the major thinkers, such as Shūzō Kuki, Hajime Tanabe, and Tetsurō Watsuji defended Japanese imperialism.[1] Kitarō Nishida's ambiguous stance was particularly significant since he was the first Japanese philosopher able not only to understand the major trends of Western thought but also to employ the Western heritage to elaborate an original philosophy of his own. He is generally considered the founder of modern Japanese philosophy.

The association between philosophy and nationalist politics was not forgotten after the war and sometimes caused the one to be rejected with the other, especially on the Left. But philosophers' enthusiasm for government policy varied widely, and Nishida was by no means the worst. As we will see below, his nationalism was primarily cultural, not military, and he was critical of racist and totalitarian interpretations of official policy. Nevertheless, his inner doubts about the war do not appear to have affected his theoretical conception until quite late, and his ideas were turned to account by thinkers far more enthusiastic about

1. For the imperialist background to Japanese thought before the war, see Dale (1986).

imperialism than he was.[2] So far as I can tell, he continued to hope until near the end that Japan would emerge from the war as the center of an original politicocultural sphere. One of his chief political essays of the late 1930s summarized his cultural ambitions for Japan as follows: "Up to now Westerners thought that their culture was superior to all others, and that human culture advances toward their own form. Other peoples, such as Easterners, are behind and if they advance, they too will acquire the same form. There are even some Japanese who think like this. But . . . I believe there is something fundamentally different about the East. They [East and West] must complement each other and . . . achieve the eventual realization of a complete humanity. It is the task of Japanese culture to find such a principle" (Nishida 1965e: 404–405).[3] Although there is much in this position that is still of interest, it gradually became so mixed up with the fate of Japanese imperialism that today it is difficult to extract its lasting significance from the circumstances of its formulation. The aim of this chapter is to explain Nishida's views, and so far as possible to identify his contribution to debates on culture and modernity that are far from resolved even to this day.

Recently there has been a revival of interest in a key intellectual event of the war that sheds some light on Nishida's position. In 1942 the theme of cultural originality inspired several seminars, the most famous of which was titled "Overcoming [European] Modernity" (Kindai no Chokoku).[4] The meeting represented a wide range of views, some irrationalist and anti-Western, others more moderate in their claims for Japanese culture. A number of Nishida's followers were present, including Nishitani Keiji, who argued that Japanese culture is an original and authentic spiritual dispensation, comparable with the Western heritage in its ability to support a modern civilization. He thus rejected the claim of European civilization to define modernity for the entire human race. As H. D. Harootunian (1989: 74–75) notes, "The problem was to find a way to conceptualize a modernity that was made in Japan, not in the West" (see also Najita and Harootunian 1988).

Also in 1942 *Chuo Koron* published several roundtable discussions

2. For an example of Nishida's doubts, see his letter to Harada of June 1942 (Nishida 1965g: 199–200).

3. Unless otherwise noted, all translations from the Japanese by Yoko Arisaka.

4. The "overcoming modernity" seminar papers were published in *Chuo Koron*, July 1942. The participants included, among others, several writers, a famous literary critic (Kobayashi) and three of Nishida's students (Shimomura, Suzuki Shigetaka, and Nishitani). For contemporary Japanese evaluations, see Hiromatsu et al. (1989) and Hiromatsu (1990).

of Nishida's students on "The Standpoint of World History and Japan" (Sekaishiteki tachiba to Nihon).[5] These discussions reflect Nishida's simultaneous defense of traditional Japanese culture *and* affirmation of modern scientific-technical civilization. This is a pattern familiar from reactionary modernism in Germany, which, as Jeffrey Herf (1984) explains, reconceptualized science and technology after World War I as dimensions of a specifically German cultural heritage and thus salvaged them from the traditional romantic critique of materialist civilization in the West. However, in Nishida's own writings the pattern remains abstract, unrelated to the Nietzschean and nihilist themes of his German contemporaries, and compatible with a variety of different political positions that were in fact explored by his students.

His students' comments in *Chuo Koron* concretize this pattern in terms of the ideas of Ernst Jünger and other German reactionaries. They celebrate the fusion of "moralische energie" and modern technology that characterizes wartime Japan. They see the struggle in China as a contest of cultures in which Japan will forcibly liberate Asia from the West. Although they have their defenders, most readers find them worrying too little about the justification of the war and showing too much enthusiasm for the moral and aesthetic dimension of total mobilization. In their defense, it might be said that the participants were endorsing an imaginary war, but this is the common mode of engagement in real warfare in an age of ideology. It is fair to say that in these conversations, militarist nationalism acquired a paradoxically anti-imperialist aura from Nishida's philosophy of culture.

The idea of "overcoming modernity" foreshadows strangely the later attempts of other non-European intellectuals in the anticolonialist movement to declare their spiritual independence from the European sources of their modernity. Today these discussions are cited with increasing frequency as a precedent for the remarkable flowering of theories of Japanese exceptionalism (*nihonjinron*) in the 1960s and 1970s. The *nihonjinron* owe a subterranean debt to these predecessors, but much of interest in the earlier formulations has been lost, along with the more embarrassing traces of nationalism.

It is important to distinguish Nishida's rather complex dialectical universalism from the particularism of these various expressions of cultural nationalism. Writing before World War II, Nishida was one of many thinkers who attempted a positive philosophical expression of

5. Participants included Kosaka, Koyama, Suzuki Shigetaka, and Nishitani. For these meetings, see Sakai (1989: 105ff.).

Japan's contribution to a world culture he experienced as still in the making. Optimistically, he believed that "a point of union between Eastern and Western culture can be sought in Japan" (Nishida 1958a: 365). And he argued, against all forms of isolationism, "To become global Oriental culture must not stop at its own specificity but rather it must shed a new light on Western culture and a new world culture must be created" (Nishida 1965e: 407).

In this context, Western culture means, of course, the specific forms of rationality associated with modern science and technology; the cultural synthesis at which Nishida aimed involved investing these with new meaning derived from the Eastern tradition. But for the *nihonjin-ron*, written after the war, the historical possibilities have been foreclosed. The highest expression of Japanese culture is now the production of difference, particularity, in those regions of life still untouched by scientific-technical rationality. Thus what was originally put forward as a hypothesis about the formation of modern world culture, in which Japan would be Europe's equal and assimilate its science and technology, is today expressed in terms of the ethnically unique deviation of Japan from universal European models. That less ambitious project has less sweeping implications.[6]

The next chapter of this book takes up the contrast between these different approaches to rationality and culture in more detail. In it I analyze the representation of modernization in a work by the great Japanese writer Yasunari Kawabata. His novel *The Master of Go* describes a famous Go match that became for him a symbol of the modernization process. The match tested the universality of modern "rationality" by contrasting the traditional Japanese style of play with a new Western-inspired style.

More effectively than the *nihonjinron*, Kawabata's novel brings into focus the inadequacy of any simple identification of rationalization with Westernization. Go was a rational system long before the arrival of Europeans. As such it inspired a whole culture of strategic action subtly different from comparable Western notions. Traces of that culture and its specific form of rationality may be seen in the traditional elements of Kawabata's story. We will find them also at the center of

6. As Naoki Sakai (1989: 105) writes, "Contrary to what has been advertised by both sides, universalism and particularism reinforce and supplement each other; they are never in real conflict; they need each other and have to seek to form a symmetrical, mutually supporting relationship by every means in order to avoid a dialogic encounter which would necessarily jeopardize their reputedly secure and harmonized monologic worlds."

Nishida's theory of action. While Kawabata drew no conclusions from his story, Nishida argued explicitly that different cultures may give rise to different types of rational social order. This aspect of his philosophy is quite contemporary and has brought about a "return" to Nishida on the part of some Japanese intellectuals who have found anticipations of a Japanese "postmodernity" in his thought, while others worry about the renewal of nationalism this return appears to imply.[7]

EXPERIENCE AND SCIENCE

Like other literate non-Western peoples, the Japanese were easily able to understand scientific-technical rationality and the material advantages it gave the West. The contradiction between that form of rationality and their own cultural tradition troubled them deeply. Should they resist modernity altogether and remain loyal to their past? Would they, on the contrary, have to abandon their way of life to acquire the technical means of resistance to the West? Or could they adopt science and technology for practical purposes such as defense while retaining their traditional spiritual values?[8]

Each of these questions implies a naive exteriority, in the first case, of a nation to its history and the encounters that irreversibly mark its destiny; in the second, of a people to its culture, which cannot be dropped like an old glove; and in the third, of a spiritual tradition to the material life of society. Nishida rejected all these illusory solutions and argued instead that Japan could forge a specifically Japanese modernity out of a synthesis of Eastern and Western elements. He hoped to accommodate modernity to Japanese tradition not by rejecting Western science but by encompassing it in a concept of experience that grew naturally out of his culture.

Nishida understood modernity on fairly standard modern terms as the emergence of rational inquiry in opposition to doctrine-bound traditions and prejudices. Since Western thought advanced through rigorous attention to facts, any similar Japanese characteristics would constitute an indigenous potential for modernization. Accordingly, Nishida

7. For an accessible example of these new approaches, see Yujiro Nakamura's interesting article in *Critique* (1983). For the major survey of Nishida and his school in a Western language, see Ohashi (1990).
8. The latter position characterized forward-looking thinking in the nineteenth century in China under the slogan "Chung-hsueh wei-t'i, Hsi-hsueh wei-yung" (Chinese learning for fundamental principles, Western learning for practical applications); but the balance at which these progressives aimed was never achieved. For this earlier experience, see Ssu-yu Teng and John K. Fairbanks (1954: pt. 3).

(1958a: 352) believed that the Japanese orientation toward "the true facts of things"—experience in its pure state—was protomodern even before the encounter with the West.

But Nishida's understanding of experience was radically different from the prevailing Western view. As Yoko Arisaka (1993) has argued, the Japanese idea of experience is neither empiricist nor romantic. Empiricism eliminates the "secondary qualities" of the object and abstracts purified conceptual entities such as "sense data" or "brute facts" from the immediate content of experience, while romanticism calls for a return from conceptual activity to pure immediacy. But for the Japanese, experience is a paradoxical kind of *cultural* immediate. It involves refining the web of associations to a universally shared remainder. Haiku, for example, are often said to be concerned with the experience of nature. But in fact they articulate the natural world poetically in all its rich emotional and historical associations without distinguishing a purely material content from the contributions of culture and the subject.

This concept of experience is incompatible with Western naturalism. It makes sense to consider nature, abstracted from culture and history, as the foundation of experience only if the object can be conceived outside of any connection to a subject. Nishida claimed, on the contrary, that not nature but experience is the ontological basis of reality. In his account, the original "pure" experience is "as yet neither subject nor object," and in it "knowledge and its object are one" (Nishida 1965a: 1). Undifferentiated into subject and object, it does not consist in material things, but neither is it individual and psychological. Experience in this sense forms a shared realm of intersubjective meanings. It is external and culturally specific, "a kind of public field," not inward and universal like the idea of experience in the West (Nishida 1970: 186). Yet like the latter, it possesses a unique foundational pathos in the context of an absolute historicism such as Nishida (1965e: 410) was eventually to elaborate.

Nishida's fame dates from the publication in 1911 of his first book, *An Inquiry into the Good.*[9] It was in this remarkable book that he proposed his concept of an all-embracing field of experience. Nishida's later writings suggest that this concept and its various successors in his thought express a peculiarly Japanese approach, not in any exclusive

9. See *Zen no Kenkyu* (Nishida 1965a), translated by Masao Abe and Christopher Ives as *An Inquiry into the Good* (1990).

sense, but simply as products of the natural sequence of development of Japanese culture. He believed that Japanese philosophy was destined to raise this feature of Japanese culture to universality much as the natural sciences had universalized Western culture.

In what did this universalization consist? In fact, in the presentation of Japanese ideas in Western dress. This becomes clear from the first page of Nishida's maiden effort, for he begins by appropriating William James's concept of "pure experience" to explain his own idea. But despite this similar starting point, real differences divide Nishida and James. For example, while pure experience for James was simply an explanatory category, in Nishida it also sometimes appears to signify a version of Buddhist "no-mind," a particular way of relating to experience. Here pure experience risks regressing to a special psychological attitude, a kind of secular enlightenment (Feenberg and Arisaka 1990: 183–185).

Although Nishida's borrowings from James call into question the authenticity of his notion of a specifically Japanese culture of experience, his procedure is less absurd than it seems. For Nishida James represented a quasi-universal logic of modernity with which Japanese philosophy would have to come to terms in its break with traditional Oriental modes of discourse. Yet the goal was not indiscriminate Westernization. It was precisely James's critique of Western metaphysics that made his thought a suitable vehicle for modernizing Japanese philosophy. As Alfred North Whitehead (1925: 205) remarked, James did not so much continue the Western philosophical tradition as introduce a sharp break in its continuity comparable with the Cartesian revolution in scope and significance: he "clears the stage of the old paraphernalia" in harmony with profound transformations taking place throughout European culture. Nishida believed that these innovations opened the doors to a broader international participation in modernity. In the early twentieth century, James was not a bad place to look for access to this emerging world culture.

The oxymoron "quasi-universal" is thus appropriate in describing Nishida's evaluation of contemporary Western philosophy. While he recognized its cultural limitations, he nevertheless rejected the idea of an external critique of modernity from the standpoint of a construct of a supposedly Eastern alternative. Instead, he chose to plunge into Western philosophy in the confidence that the originality of his peculiarly Japanese insight would shine through. As Torataro Shimomura (1966: 16) explains, he took "Western philosophy as a mediation to be used in challenging Western philosophy itself." Nishida's confidence was not misplaced, but the operation in which he was engaged was far more difficult than he imagined in 1911. For over thirty years he was occupied in the construction of one after another version of his system, none of which ever satisfied him. In any case, his choice enabled him to steer a new course between both imitative Westernization and Eastern exoticism.[10]

In Nishida's later work, his already cultural concept of experience became the basis for a historicist ontology. He argued that insofar as the knowing subject is a human individual, it is not only a knower but also an actor, related not only to things but also to history. If one sees knowing as more than a contemplative encounter of a cogito with truth, but also as a practical social activity, then it is plausible to ask *what else* this activity entails besides pure knowledge. In question is not merely the validity of theory or the goal of the activity it orients, but even more its place in a life-form. Nishida (1965e: 408) called this his "fundamental idea": "Ordinarily, we think of the material world, the biological world, and the historical world as being separate. But in my view the historical world is the most concrete, and the material and biological worlds are abstractions. Thus, if we grasp the historical world, we grasp reality itself."

Today such formulations resonate with the notion that the universality of reason is an illusion. Following Foucault, feminist theory, and constructivist sociology of knowledge, a case can be made that our science is really only one "ethnoscience" among others (Harding 1994). However, in his historical situation, Nishida could not simply call for a full-scale return to ethnoscientific traditions without surrendering to reactionary obscurantism.[11] Nativist ideas of "Japanese science" seemed to him an excuse to resist the sincere confrontation with the cultural achievements of the West required by the globalizing process of mo-

10. This aspect of his achievement is lost, however, in much recent scholarship. Because Nishida attempted to reformulate a putatively Japanese worldview in the language of Western philosophy, students of his thought often read it as an elaborately encoded version of traditional Mahayana metaphysics (Carter 1989). While decoding Nishida's writings in Eastern terms can be useful, unfortunately this approach has also contributed to the widespread impression that Nishida was an antimodern, traditionalist thinker; but in fact, like most of his generation, he evaluated modern science and civilization positively on the whole (a view, be it said, that is not incompatible with a sympathy for Buddhism).

11. A Western reader who wants to understand the liberating impact of modern science in Japan (as opposed to the fear of its military technology) should look at Genpaku Sugita's famous book *Dawn of Western Science in Japan* (1969). Sugita recounts his experience (in 1771!) examining the dissected body of an executed criminal while compar-

dernity. Instead of proposing a return to an ethnically rooted "local knowledge," Nishida attempted to put science in its "place" in a historical framework that reflected the values of his culture. Science was to be given a new meaning in this context, not merely employed to secure material wealth and national independence. Such ideas were widely accessible to Japanese writers and intellectuals, caught in the midst of a modernizing movement they lived simultaneously as a response to both the universal—scientific truth—and the particular—Western power.

Nishida sought the principle of an absolute historicism in the underlying assumptions of Eastern culture. However, in turning to these Eastern sources, he believed himself to be advancing forward rather than backward in accordance with the tendencies of modern science. This apparent paradox makes sense if we share Nishida's view of the revolutionary character of modern science along lines already anticipated less self-consciously in his earlier appropriation of James. He believed that recent physics and mathematics had already broken with the West's own most parochial limitations, such as Christian transcendentalism and the substantialism inherited from the Greeks. But these traditional views hung on in the historical sciences where they would inevitably be overcome as other cultures appropriated modernity.

Eastern thought was uniquely qualified to contribute to this revolution in historical understanding. Like Greek thought, it defined reality in this-worldly terms, but it lacked the substantialist prejudice of the Greeks. Through its intervention, the historical world was to be swept up in the same sort of whirlwind as nature; not Aristotelian "things" or Cartesian "cogitos," not even Newtonian "laws," but tumultuous processes of conflictual structuration operate over the abyss of nothingness. To Nishida, Japanese modernity promised just such an up-to-date vision.

DIALECTICS OF PLACE

Under Hegel's influence, Nishida's argument for this approach took the form of a dialectical system. As a good Hegelian, he believed that

---

ing Chinese and Dutch anatomy books. All that he had been taught as a doctor was suddenly overthrown, and he devoted the rest of his life to translating the Dutch book in which he had found the truth his eyes confirmed. Naturally, this does not exclude a later recovery of a different level of meaning from Chinese anatomy once it is no longer taken literally as an image of bodily organs.

"the truth is the whole." Isolated parts are "abstract moments" of the "concrete universal," that is, the totality to which they belong. His system began with the abstract parts and worked toward the reconstruction of the whole by continually shifting point of view to broaden the context of explanation, moving from abstractions to the life-forms that animate them. This method yielded a dialectical progression of levels of knowledge, reflection, action, and experience, each of which represented a more or less abstract dimension of the concrete totality of experience; that totality itself was conceptualized, however, in a more Heideggerian than Hegelian style as the absolute activity of presence.[12] At this highest level, Nishida located something he called the "place of absolute nothingness," a philosophical concept derived from his earlier concept of pure experience and retaining its Buddhist allusion.

Here, schematically presented, are the four basic levels of Nishida's dialectic:[13]

1. Judgment, or knowledge of nature: the known abstracted from the knower.

2. Self-consciousness, or the psychological self of knowledge and action: the knower/doer abstracted from culture.

3. The world of meaning or values as ground of action: the self considered in its cultural significance.

4. "Absolute nothingness": experience as a field of immediate subject-object unity underlying culture, action, and knowledge and making them possible as objectifications of this prior unity.

Nishida called each level a *basho*, a "place" or "field." Within the various *basho*, he distinguished between an objective and a subjective aspect. What is subjective at one level appears as objective at the next level, and vice versa. For example, the subjective side of the level of judgment is the "field of predicates," the universal concepts employed in describing things. To these predicates corresponds the specific objectivity of the Aristotelian thing of which they are predicated. But what is this thing? Its individuality is inconceivable from the standpoint of a judgment that works exclusively with universals. Only an individual can relate to an individual. An adequate approach to the thing known

12. That this similarity is no accident is argued in Parkes (1992).
13. The originator of this sort of systematic interpretation of Nishida is Koyama (1935). See also Abe (1988).

requires us to go beyond the horizon of logical predication to identify a knowing thing, a subject that knows. This transition marks the passage to self-consciousness, the next level of the dialectic. The objective side of the dialectic of predicates—the thing—is now thematized as the knowing subject which transcends its predicates through embracing them on the field of knowledge. The predicates which first inhered in the thing now inhere in the consciousness that knows them. We have in a sense moved from Aristotle to Kant.

But the dialectical progression continues. As we saw in the last section, the knowing subject is more than a knower; it is a human being necessarily situated in a cultural world. "'Knowing' itself," Nishida (1970: 96) wrote, "is already a social and historical event." Paradoxically, although knowing is a culturally situated activity, culture appears arbitrary to it. Mere facts cannot determine the values that move the person to action, or discriminate between the good and the bad, the beautiful and the ugly. This is the function of culture, which can only be explained by a theory of the will in its relation to meanings. At that level consciousness appears to be determined by moral and aesthetic values which embrace it and provide the wider context for its actions. The subject—consciousness—becomes object in the framework of the cultural system of which it is a manifestation or "self-determination." This notion refers us not to a scientific theory of culture, but to a cultural theory of action.

At each level, Nishida's dialectic moves toward greater concreteness, away from abstract knowledge toward "existence," toward an experience so familiar we constantly overlook it in our attempts to categorize and explain. That experience is the immediate unity of subject and object in action. In most Western thought this unity is regarded as the effacement of consciousness in mere reflex. Philosophy, as a form of knowledge, quite naturally considers the objects of knowledge to be the primary reality. But for Nishida, the reverse is true: the engagement of the actor with the environment is more fundamental than cognition. Knowledge must dethrone itself and learn to see through the eyes of action.

That vision is not thoughtless, but the concept of self-consciousness is inadequate to represent it. This is another reason why Nishida's cultural theory moves beyond the stage of self-consciousness to a unifying intuition that is neither a knowing nor a doing as we usually conceive them, but the knowledge implicit in action itself. At that level, we find ourselves again in the world of pure experience, in which meaning and being are joined in cultural immediacy prior to the abstract distinction of fact and value, situation and will.

This "action-intuition" is similar to Heidegger's concept of "circumspection" (*Umsicht*) in that it too aims to liberate the subject-object relation from the limitations of rationalistic models. That means, among other things, overcoming a voluntaristic view of action as mere implementation of preconceived plans in pursuit of subjective ends. And like Heidegger, Nishida rejected the privilege of knowledge over the culturally defined world of action in which it finds its roots and instead asserted the relative priority of culture over knowledge.

However, Nishida believed that Heidegger's approach was insufficiently dynamic. He claimed that "even though Heidegger's idea of existence is historical, it is without movement or action" (Nishida 1970: 40). Here Nishida is at least partially unfair. Heidegger undoubtedly attained the standpoint of action, but it is true that he concerned himself only with the circumspective understanding of things as objects of practice and failed to grasp the self-constitution of the human subject in interaction with the Other. Nishida's philosophy, unlike Heidegger's, focused on the objectivity of the acting subject, its essential situatedness in a "place" (*basho*) out of which it must act and in which it is acted on and shaped.

This focus points beyond hermeneutics toward dialectics. But here too Nishida was unsatisfied with Western formulations. He believed that Hegel, while developing all the basic categories of dialectics, had remained stubbornly at the level of self-consciousness. "Hegel," he wrote, "sought reason behind reality rather than seeking reality beyond reason. In this his dialectical method was subjective and fell into mere formalism in trying to understand concrete reality. . . . We should not understand reality through logical formulas. Rather, reason must be interpreted historically as one aspect of our lives. Instead of understanding Hegel's logic in terms of its developmental process, it should be understood as an abstraction from concrete life as the self-determination of nothingness" (Nishida 1965f: 80). In sum, Nishida introduced action-intuition into Hegel's dialectic and reconceptualized it from the standpoint of practice, while introducing dialectics into the hermeneutics of historical practice he had found in Wilhelm Dilthey and Heidegger. As he put it elsewhere, "In the true historical world, the world of true objectivity, the approach to things and the approach to the Thou have become one" (Nishida 1970: 95 [translation modified]).

This unusual synthesis yields a kind of anticipation of systems theory. History is a process in which the "formed" becomes the "forming." Nishida deconstructed it into various circular processes of self-production and self-transformation. The subjects whose actions create history are themselves historical products. Values are at once objective historical givens and dynamic principles of action. So understood, history cannot be reduced to a concatenation of stable naturelike things, because it is composed ultimately of actions. Knowledge of the natural scientific sort cannot comprehend this historical world, which must be grasped instead by dialectics (Nishida 1970: 216ff.).[14]

So far in this exposition of his system I have emphasized the relationship between Nishida and the Western thinkers who influenced him and through whom his ideas become comprehensible. However, as with James, here too Nishida's thought cannot be reduced to its Western sources because the Eastern tradition to some extent shaped his use of them. This is especially apparent in the final stage of Nishida's dialectic. This stage, the "place of absolute nothingness," is not some sort of mystical intuition, but it is indeed difficult to understand without reference to Buddhism.[15] It was here that Nishida most clearly attempted to validate his notion of a unique contribution of the East to modern culture. I can only sketch an approach to this difficult concept, taking off from the historical and cultural problems that are my principal concern.

There is a dimension of Nishida's view of history that transcends mere theory of practice toward existential realization. In Nishida, actors necessarily posit an environment against which they must assert themselves to live, yet as they express their life they objectify themselves in the struggle and become the environment of each other. This is the "identity of opposites" or "contradictions": "Action means negation of the other, and means the will to make the other [an expression of] oneself. It means that the Self wants to be the world. But it also means, on the other hand, that the Self denies itself and becomes a part of the world" (Nishida 1958b: 171). "Acting," in sum, "is essentially 'being acted'" (Nishida 1958b: 186).

The Leibnizian image of a community of monads each reflecting the world in itself suggested a model of this dialectic of self and other.

14. For a different reading of Nishida's conception of history (and the only other one I have found in English), see Huh (1990).

15. Although he does not cite Nishida in this connection, Nishitani's interpretation of Sunyata could almost be a commentary on the Buddhist background to his concept of absolute nothingness (Nishitani 1982). For further explanation, see also Nishitani (1991).

According to Nishida (1987: 58), "Each existential monad originates itself by expressing itself; and yet it expresses itself by negating itself and expressing the world. The monads are thus co-originating, and form the world through their mutual negation. The monads are the world's own perspectives; they form the world interexpressively through their own mutual negation and affirmation. Conversely, the concrete matrix of historical actuality that exists and moves through itself enfolds these monadic perspectives within itself." The objectivity of history thus arises from the mutual perceptions of the individuals engaged within it. Put another way, its objectivity is simply the necessarily reciprocal relations of these actions because actor and object have become perspectives on each other rather than distinct species.

The inner realization of this truth is the existential discovery of the "field" (basho) on which self and other deploy their identity and difference. When the self identifies concretely with that field, it "discovers the self-transforming matrix of history in its own bottomless depths" (Nishida 1987: 84). That field is a scene of struggle understood in traditional Buddhist rather than Western individualist terms: one plays one's role without reserve but also with an immediate sense of the system formed by one's interactions with other individuals. The more one identifies with the system as a whole, the more one is properly in one's own place within it and vice versa. This peculiar double structure of action, operating as an ontological postulate, provides an original image of the concrete totality as the "place of nothingness."

Nishida's conclusion is profoundly paradoxical. He founded an absolute historicism that encompassed modern science in an account of experience derived from the Eastern tradition. That account is itself modern in the sense that it responds to the thoroughgoing epistemological atheism that underlies twentieth-century science and philosophy. Yet in demonstrating that history is the ultimate reality, Nishida brought back the science question from a different angle. As I will argue in the next section, his own Eastern logic forbade a nativist regression. Scientific knowledge, as the culture and action of the West, cannot be dismissed, but must be encountered authentically in the struggle for modernity. The dialectical system was intended to engage Japan in that struggle.

In sum, Nishida grasped the cultural connections that threaten scientific self-certainty and the social reciprocities that undermine subjective autonomy and yet affirmed science and subjectivity. He refused the transcendence of culture in knowledge without adopting a comforting relativism that would at least allow disengagement from the hegemony of Western science. Nishida seems to have been determined to leave himself no resting place. This ambivalence is related to Japan's difficult place in the system of world culture.

CULTURAL SELF-AFFIRMATION

Nishida's philosophy of culture attempted to vindicate the self-assertion of Japan as an Asian nation against European world hegemony. The new order emerging from the war would restore Japan's historic "world mission," lost so long as "Asian nations were suppressed by European imperialism and viewed from a colonial standpoint" (Nishida 1965d: 429).

All modern cultures, including the Japanese, are equal, according to Nishida, in the sense that each has a contribution to make to an emerging world culture (Nishida 1965b: 267–268). There can be no single universal replacement for national culture, for "when they lose their specificity they cease to be cultures"; but neither does the uniqueness of each culture authorize "a merely abstract advance in an individual direction" (Nishida 1970: 254). "A true world culture will be formed only by various cultures preserving their own respective viewpoints, but simultaneously developing themselves through global mediation" (Nishida 1970: 254). All modern cultures must participate in a fruitful intermingling and mutual contamination. World culture consists in a field of dialogue and conflict rather than a specific substantive way of life, comparable to the existing cultures. "Each people stands on its own historical ground and has its own world mission, and that is how each nation possesses a historical life. When I say that each nation must realize itself while transcending itself and creating a world culture, I mean that each nation must realize itself through its own particular culture. It is in this way that particular cultures emerge from the foundation of history and constitute a world culture. In such a world each national culture expresses its own unique historical life and, at the same time, through their world-historical missions they all unite to form one world" (Nishida 1965c: 428). This dialectic of world culture is consistent with Nishida's conception of action. The Oriental engagement with the West embraced a deeper collaboration under the surface conflict; it was to be a productive transformation of modernity with global consequences.

Because modern cultures all share science, they now subsist generally in the "truth" and can no longer be described as mere errors or diva- gations. But what then explains their multiplicity? Nishida's historicist ontology promised a "multicultural" bridge between national particu- larity and rational universality. The categories of the various stages of his dialectic can each be employed to describe the unique emphasis of a cultural type. Cultures consist in horizons of thought and action, paradigms or "archetypes," in which one or another category is unilat- erally absolutized (Nishida 1958a: 353–354). National struggles man- ifest conflicts between the diverse conceptual frameworks of social ontology at the level of whole peoples and their ways of life. In sum, ontological and cultural categories are mutually translatable. Presum- ably, cultures communicate and complete each other through the pro- cesses of exchange and discussion in which ontological visions are elaborated.

This view certainly owed something to Hegel's *Phenomenology*, al- though Nishida refused the final synthesis at which Hegel was tradi- tionally said to aim. In this regard, Nishida was actually closer to con- temporary Hegel scholarship, which argues that the ultimate "Begriff" (concept) does not resolve contradictions metaphysically in a substan- tive totality but embraces them methodologically, maintaining the op- position between them. Such antimetaphysical readings of Hegel re- spond to skeptical and neo-Kantian currents in contemporary thought (Pippin 1991: 66–79).

Nishida's reasons for rejecting synthesis were quite different: his em- phasis on action excluded a purely conceptual resolution of the contra- dictions. This would explain why his writings do not offer third terms but rather endlessly alternating emphases among the fragmented field of historical and cultural contradictions and their corresponding ac- tion positions in the world system.

Alongside this affirmation of multiplicity, Nishida defended the ap- parently contrary notion that Japanese culture has a global character. Since modern culture is scientific in character, Japan's global mission cannot be merely religious or aesthetic as is sometimes supposed, but must include a unique intellectual content, a "logic," with the sort of universal value attributed to other achievements of modern thought (Nishida 1958a: 363). This logic was Japan's culturally specific appro- priation of modernity in terms of the "identity of contradictions" as described in the previous section.

This is the same logic that underlay Japan's long history of flexibil- ity and assimilation of alien influences. In ancient times, Japan absorbed Chinese culture, and so today will it assimilate Western culture, serving thereby as a global point of junction (Nishida 1965e: 417). According to Nishida, the "formlessness" or "emptiness" of Japanese culture enables it to harbor unresolved contradictions in itself. This formlessness reflects at the historicocultural level the philosophical notions of pure experience and absolute nothingness. Here these apparently abstruse philosophical categories turn out to signify a unique cultural identity and role.

It is difficult to be sure what Nishida thought of the function of philosophy in modern life, but it seems to serve as a cultural crossroads, an essential point of translation and communication in an era characterized by intensifying interactions between peoples. Nishida saw his own thought as the product of the confrontation of cultures in the new era of world culture. It did not offer a final synthesis but a language in terms of which the philosopher can be at home in a multiplicity of forms of thought. Nishida's ambition was not to resolve these contradictions, but to devise a method for thinking each moment in its relation to its Other. In this his philosophy reflected the emptiness which opened Japan to universal experience (Nishida 1965e: 407).

But unfortunately, Nishida's conception of cultural self-affirmation seems to have gone well beyond the search for fruitful dialogue and embraced military struggle as a positive moment. In conclusion, I must discuss this disturbing aspect of his thought. This discussion is, however, limited by the confusion that surrounds Nishida's role in the war; he does not appear to have had any official or even semiofficial post, and the texts from the period are so abstract they might be accommodated to rather different political positions. Hence the inconclusive controversy between those who hold Nishida, as a leading intellectual, in some measure responsible for Japanese imperialism and those who see him as a moderate who dissociated himself from the worst ideological excesses of the time (Hiromatsu 1990: 207–208; Lavelle 1994; Yusa 1991). Nevertheless, I will argue that his late texts point at least to provisional conclusions which I put forward below in the hope of provoking further research and discussion.

GREEKS OR JEWS?

Hegel argued that war is a means of spiritual self-affirmation for modern nations. Today this view has become shocking, but for several generations Hegel's doctrine merely articulated the common sense of nations in Europe and North America. Recall, for example, the vulgar Hegelianism of our own concept of "Manifest Destiny." In a later time, conservative Japanese philosophers defended war on just such Hegelian grounds without understanding that it was too late in the day to launch a colonial enterprise and carve out a sphere of influence of the old type.

It seems that Nishida shared this view. Several future national leaders (Konoe, Kido) attended his classes, and in 1941 he was even invited to give a speech to the emperor (Nishida 1965b).[16] It is not surprising then that he was consulted by the government. He opposed war with the United States and he emphasized the importance of cosmopolitan cultural interaction to an unusual degree, but otherwise his occasional comments on world politics appear to follow the conventional opinion of the day (Nishida 1965c). Although he never explained how to achieve it, he supported Japanese hegemony in Asia, and he was an enthusiastic advocate of the emperor system. Indeed, for Nishida the imperial house lay at the center of both the political and cultural systems. As such, he called it the "identity of contradictions," situating it mysteriously beyond the reach of his own concept of action as a system of reciprocities (Nishida 1965d: 336).[17] This would seem to absolutize the state as an expression of the emperor's will; only the sustained ambiguity of politics and culture in Nishida's thought distances it somewhat from the crude statist nationalism of the day by signifying that will as a place (basho) of nothingness without particular content.

The flavor of his position, and much of the reason for our difficulty in evaluating it today, is clear from the following thoroughly symptomatic passage from his speech to the emperor:

> Today, due to the extensive development of global transportation, the world has become one. Today's nationalism must be conceptualized from this standpoint. It is not a nationalism in which each nation turns in on itself, but rather in which each nation secures a position of its own within the world, that is to say, each nation must become globally aware. When diverse peoples enter into such a worldhistorical (sekaishiteki) relation, there may be conflicts among them such as we see today, but this is only natural. The most worldhistorical (sekaishiteki) nation must then serve as a center

16. This was a great honor but not quite the union of philosopher and statesman a Straussian might imagine. Other prominent intellectuals were given a similar opportunity to educate the emperor in what was essentially a ceremonial occasion.

17. In Heideggerian terms, this is to ignore the ontological difference and to identify Being itself with a particular being. As we know, Heidegger himself was not above making a similar mistake.

to stabilize this turbulent period. What do I mean by a nation having a global character? It means that this nation embraces holism yet at the same time does not deny the individual and, indeed, takes individual creation as its medium. Today we usually conceive of individualism and holism as opposed to one another, but by itself, individualism is outdated, and any holism which denies the individual is also a thing of the past. (Nishida 1965b: 270–271)

In the context of the ongoing war, these remarks can, but need not necessarily, be read as a euphemistic defense of Japanese imperialism, yet at the same time Nishida also appears to contest totalitarianism in the name of individual and cultural creativity.

On reading Nishida's war writings, the comparison with Heidegger immediately springs to mind. But this comparison is misleading. It is true that like Heidegger in his Nazi phase, Nishida could be heard repeating imperialist slogans. But unlike Heidegger, whose "private National Socialism" was expressed for a time in the official language of the Nazi state he represented as a government official, the private thinker Nishida always qualified offensive expressions of nationalism from his own culturalist standpoint. Here, for example, is a passage in which, without actually questioning the Imperial Way ideology that justified the Pacific war, Nishida (1965d: 341) attempted to reformulate it culturally: "Japan's formative principle must become the formative principle of the world as well. . . . But it is most dangerous to subjectivize Japan. That merely militarizes the Imperial Way (kodo) and transforms it into imperialism (teikokushugika). . . . In contrast we must contribute to the world by discovering our own principle of self-formation in the depths of our historical development; that principle is the identity of contradictions. This is the authentic . . . Imperial Way. This is the true meaning of 'Eight Corners of The World Under One Roof' (hakko ichiu)."[18]

There is an even deeper distinction to be made between Nishida and Heidegger in terms of their historical situation. Although Heidegger claimed to look toward the future, he was unable to give any positive content to his notion of a distinctively authentic modernity, and eventually he fell victim to the deluded hope that Germany could be the

18. Lavelle (1994) dismisses this apparently antiwar statement and assimilates Nishida's views to the moderate ultranationalism of the Konoe faction on the grounds that anti-imperialist rhetoric was common even in the military at the time. I believe this goes too far toward disambiguating the ambiguities Nishida appears to have purposely introduced into his public statements.

agent for his reactionary program of affirming man against technology and mass society. This was the basis of his Nazi adventure, to which he never counterposed another comprehensible, much less credible, alternative (Herf 1984: 109ff.). Heidegger's later thought of Being offers an oracular discourse that strives nobly to reenchant the world, but it falls far short of a concrete alternative.[19]

By contrast, as a non-Westerner in a newly developed country Nishida seems to have experienced no particular anxiety about scientific-technical progress. He was untouched by the gloomy mood fostered by Weber, Jünger, and Spengler and looked hopefully to the emergence of an alternative modernity defined in the rich terms of his own living Japanese culture. Accordingly, he had no need of a "politics of being" to break with a despised present.

One might also recall Marcuse's position, which offers a third point of comparison. His early philosophy was in large measure a left Hegelian reaction to Heidegger's thought in contrast with Nishida's right Hegelian turn toward national culture. Like his teacher, Marcuse sought to reframe the "question of technology" in terms of an ontology of practice. Methodologically, he too agreed on the need to found reason phenomenologically in the world of everyday experience. But Marcuse was also influenced by Hegel, who offered a historicized notion of that world and hence suggested the necessity of a far more concrete foundation than anything in Heidegger.

The search for a historical foundation becomes complicated due to the hegemony of technology in the West. One could no longer look to traditional culture for a solution, and only a political fool, which Heidegger certainly was, would imagine that crude nationalism could introduce a new ontological dispensation. Nor could one simply turn to the culture of the present, which was already so colonized by scientific-technical rationality that it offered no alternative. Thus Marcuse could rely on no specific geographically situated culture for a framework, as could Nishida.

As a Westerner, his sights had to be turned toward the future. The notion of socialist revolution appeared to serve his purpose by widening the historical context of scientific-technical rationality to encompass its potential transformation in a pacified society. But given this approach, Marcuse would have had to be naive indeed not to notice

19. Unbelievably, Heidegger's last interview expresses his conviction that "only a God can save us" from modern technology. For a thorough study of Heidegger's views on technology, see Zimmerman (1990).

that the Soviet Union was engaged in modernizing along Western lines, and in fact he kept his utopian distance from the Soviet experiment. Resistance to a historicist unification of idea and actuality was more difficult for Nishida. He had identified the principle of absolute nothingness with the essence of his own national culture, which, in his view, still maintained significant autonomy despite two generations of development.

It was this hopeful conception that became entangled with Japanese imperialism in his 1943 response to the War Cabinet's request for a paper on the New World Order. There he can be found telling the old Hegelian story of national identity. According to this text, the Pacific war would lead to the appropriation of modernity by Eastern cultures that had so far participated in the modern world only as objects of Western conquest. The war was interpreted here as a kind of struggle for recognition out of which a new form of global community should emerge.

Nishida did not explain why Japan would have to mimic Western colonialism to achieve this laudable goal, and his understanding of events appears strangely anachronistic. He naively compared the war to the Greek struggle with Persia, as the military precondition of a triumphant cultural self-affirmation of world-historical significance: "Just as the victory of Greece in the Persian War long ago set European culture on a path it has followed up to this day, so too the contemporary East Asian war determines a path of development for the coming epoch of world history" (Nishida 1965c: 429). From that standpoint Japan's defeat would seem to represent the destruction of a cultural universe, indeed of the very possibility of cultural plurality in the modern world.

There is something of the Meiji man in this position. In the Meiji period Japanese militarism had a much clearer anti-imperialist content than later on. It is easy to sympathize with Nishida's enthusiasm for Japanese victories against the Russians in 1905, when Japan was still subject to national humiliation by the Western powers. It is not so easy to understand his apparent support for the war with China in the 1930s and 1940s when Japan was a great power.

Perhaps Nishida's understated position reflected awareness of this difference. No doubt he hoped that emphasizing Japanese cultural rather than military leadership in Asia would contribute to an early end to the war. But he continued to think in terms of power blocs; his writings do not reflect until quite late a clear understanding that

Japanese colonial policy was not simply a normal mode of participation in global politics, but the very death of his own cultural program.[20] In our time freedom, equality, and trade have cultural implications, not the military conquest of weaker neighbors.

We can hardly miss this point today, given the postwar experience of decolonization. Had Japan won the Pacific war, it would have founded an immense Asian empire at precisely the moment when Europe was giving up on colonialism. As honorary Europeans, the Japanese would have arrived too late at this banquet table to enjoy the fun. One imagines the consequences: Japan would have spent the next generation fighting guerrilla wars all over Asia; fascism would have remained in power for another generation. Far from the conquest of Asia fulfilling Nishida's cultural program, it would have resulted in a terrible cultural catastrophe.

Toward the end of the war, Nishida seems to have understood his epoch better. He and his circle engaged in intense discussions of postwar policy in view of national-cultural survival. Several months before the surrender, he wrote a final essay entitled *The Logic of Basho and the Religious Worldview*, which hinted at a very different understanding of Japan's situation. This extraordinary essay sharply distinguishes between the political and the religious dimension of human experience. The nation is an ethical-political unity in the Hegelian sense of *Sittlichkeit*, but as such it belongs to the "corrupt" world of everyday existence. Hence "the nation does not save our souls" (Nishida 1987: 122). Yet by the logic of the "identity of contradictions," immanence *is* transcendence and national life therefore also relates to the absolute. "The reason that a nation is a nation lies . . . in its religious character as a self-expression of historical life. A true nation arises when a people harbors the world-principle within itself and forms itself historically and socially" (Nishida 1987: 116). The religious essence of nationality is both culturally specific and global, and as such it contains the secret of international coexistence in the modern age.

These ideas represent a radical break with contemporary Japanese nationalism. Nishida's earlier political writings had followed conventional opinion in overestimating the philosophical significance of the state, a natural enough tendency given the centrality of the state in re-

20. Power-bloc thinking was not of course confined to Japan. As late as 1949, George Kennan could write that "realism will call upon us not to oppose the re-entry of Japanese influence and activity into Korea and Manchuria" to hold back Soviet expansion in Asia (quoted in Cummings 1989: 16).

shaping Japan from the Meiji period on. However, this state nationalism had proven a false path, and Nishida's attempt to infuse it with his own culturalism was a disastrous failure, as he would no doubt have conceded had he survived the war.

As imminent defeat clarified the situation, Nishida innovated a new nationalist discourse based not on the state but on culture. That discourse was still continuous with the old state nationalism in many particulars, and may, through the postwar influence of his followers, have helped to provide the basis for the conservative reconstruction of Japan as an unarmed culture-nation. The important point was the shift to a principled affirmation of ethnic identity, not of course on a primitive racialist basis but in terms of a global cultural mission that excluded militarism. This shift showed up in a change in historical metaphors for Japan's position in the world.

The implicit point of comparison was no longer the Greeks but the ancient Jews. Their defeat and occupation by the Babylonians is recorded in the Bible, particularly in the prophetic Book of Jeremiah. Nishida (1987: 116) noted that despite their conquest, the Jews maintained their "spiritual self-confidence" and transcended their merely ethnic limitations to create a world religion.[21] Just so, he argues, "the Japanese spirit participating in world history . . . can become the point of departure for a new global culture," but only if Japan overcomes its "insular" and "vainly self-confident" outlook (Nishida 1987: 112). Then Japan would no longer have to compete with the West by violence to make its cultural contribution, but could, like the Jews, learn to defend and spread its values from inside a system defined and dominated by the Other.

Nishida found in the biblical texts a coded way of referring to the impending defeat he predicted more openly in his letters of the period. One easily understands the appeal of the Prophecies in the midst of the bombing attacks of 1945: "For I have set my face against this city for evil, and not for good, saith the Lord: it shall be given into the hand of the king of Babylon, and he shall burn it with fire." Astonishingly, as MacArthur's ships approached, Nishida (1987: 116) cited Jeremiah's warning that Nebuchadnezzer is also a servant of Yahweh. Even the enemies of the chosen serve God's ends by chastening his people. In

21. Cf. Nishida's (1965g: 426) letter to D. T. Suzuki of May 1945: "Lately, reading the history of the development of Jewish religion has made me think a lot. The Jews built the foundation for the direction of development of their world religion in the Babylonian captivity. The true spirit of the people must be like this. The nation which combines self-confidence with militarism perishes when the military power perishes."

this bizarre passage Nishida seemed to anticipate a *meaningful* occupation, which indeed it proved to be.

And none too soon! Japan's role in the modern world could not possibly conform to the old Hegelian model, but required a new one the outlines of which were only barely visible in the months preceding the defeat. The Jewish example indicated a way out through cleanly separating cultural from politicomilitary self-affirmation. Nishida's surprising reference to the Jews suggests that he wanted Japan to accept its defeat and choose its fate. He seemed to promise that if it did so Japan would rise from the ashes as a great cultural force in the postwar world.

CONCLUSION

For Nishida the globalization of world culture challenged philosophy and science to recognize the contributions of non-Western peoples. He believed that Oriental culture could offer a new paradigm of historical understanding that would respond not only to the theoretical problems of the times but also to the pressing need for a new mode of coexistence between nations and cultures. That paradigm was based on the notion of the identity of contradictions, global conflict grasped as a process of self- and world-formation. Japanese culture seemed to Nishida exemplary in this regard and capable of representing the new paradigm as a specific national instance, much as Europe represented the universal achievements of natural science to the world at large.

The contemporary relevance of these ideas is clear. The gradual decentering of the world system calls for renewed reflection on the equality of cultures. But it is not easy to reconcile that moral exigency with the powerful cognitive claims of the hegemonic science and technology. This is the dilemma Nishida faced. In responding to it, he showed that world culture is plural not simply in the variety of its dying traditions but in the very spirit of its distinctive modern experiments.

CHAPTER NINE

Alternative Modernity?

Playing the Japanese Game of Culture

If games both fashion and reflect culture, it stands to reason
that to a certain extent a whole civilization and, within that
civilization, an entire era can be characterized by its games.
                                        —*Roger Caillois 1955*

The writer's irony is a negative mysticism to be found in
times without a god.
                                        —*Georg Lukács 1968: 90*

GAMES AS RATIONAL SYSTEMS

In 1938 the great Japanese novelist Yasunari Kawabata witnessed a
turning point in the history of the game of Go. Kawabata was then
a young reporter covering the championship match sponsored by his
newspaper. Honnimbō Shusai, the "Invincible Master," who had reigned
over the world of Go for a generation, was pitted against a young challenger. So popular was Go that Kawabata's newspaper could offer the
players substantial sums for participating and pay all their expenses.
These were considerable as the match lasted many months.

Kawabata felt he had witnessed the end of an era at that Go match
in 1938. Many years later he brought out his old newspaper articles,
added new fictional material, and published a novel called *Meijin*, later
translated into English as *The Master of Go*. This novel is an elegy for
the world the Japanese lost as they modernized. But Kawabata's rather
sentimental traditionalism is not so simple as it appears at first; nostalgia is a moment in the structure of modern consciousness, and a for-
tiori, novelistic form. This is why his story has much to tell us about
the nature and possibilities of modern society.

It may seem strange that Kawabata's most sustained investigation
of modernity should be the story of a board game, but in fact games
exemplify formally rational systems. Like markets, law, and scientific

and technical research, games break loose from the continuum of social life to impose a rational order on a sector of experience. Modern
institutions too are characterized by explicit rules, unambiguous measures, defined times and places of action, absence of predetermined content, equalization of participants' positions. Their gamelike structure is
contrasted favorably in modernizing ideology to irrational, dogmatic,
and biased traditions.

We will see how Kawabata, through his narrative of the great Go
match, turns the argument around and develops an implicit critique of
the particularity and bias of formal rationality. He accomplishes this by
the peculiar literary technique of unfolding layer after layer of meaning in the moves of the game. The apparently neutral forms of play
turn out to be loaded with social, cultural, and historical content. The
Go match can stand for the whole range of modern institutions invad-
ing Japan, each of which delivers far more in the way of social change
than appears on the surface.

In the concluding portion of this chapter, I attempt to enlarge the
scope of these reflections in three directions. I will first compare the
layered structure of Kawabata's novel with the order of Nishida's dialectic, discussed in the previous chapter. Second, I will compare his
literary technique with Lukács's early theory of the novel. Using different means derived from his own culture, Kawabata achieved a form
based on the same sort of double meanings Lukács analyzes in terms
of the category of irony. It is this form which structures Kawabata's
critique of Western modernity. Third, I will discuss the larger implications of Kawabata's novel for the question of modernity. Japan's cultural specificity is often mentioned as a factor in its rise to industrial
power. Kawabata's novel suggests a new way of thinking about why
this might be so.

THE RULES OF THE GAME

Millions of Japanese play Go much as Westerners play chess. Kawabata's novel assumes a passing familiarity with the game and, unfortunately, we will not be able to discuss it without at least that degree of
acquaintance. I must therefore ask the reader to bear with me for a
brief description of the rules.[1]

Go is said to be more difficult than chess. Although the rules are

1. For more on Go, see Korschelt (1965).

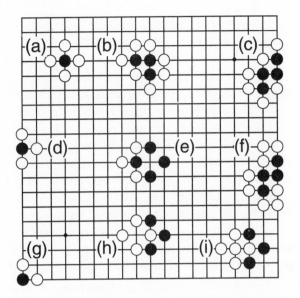

Figure 1. Typical configurations of stones on a Go board.
From O. Korschelt, *The Theory and Practice of Go* (Tokyo:
Charles E. Tuttle, 1965), 34. Reprinted by permission.

simpler, the play is more complicated if only because the board is more
than four times as "big" as a chess board. Black and white stones are
placed on this board at the intersections of a grid nineteen by nineteen
lines (see fig. 1). The number of possible moves is the factorial of 361,
more than the number of atoms in the galaxy.

The aim of play is to capture territory and enemy pieces by surrounding them with one's own pieces. Once placed on the board, pieces
cannot be moved; they remain where they were played until they are
captured. Every piece covers the intersection of two lines, which themselves intersect with other lines at four adjacent points. Each of these
points counts as an "eye" or "breathing space." Adjacent pieces of the
same color share "eyes." So long as a piece or a group of pieces has at
least one such "eye" uncovered by the opponent, it is "alive." Once all
its "eyes" have been taken, it is captured and the space it occupied belongs to the opponent's count (see fig. 1, a–d).

Because the board is so large, it is impossible to concentrate on any
one portion of it for long without losing the initiative to a more mo-
bile adversary. Thus contests break out everywhere and the players periodically return to one or another of them, advancing battles toward
an eventual conclusion a few moves at a time. Beginners are bewildered

by the frequent interruption of these apparently inconclusive struggles, but this is the essence of the game.

The game moves through roughly three phases. At first territory is staked out by posting isolated pieces around the board. Gradually battles emerge around conflicting claims, none of which are entirely secure in the early phase of the game. Finally, the board is filled in, the last ambiguities removed, and the captured spaces and pieces counted. Until the last phase, there are always many incomplete conquests, broken lines, lost pieces left in place, and so on. Although significant stakes ride on clearing them up properly, these housekeeping tasks are generally left till the end while the players confront more serious challenges.

The rules of Go are a model of simplicity and clarity, but they contain one logical flaw. An oscillating pattern can emerge in which both players have a disproportionately large incentive to repeat their last move. This situation occurs when the piece used to take an enemy piece is itself exposed to immediate capture, reproducing the status quo ante (see fig. 1, e and h). This situation is called a *kō*, from the Sanskrit *kalpa*, meaning an epoch or eternity. To prevent endless repetition, the second player is obliged to play away from the *kō* for a turn, breaking the pattern. Then the first player can fill it in. (If white plays in the space on figure 1, h, after removing the black piece, the *kō* disappears, as in figure 1, i.) We will have to return later to this idea of "playing away."

THE WAY OF GO: AUTONOMY AND REFLECTION

Go was introduced into Japan from China thirteen centuries ago. In Japan, it gradually evolved into a discipline, a kind of sedentary martial art. As such Go came to be seen as a *dō*, or Way of self-realization, and not primarily as a contest, although obviously the best player was honored. Kawabata writes, "The Oriental game has gone beyond game and test of strength and become a way of art. It has about it a certain Oriental mystique and nobility" (p. 117). And he compares it to the Nō drama and the tea ceremony as belonging to "a strange Japanese tradition" (p. 118).[2] With this background in mind, one is less astonished to learn that the champion of the leading school of Go took Buddhist orders and was called the Honnimbō.

2. For Kawabata's relation to this tradition, see his Nobel Prize acceptance speech (1969), and Petersen (1979: 129–132). Quotations from *The Master of Go* in this chapter will be indicated by page number only.

This characteristically Japanese concept of Way has a two-tiered structure. For an activity to support a Way, it must be abstracted from the contingencies of everyday life and constructed as an autonomous "field" with its own logic. Then, this field must become a locus of reflection and self-transformation for the agent engaged in activity on it.

The autonomization of Go involves the following features which it shares with other board games:

1. Every move in the game must conform to an explicitly formulated, unambiguous rule.

2. Moves are stripped of semantic content and reduced to unambiguous acts that can be represented diagrammatically with precision.

3. The purpose of each move and of the game as a whole is clearly defined and immanent in the rules.

4. The game discriminates between winners and losers by a precise quantitative measure, leaving no room for doubt about the outcome.

5. Moves can always be clearly distinguished from other events in the social surroundings of the game, and can therefore be assigned a specific "space" and "time" of play.

6. Insofar as the rules are concerned, players' positions in the game are equivalent in every possible respect, the major and unavoidable exception being the first move.

7. The game is a collaborative performance requiring various forms of reciprocity, from the simplest—alternating and mutually responsive moves—to the most complex—attention to the competitor's state of mind or physical needs.

Two features of this list seem particularly significant. They are (1) the care with which ambiguity has been eliminated from the field of play through such means as explicit rules and quantitative measures and (2) the artificial equalization of the players who, in everyday life, are sure to be subtly differentiated in ways the game ignores. These features of the game indicate its remoteness from the surrounding social world in which ambiguity and inequality are the rule. And by this very token, these features seem to echo strangely our modern notions of scientific and political rationality. We will return to this surprising coincidence.

Autonomy is not an end in itself, but is linked to reflexivity. Because the game can be separated from its environment, its characteristic situations can be endlessly retrieved and studied. Self-criticism, repetition, and practice can refine specialized abilities. Performance can be judged, play can be perfected, degrees of competence can be measured in matches. Reflection not only improves performance but also recontextualizes the autonomous game in the player's life process. Play is a practice of self-realization modifying the player through discipline. This is the core of the notion of Way; in Western societies the idea of "vocation" plays a similar role, describing the effect on the subject of activity in a relatively autonomous domain such as a profession.

The recontextualizing practice of the game as a Way has the paradoxical effect of reinforcing its autonomy. The game is wholly absorbed in a way of life that is itself wholly absorbed in the game. As Kawabata says of the old Master, he was "a man so disciplined in an art that he had lost the better part of reality" (p. 32). What Erving Goffman (1961: 20) calls "rules of irrelevance" that anchor attention on play and abstract it from the social surround have taken over his whole life.

This is a well-known hazard of Go. There is an ancient Chinese tale of a woodcutter who comes upon two old men playing in the forest and stops to watch. Eventually the game ends and the players disappear into thin air. The astonished woodcutter discovers that his own hair has turned white during the play, and the handle of his axe has rotted through. For Kawabata the game has a demonic quality. "From the veranda outside the players' room, which was ruled by a sort of diabolic tension, I glanced out into the garden, beaten down by the powerful summer sun, and saw a girl of the modern sort insouciantly feeding the carp. I felt as if I were looking at some freak. I could scarcely believe that we belonged to the same world" (p. 27).

NO-MIND: THE STRUCTURE OF CONFLICT

The Way of the game is not about victory but about self-realization through discipline. But paradoxically, self-realization through discipline yields victory. Kawabata tells the story of two high-ranking young players who ask the advice of a clairvoyant on how to win. "The proper method, said the man, was to lose all awareness of self while awaiting an adversary's play" (p. 42).

One immediately recognizes here the Zen concept of "no-mind" as it appears in Japanese martial arts, the peculiar form of self-forgetfulness involved in effective sport or combat. But this is surely an odd application of Buddhism, a religion of ascetic detachment from the world. As

Suzuki (1970) explains it, the principle of "nonattachment" can be extended down to the level of attentive processes, freeing the actor from inhibiting concentration on either self or other. This loosening of focus banishes hesitation and fear and improves fighting performance. "'From this absolute emptiness,' states Takuan, 'comes the most wondrous unfoldment of doing'" (Herrigel 1960: 104).[3]

This is not the place to discuss the religious implications of no-mind. What interests me more in any case is the structure of the concept which is derived, by a subtle transformation, from the traditional Hindu and Buddhist notion of nonduality. According to that notion, conflict is illusory, as in Ralph Waldo Emerson's famous poem "Brahma":

> If the red slayer think he slays,
> Or if the slain think he is slain,
> They know not well the subtle ways
> I keep, and pass, and turn again.
>
> (quoted in Suzuki 1970: 207)

Jorge Luis Borges's story "The Theologians" reaches a similar conclusion. Here is the heavenly coda to this account of a metaphysical dispute that ends tragically with one of the disputants burned at the stake at the instigation of the other: "In Paradise, Aurelian learned that, for the unfathomable divinity, he and John of Pannonia (the orthodox believer and the heretic, the abhorrer and the abhorred, the accuser and the accused) formed one single person" (Borges 1964: 126).

These works appear to invite us to occupy a "third" position above the fray: the "I" of Brahma or the theologians' God. Presumably, if the swordsmen and the theologians could occupy this position themselves, their strife would cease and they would be reconciled in perfect understanding.

The doctrine of no-mind agrees that apparent dualities reveal a more fundamental unity. But what makes it so interesting is the elimination of the third position. Struggle itself is shown to be prior to the parties it joins, an underlying unity of which they are mere projections. True nonduality therefore cannot be achieved by *observing* the conflicts in which others are plunged, no matter how dialectically. Such an observer would still stand in dualistic opposition to an object. Rather, no-mind is a particular way of *living* duality, an existential position *within* it, and not a modality of knowledge transcending it. Hence the

---

3. The reader interested in the concept of no-mind should consult Suzuki (1973), the chapters on swordsmanship in Suzuki (1970), and Herrigel (1960). See also Loy (1988), especially page 123, for the issue of the "third" point of view discussed below.

Zen master's reply to the impertinent question of how the enlightened deal with hunger and cold: "When hungry, I eat, and when cold I put on more clothes" (Suzuki 1973: 75).

This reply indicates why Zen turned out to be peculiarly available to the martial arts, and ultimately, I will argue below, to literature as well. For this doctrine, the goal is not to rise above conflict in reconciliation but to achieve total identification with the context of struggle in the very midst of struggle. If conflict can be transcended, it must be from within, without setting up a "third" consciousness above the fight. This no-mind is not a mystical state, but a consciousness that has become one with the formal requirements of the activity frame and that sees its role within that frame as in some sense "logically" entailed rather than psychologically motivated.

The same point can be made in relation to Go. Insofar as the players identify completely with the situation on the board—that is, with the "whole"—they assume their role unreservedly and carry it out without concern for survival or victory. Good play thus has nothing to do with one-sided personal aggression; at the height of the most intense competition, the players are joined in harmony in the construction of the board, much as singers respond to each other in a piece of complex choral music. Their collaboration, expressed in mutually responsive moves, takes precedence over their struggle. Ultimately, they "form one single person."

THE PATTERN DISTURBED

In Japanese culture, the pursuit of self-realization through a Way manifests itself aesthetically, in this instance as the beauty of the board on which the dance of adversaries produces a magnificent and complex pattern. Of course, the aim of Go is to win; however, Japanese commentators always note that this aim is transcended by a higher interest in the aesthetic achievement of "harmony" and pattern. Go is the collaborative production of aesthetic form through competitive play. Both moments, collaboration and competition, are equally important, for without struggle there is no beauty. The weak player who offers no resistance cannot share in the production of a satisfying board, full of symmetry and surprise. There is thus a promise of aesthetic redemption contained in the hard-fought game; Kawabata's novel is the story of the betrayal of that promise by the modern focus on victory and defeat for its own sake.

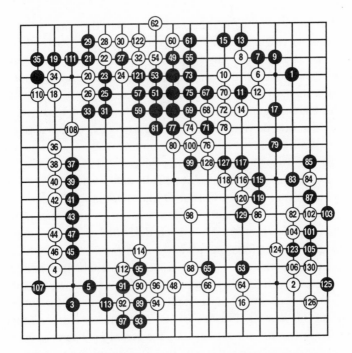

Figure 2. 1938 match between the Master (White) and the challenger Otaké (Black).

That new focus becomes apparent in the climactic move of the great 1938 match. After many months of difficult play, interrupted by the illness of the Master, the game seems perfectly poised with no advantage to either side. A decisive struggle breaks out in the center of the board. As the day comes to an end, the challenger, Otaké, seems unsure of his course. He writes his final play of the day—move 121—on a card and seals it in an envelope, to be opened by the referees the following morning, and with that the players retire (see fig. 2).

When the seal is broken at the next session, the move is not in the central battlefield at all, but strikes at the Master far away near the top of the board. Yet it compels at least a brief response of the housekeeping sort; it resembles the move the disadvantaged player makes away from a *kō* to distract the adversary with a sharp diversionary blow. Soon the players return to the center of the board where the Master plays poorly, making the mistake that costs him the game.

What is the meaning of this incident? The organizers of the match granted each player a total of forty hours to consider their moves. Sealing the final move of the day is supposed to prevent the players from adding the time between sessions to this already generous total. But by tying the master up for a turn with his trivial sealed play, Otaké appears to have frozen the most important action so as to have a leisurely look at it overnight. The Master is convinced that Otaké used the sealed play to gain time to reflect on the difficult position in the center of the board, time he desperately needed, as he was rapidly using up his allotment.

Despite the suspicious appearance of move 121, it is not certain that the challenger actually used it to gain unfair advantage. Although at one point the narrator says that Otaké "would avert defeat even if in the process he must chew the stones to bits," he is not portrayed unsympathetically (p. 178). He is even described as reading the *Lotus Sutra* to calm himself before playing. And the narrator, who is full of admiration for the Master, also respects his challenger and, at one point, intervenes effectively to prevent him from forfeiting the match.

This ambiguous situation crystallizes the action of the novel. And because the human significance of the climactic move is ambiguous, the specificity and the concreteness of the actual play persists even after the novel appears to assign it a meaning. It remains in fact a permanent stumbling block to final interpretation, an ambiguous intersection of the multiple codes that structure the novel.

But whether Otaké made good use of the extra hours or not is ultimately irrelevant since the Master is so upset by the sealed play that he can no longer concentrate properly on the game. The challenger's apparent thrust toward victory disturbs the pattern and undermines the spiritual significance of the game. It is as though the delicate work of producing the board, which has as its secondary consequence victory and defeat for the players, was interrupted by a mere tug of war between roughnecks who have no conscious relation at all to the combined effects of their labors and no purpose other than winning. The incident brings out into the open the potential conflict between collaborative and competitive dimensions of the game and thus between its roles in supporting a Way and in discriminating between winners and losers.[4]

Because the Master is upset, his feelings come out momentarily in the presence of the reporter who narrates the tale. Kawabata writes,

4. It is important not to miss the specific emphasis on winning characteristic of traditional play. Ritual is of course significant for it to a degree that differentiates it from modern play, but it would be wrong to describe it as merely formalistic in opposition to

"The Master had put the match together as a work of art. It was as if the work, likened to a painting, were smeared black at the moment of highest tension. That play of black upon white, white upon black, has the intent and takes the forms of creative art. It has in it a flow of the spirit and a harmony as of music. Everything is lost when suddenly a false note is struck, or one party in a duet suddenly launches forth on an eccentric flight of his own. A masterpiece of a game can be ruined by insensitivity to the feelings of an adversary" (p. 164).

Later the Master has his doubts or in any case is more reticent. His published account of the game, like that of the new champion, contains no criticism of this decisive move which, despite its odd timing, is perfectly ordinary in other respects. Thus the waves quickly close over the suspicions that ruined the match; all rally around to protect the image of their art.

METARULES: ETIQUETTE OR EQUITY

Rationality does not enter social life for the first time in the modern era. Every culture has domains governed by formal rules. These rules can be considered "rational" in the sociological sense of the term on two conditions: first, that they employ tests of experience or impose principles of equivalence, implication, or optimization on thought and action, and second, that they do so with an unusual degree of precision. So it is, for example, with accounting rules designed to ensure the equality of income and outgo, or legal rules that affix punishments to crimes. Or the rules of Go that create a domain in which the difference between better and worse play is not open to dispute.

Although all societies produce such domains, modernity can nevertheless be clearly distinguished from every other type of society by its unique way of dealing with rationality. In modern societies certain formally rational activities are liberated from traditional recontextualizing strategies that reconcile them with rituals and the social hierarchy. In the case of a game like Go, potential conflicts between the requirements of the one and the other are resolved in advance by what I will call "metarules" that regulate the social relations of the players congruent with the requirements of play.

---

a modern instrumental orientation toward victory. One would have the same problem distinguishing formal from instrumental motives in evaluating bullfighting. And the same problem Kawabata's novel describes would arise, but in a ridiculous form, if a new "modern" style were introduced that consisted in shooting the bull.

In the old Japan, etiquette inscribed agents' identity in all their activities without exception. The constraints of etiquette were perhaps more strongly felt in this society than one can imagine in the West. True or not, only in Japan could the story be told of the feudal general who washed and perfumed his hair before battle in case, in the event of defeat, his decapitated head were to be presented to the victor and the ladies of his court.

Etiquette recontextualizes formally rational activities to ensure that they take a subordinate place in a world ordered according to quite different principles, for example, ranking by age, which relates all human activity to the mortality of the agents and their role in family life. Deference in this context not only expresses a social prejudice but *contains* the socially dangerous equalizing potential of formal rationality.[5]

This cultural framework had completely enveloped Go in complicated quasi-religious rituals until the match of 1938. That match marks the breakdown of an older vision of the game as a spiritual discipline and the emergence of a new one in which it is essentially a test of strength. The modernization process that had been gnawing at traditional Japanese culture in every domain since the Meiji Restoration finally reached this odd holdout.

The modalities of this shift are linked to what I will call the textuality of Go as a board game. The decontextualized character of the play, which suits it to be a Way, also makes it possible to define the state of the game at any moment by simply recounting the sequence of moves. In fact, games resemble writing in producing an object that can be separated from any particular material support, such as a piece of paper or a board, and circulated as a system of signs.

The quasi-textual nature of the game suits it for dissemination through a newspaper. Like his earlier reporting, Kawabata's novel dramatizes the Go match, the twists and turns of which it follows exactly despite the poetic license he took with many human details. This exactitude is in itself significant: the narrator is a reporter, like Kawabata, and the same kinds of charts that appeared in the newspaper articles are reproduced in the novel.

The involvement of a newspaper in the championship match results in a significant shift in emphasis. The game, which used to be a unique

---

5. Other recontextualizations are of course possible. For example, technical systems were incorporated into social life through guilds in premodern Europe. Socialism might be interpreted as the demand for a similar recontextualization of modern technology in democratic forms. See Feenberg (1991: chap. 7).

spiritual performance, is reduced to a mechanically retrievable spectacle, a "match." Of course, there was always an element of show in it, but a transformation occurs when mediated mass spectatorship replaces the burdensome ritual of personally following the players to their meeting place and remaining silent in their presence. Newspaper readers are in immediate contact only with the contextless chart of the unfolding game, the thrust and parry of successive moves, the final drive toward victory, all of which can be printed exactly as played. This change, made possible by the formal autonomy of the game, eliminates its "aura" and diminishes interest in it as a Way, which now becomes a kind of folklore or ornament of the record in the press (Benjamin 1969: 224–225).

The newspaper and its readers are less interested in these traditional aspects of the game than in its fairness, so new metarules are introduced to ensure the victory of the better player. "The modern way was to insist upon doing battle under conditions of abstract justice, even when challenging the Master himself" (p. 52). The uniformity of the game, in which nothing distinguishes the players but the color of their stones, must be reflected in their roles in play. The social institution that corresponds to this notion of equity is the contract, and the organization of the match is therefore settled contractually.

Several of these new rules are imitated from Western chess, such as time limits on play and sealed plays at the end of the day. The players are even sequestered to prevent outsiders from contributing advice. Of this code, with its cold rationalism, Kawabata says, "It later came to seem like a foreshadowing of death" (p. 58).

There can be no objection to such rules, especially not if one wished to receive the generous rewards for playing the game under conditions that would increase newspaper sales. Yet these rules ran roughshod over precious Japanese sensitivities in their exclusive concentration on the question "Who is the best player?"

Traditional etiquette prescribed not an equal but an unequal relationship between the older and the younger player, the champion and his challenger. Accordingly, the Invincible Master had the right to expect that his age and eminence would be recognized not merely through outward signs of respect but through obedience to his decisions about the play, the length and timing of sessions, and related matters. There is a certain conflict of interest implied in this arrangement, but presumably the Master's position is too visible and his responsibility too heavy for him to abuse his discretion. Considerations of honor limit the asymmetry between the players. Was it not rude then to place them both on an equal footing? Was it not demeaning to the art of Go to imply, by imposing these rules, that the players are mainly interested in victory? Was finding out who plays best important enough to excuse these offenses?

In one sense the answer is obvious. Kawabata's narrator is a good newspaperman and knows all the dirt, even on the old Master. He does not hide from us that the Master dodged a match with his challenger's teacher, Suzuki, who might well have beaten him. One of his disciples is suspected of having whispered the winning move to the Master in a previous match. And worst of all, he treated his own position as "a commercial asset" and "sold his last match to a newspaper at a price without precedent" (p. 53). So much for virtuous old Japan!

And yet the narrator nevertheless describes the Master as "forever true and clean," which he is by comparison with slick modern players (p. 109). Kawabata explains that the disappearance of favoritism is not the innocent gesture it appears to be, for "new rules bring new tactics" (p. 165). And he notes, "When a law is made, the cunning that finds loopholes goes to work. One cannot deny that there is a certain slyness among younger players, a slyness which, when rules are written to prevent slyness, makes use of the rules themselves" (p. 54). The sealed play containing move 121 is an example.

Rules that claim universality in the equal treatment of all are applied in a world of particular circumstances. Far from standing above the struggle, they end up being instrumentalized in individual strategies as means to the end of victory. The shrewd grasp of loopholes in the new rules replaces the honest subtlety of the really insightful player. Thus the ideal of fairness as a quasi-mechanical equality between players is never achieved. Once again, therefore, one must rely on honor to restrain abuse. But now honor has been weakened by the alibi of conformity to the letter of the rules which takes its place in the modern mind.

There is a further unfortunate consequence of the introduction of the new rules: the loss of aesthetic values. Etiquette is of course extrinsic to the play itself and as such may interfere with the logic of the game. But in fact the novel is not about the Weberian struggle between ascriptive values such as age and a new achievement-oriented ethos. Far from emphasizing the unfairness and distortions deference causes, the novel presents etiquette as a context of play uniquely suited to bringing out the aesthetic achievement of a truly heroic match. Meanwhile, it is the orientation toward success that is shown to distort play through relying on mere technicalites. The narration thus deconstructs the familiar opposition of ascription and achievement.

The novel lets us understand that the mere establishment of the bureaucratic framework already marked the Master for defeat. It is not just that he is bound to be less clever than a younger man at manipulating the system. No, it is the distrust embodied in the very nature of the rules which was bound at some point to demoralize and upset him beyond endurance. Against this background some event was sure to cast doubt on the position and lead to the collapse of the Master's spirit. Kawabata writes, "It may be said that the Master was plagued in his last match by modern rationalism, to which fussy rules were everything, from which all the grace and elegance of Go as art had disappeared, which quite dispensed with respect for elders and attached no importance to mutual respect as human beings. From the way of Go the beauty of Japan and the Orient had fled" (p. 52).

Because etiquette privileges the collaborative over the competitive dimension of play, it opens up a space within which the aesthetic ideal of Way can flourish. But in the new Japan, the social context of play is a matter of simple fairness abstracted from personal considerations. Fairness projects other aspects of the game, such as equality and struggle, into the social environment. When social activity is treated as a mere competition, the structure of the game, with its clear decision between winners and losers, reaches out to simplify life itself.

LAYERS OF MEANING

This approach has a remarkable (if no doubt coincidental) similarity to Nishida's dialectic. Nishida attempted to accommodate modernity to Japanese tradition in an original way. Rather than focusing on the obvious sociohistorical issues, he sought their basis in the relation between Western scientific knowledge and a more fundamental level of concrete practical engagement with the world. As we saw in the previous chapter, his theory of practice culminated in something he called the "consciousness of absolute nothingness," a philosophical version of the concept of no-mind discussed above. Nishida's project was to encompass knowledge in practice through situating the Western contribution—scientific rationality—in a larger scheme with Eastern foundations.

Of course Kawabata need not have read Nishida to share a similar perspective. The Japanese intelligentsia confronted a confusing juxta-position of levels of meaning derived from East and West, past and present. There were only a limited number of ways to order the confusion and give it form. At a certain point in their careers Nishida and Kawabata, like many others, approached this task in a similar spirit in the otherwise quite different media of philosophy and literature.

This difference between the forms of expression has perhaps a historical significance of its own. As we have seen, Nishida's philosophy was an expression of cultural ambitions that seemed justified before the war. For Kawabata, writing after the war, the highest expression of Japanese culture was the production of what he called "elegies," literary works recounting its fall. Placing these elegies in the context of Nishida's philosophy explains many things.

How does Kawabata develop the dialectic in his novel? The *Master of Go* is based on multiplying codes in terms of which to interpret an apparently simple move in a game. The order and connection of meanings at each level parallels that at the other levels. The same action can be identified at all levels, unchanged except in terms of its contextualization and significance. It is not possible to relate these levels causally, to explain one level by another, because each has its own "logic." Such multilayered entanglements are characteristic of formalized fields. Any act that has an apparently technical or formal motive reveals double or triple meanings when placed in its social context.[6]

Kawabata's novel is an attempt to understand and encompass the increasingly intrusive lower levels of the dialectic, privileged by modernity, in a higher aesthetic form. In Nishida's terms, the game is a formal-rational system, a "field of predicates" that can be isolated from its practical context as a set of spatial coordinates, a chart. This representation of the game abstracts from the process of production in which it appears as the object of individual action, that is, of "self-consciousness." Recontextualized as a performance, the abstract chart is animated by a practice of play; it becomes *this* particular game played by these players in a definite time and place. A completely self-

---

6. See Latour (1987: 138): "If you take any black box and make a freeze-frame of it, you may consider the system of alliances it knits together in two different ways: first, by looking at who it is designed to enroll; second, by considering what it is tied to so as to make the enrollment inescapable. We may on the one hand draw its *sociogram*, and on the other its *technogram*." "Black box" here refers to facts and artifacts produced by scientific and technological research and development. Their social and scientific-technical logic are inextricably intertwined. The equivalent in Go would be the results of a match.

sufficient account of the action is possible at the level of the game, its rules, and the strategy of play, and such an account is plausibly offered in published descriptions of the game.

Of course, there is always more going on than is deemed fit for presentation in such publications. The novel takes us behind the scenes by revealing the psychological meaning of the player's actions. At this level the game appears as a structure of social relations, mixing respect, fairness, aggression, and anxiety in a surprisingly complicated narrative flow.

But even this description is incomplete; it abstracts from a still wider context: the social background. The players, after all, are not isolated beings but members of a society. The game is thus further encompassed in the wider practical field of social, cultural, and historical meanings. These meanings are embodied in the different metarules of etiquette and equity with their different emphases on Way and winning. Here we reach the third level of Nishida's dialectic where rationality and individuality are encompassed in history.

The conflict between the newspaper's rules and the old etiquette reflects a larger historical conflict dramatized in the match. The Honnimbô Shusai was not just a Go master, but the champion of a dying civilization, the old Japan, a world in which a certain kind of aristocratic idealism and aestheticism prevailed over modern worries about success and money. For the Master, the game is the occasion for an aesthetic revelation beyond any merely personal contest. But in modern times there is no longer any "margin for remembering the dignity and the fragrance of Go as an art," and the challenger plays simply to win (p. 52). As Kawabata writes, "The Master seemed like a relic left behind by Meiji" (p. 63). In fact he died shortly after the finish of the match. His challenger, however decent a man, was the agent of the modern world. His victory meant the end of the old Japan and the emergence of a new spirit, dominated by business and the media.

For Kawabata the 1938 championship match was emblematic of the modernization of Japan. He repeats the usual contrast between modernity and tradition familiar from Japanese literature: the struggle between ideals and interests, feeling and reason, beauty and power. But despite the clichés, his narrator cannot entirely disapprove of the modern; it will bring, he says, "new vitality in the world of Go" (p. 145).

In fact the novel seems to soften the epochal differences between its two principal characters. No doubt we are intended to discount the rumors about the Master and to believe the worst of his challenger. But the ambiguities indicate that the problem of modernization is not just about psychology or ethics; the game has different potentialities that are reflected in historically typical forms of personality. The personal level thus depends on an underlying change in the place of the game—of rationality—in social life.[7] A perfectly respectable move from one standpoint is an outrage from the other. The players are in effect playing different games. Their encounter must lead to a profound misunderstanding, a conflict of "doubles" in which each participant operates according to a different code.[8]

It is the journalist narrator who carries the burden of explaining these larger implications. He can do so because he embodies in his person the very ambiguity of the match. On the one hand, just as the Master reduces himself to nothing before the game, so the narrator says, "I reduced myself to nothing as I gazed at the Master" (p. 115). On the other hand, his relation to Otaké is characterized by egalitarian affection and esteem. His doubleness reflects the doubleness of Japan itself (Pilarcik 1986: 16–17).

Yet it would be a mistake to see the narrator as passive. His actions flow from the logic of the situation with grace and immediacy, and he plays an essential role in the unfolding match through the comfort and advice he gives the players. It is through this practical engagement that his consciousness, as pure receptiveness, embraces the whole.

The profound ambiguity of the narrator's identity opens a space that encompasses all the lower fields in a sort of literary no-mind, a Nishidan "absolute nothingness." In his Nobel Prize acceptance speech, Kawabata (1969: 42) endorses such a view of his writing. He quotes the poet Saigyô: "Confronted with all the varied forms of nature, his eyes and his ears were filled with emptiness. And were not the words that came forth true words?" And he concludes, "My own works have been described as works of emptiness" (Kawabata 1969: 43).

AESTHETICISM, EAST AND WEST

The Master of Go represents a type of aesthetic critique in which Japanese spirit survives outside of history as a peculiar and quite con-

---

7. Pilarcik (1986) offers a skillful analysis of the various ways in which characterization is used to express the epochal transition. See especially her description of the players' use of time (pp. 12–13) and their strategies (pp. 14–15). Cf. Thomas Swann (1976: 105–106). But for a novel in which the same transition is treated as *essentially* a matter of changing character, compare Endo (1980).

8. The concept of doubles employed here derives from René Girard. For an application of his approach to the role of economics in the novel, see Feenberg (1988a).

tingent doubt haunting triumphant modernity and revealing its limits. Perhaps this is the sort of thing Jun'ichiro Tanizaki foresaw already in 1933 when he wrote his famous essay *In Praise of Shadows*. Despairing of the survival of traditional Japanese culture under the brightness of electric light, he writes, "I have thought that there might still be somewhere, possibly in literature or the arts, where something could be saved. I would call back at least for literature this world of shadows we are losing. In the mansion called literature I would have the eaves deep and the walls dark, I would push back into the shadows the things that come forward too clearly, I would strip away the useless decoration. I do not ask that this be done everywhere, but perhaps we may be allowed at least one mansion where we can turn off the electric lights and see what it is like without them" (Tanizaki 1977: 42).

The aestheticism of these Japanese writers has interesting similarities with Lukács's early pre-Marxist theory of novelistic irony as a kind of "negative mysticism."[9] The coincidence is important because it suggests a wider context for Kawabata's critique of modernity: the novelistic tradition. Furthermore, Lukács's theory indicates a way of distinguishing Kawabata's novels, as aesthetic forms, from mere sentimental nostalgia for the past.

According to Lukács, the novel is the original and most profound critique of modernity. That critique, at least in the French and Russian novels Lukács took for typical, is aesthetic rather than moral or political. These novels are the product of an irony that is half within, half without the conflicts of the world. The novelist neither stands in polemic opposition to modern society on the ground of tradition or passion—usually exemplified in the hero—nor justifies modernization and its costs with what Lyotard would call a "grand narrative" ending in the present or leading to a shining future. Indeed, were the writer to identify purely and simply with either the world or the hero, the novel would lapse into the pamphlet or the lyric.

Novelistic irony is thus peculiarly ambivalent. On the one hand, it demystifies modernity's claim to universality by revealing the contrast between the facade and the realities of economic, political, and legal

9. "The writer's irony is a negative mysticism to be found in times without a god. It is an attitude of *docta ignorantia* towards meaning, a portrayal of the kindly and malicious workings of the demons, a refusal to comprehend more than the mere fact of these workings; and in it there is the deep certainty, expressible only by form-giving, that through not-desiring-to-know and not-being-able-to-know he has truly encountered, glimpsed and grasped the ultimate, true substance, the present, non-existent God. This is why irony is the objectivity of the novel" (Lukács 1968: 90). For a critical discussion of this passage, see Bernstein (1984: 195ff.).

institutions. Often (in Dickens or Balzac, for example) this leads to a certain sentimentalizing of tradition. On the other hand, the novel's ironic structure subverts any idea of a return to the past by showing how deeply tradition has been intertwined with modernity. Indeed, tradition, like other hopeless ideals the heroes oppose to modernity, serves primarily as a marker for an impossible transcendence that can be indicated only *from within* the tensions and oppositions of society. The novelist may seem to take sides, but his irony nevertheless situates him in what Lukács calls a "transcendendental place" from which alone the whole is visible.

Formally, this ironic stance resembles the consciousness of Way, the no-mind that plays its role to the fullest while identifying with the whole to which it contributes its conflictual share. Just so, Kawabata's narrator sides nostalgically with the old Master and yet manages to depict the contradictions of Japanese tradition and Western modernity in a way that avoids tendentious polemic. He is a mysteriously neutral observer of the real struggle of the book, which produces the aesthetic patterns suitable to literary representation, the graceful move and countermove in a conflict of cultures. To depict this struggle in a "work of emptiness" is to transcend the opposition of tradition and modernity aesthetically. Lukács's remarkable intuition of the novel's religious content is confirmed by this echo from another culture.[10]

There is, however, an important difference between Western and non-Western forms of ironic consciousness of modernity. In the West, one typical heroic type embodies ideals from the past that are doomed by social advance. But the old Master, a similar heroic type depicted in a non-Western setting, exemplifies not merely the tragedy of historical lag, but a contemporary clash of cultures in geopolitical space. That clash takes place in the context of Western cultural imperialism in which Japan appears doomed to defeat not so much because its time

---

10. In the larger context of contemporary world literature, the novelistic turn is reached by different peoples at times reflecting comparable levels of development and carried out with means supplied by their cultures. Thus behind the similarity of the Hungarian Lukács and the Japanese Kawabata, writing a generation apart, lies a deeper cause in the rhythms of modernization in different parts of the world. It is perhaps no coincidence that the Iwakura mission, which visited Europe from 1871 to 1873 in search of insight into how to modernize Japan, focused on the example of Hungary, a country which seemed to point the way. Their report notes: "The various nations who today are delayed in their enlightenment will be deeply impressed by studying the circumstances of Hungary" (Soviak 1971: 15). The artistic and theoretical opening made possible by the novel corresponds to a moment of critique in a process of development undergone by both countries.

has come as because it has met a superior force that has acquired a corresponding but perhaps undeserved prestige. The later development of Japanese society shows how important it is not to overlook this difference.[11]

Today, in a world in which Japan has become a leading industrial power, we can ask whether the continuing signs of the vitality of Japanese culture do not refute the aestheticizing pessimism of authors such as Tanizaki and Kawabata. Their position belonged to the period of cultural trauma that began with the Meiji Restoration and culminated in the occupation. The novel prospered as a literary form during this period. It opened a space within which Western modernity could be exposed in its particularity without regression to discredited theological or ideological prejudices. Its structure was thus modern even though the surface message was often traditionalist. But if the novel, an imported form after all, could achieve such critical distance from its Western origins, why despair of the possibility that similar adaptations and amalgams might occur in other spheres, giving rise to a specifically Japanese modernity?[12]

This speculation recalls a rich tradition of reflection on the possibility of alternative modernities that has been invoked since the 1930s to explain how Japan can preserve its cultural originality inside the modern project rather than through reactionary retreat (Nishida 1958a; Ohashi 1992). Despite Kawabata's despair over the apparent defeat of this prospect, it finds ambiguous support in the underlying structure of his novel. The Master of Go shows us that modernity too is a culture, or, as we will see, several possible cultures confronting each other through a process of generalized "contamination" (Vattimo 1991: 158).

CULTURAL GENEALOGY

What is meant by the notion of an alternative modernity, and is it really plausible? What I will call the "content approach" to alternative modernity emphasizes such ethnic and ideological differences as the kinds of food people eat, the role of family or religion, the legal forms

11. Explaining the philosophy of history of Nishida's student Koyama, Sakai (1989: 106) writes, "History was not only temporal or chronological but also spatial and relational. The condition for the possibility of conceiving of history as a linear and evolutionary series of events lay in its not as yet thematized relation to other histories, other coexisting temporalities."

12. On the culturally specific modernity of the Japanese novel, see Miyoshi (1989).

of property and administration, and so on. These are weak bases for an alternative because modernization, as we should know since Marx and Weber, consists precisely in erasing or incorporating such ethnic and ideological contents in a convergent model of civilization. The universalist view, which uncritically confounds Westernization and modernization, is still persuasive compared to this.

If an alternative modernity is possible, it must be based not on contents but on deeper differences in cultural forms. Nietzsche's "genealogical" method suggests an approach through following the progress of a way of life from one historical period to the next. Judeo-Christianity in this Nietzschean sense is not a particular religion but a way of being in the world that can reappear in different ideological and institutional guises over thousands of years of history. Nietzsche would claim that this form is still active in the West as capitalism, socialism, and democracy.

Inspired directly or indirectly by Nietzsche, other philosophers such as Heidegger and Derrida have developed far-reaching models of the most fundamental metaphysical assumptions of Western culture. These philosophers tend to assume tacitly that since modern institutions and technical rationality arose in the West, they are essentially incompatible with other cultures.[13] As "postmodernity" or "multiculturalism," this view leads to a revalorization of tradition and ethnic particularity, and in the worst case it collapses back into the content approach.

The Master of Go practically invites such a traditionalist reading, at least to Westerners who tend to see in it a struggle between Japanese particularity and the universality of modern culture. On those terms, Kawabata would be arguing that etiquette, self-realization, and aesthetics are substantive ends that must be sacrificed for instrumental efficiency in a modern society.

This interpretation of the novel agrees with a commonplace universalist view of Japanese culture as different precisely insofar as it is still marked by feudal survivals which presumably will dissipate as modernization proceeds (Morley 1971: 19). Of course, it is harder to believe this today than it was when the theory was originally proposed by Marxists in the 1930s. Now that Japan is the most advanced capitalist country, it seems unlikely that feudalism could be alive and well there, but the universalist view is still popular among observers who find Japanese culture oppressive and authoritarian.

13. For a useful evaluation of related issues, see Arnason (1992).

Kawabata's novel appears deceptively compatible with this univer-salist framework because the old Japanese values it endorses share the pathos and fragility of the Master whose defeat marks the entry of Japan into modernity. But the novel is nevertheless incompatible with the Weberian framework. Its Japanese elements are not merely sub-stantive "contents" sacrificed to formal rationality since they include a specific strategic practice of the game. Thus the fateful necessity of the outcome does not flow smoothly from an Enlightenment grand narra-tive of progress, even in Weber's disillusioned version. In sum, it is not easy to fit Kawabata's novel into the currently fashionable paradigm of ethnic protest against totalitarian rationality. I believe that Kawabata is not so much a defender of particularity against universality as he is a critic of the pretensions of false universality. In this too he is true to the novelistic tradition as the early Lukács defined it.

The reorganization of Go around Western notions of fairness is not a move from particular to universal but merely shifts the balance of power in favor of a new type of player. As deference falls, it carries down with it the values of self-realization and aesthetics that flourish in the context of traditional etiquette. Henceforth Go will be a business rather than a spiritual discipline. The best player, in the sense of the one who produces the most perfect game, will be replaced by the player who is best at winning—not precisely the same thing as we have seen.

Reflection on Kawabata's novel thus suggests the limits of the iden-tification of rationality with Western culture and offers starting points for a genealogy of non-Western modernity. From that standpoint, the progress of Japanese modernity would roughly parallel Western devel-opments, that is, the emergence of new secular expressions of basic cultural forms amidst the gradual decline of the feudal-Christian tra-dition that had once been a vigorous expression of that same culture (Dore 1987).

Admittedly, given the recentness of the opening and modernization of Japan, it is often difficult to distinguish survivals from modern in-stances of deeper cultural forms. That ambiguity emerges as a central theme of Kawabata's novel. I want to turn now to the task of unravel-ing it.

THE CULTURE OF PLACE

To this end, I will focus briefly on the category of "place," which plays such an important role in Japanese philosophy and social thought.[14] This notion underlies the concept of no-mind that we have seen at work in Kawabata's novel. As a general cultural phenomenon, it articulates an everyday experience available to every member of the society. This is the experience of seeking one's "place" in the system of social relations in which one finds oneself.

It would be easy to assimilate this category to the notion of social status and to treat it as evidence of the persistence of hierarchy in Japanese culture. This is Chie Nakane's (1970) famous theory of the *tate shakai* (vertical society), which she proposed to explain Japan's success in the modern world. This theory has come in for much criticism because of its implicit appeal to culture to justify submission to authority (Dale 1986: 44–45). It is tempting to reject the whole notion of place as an artifact of an ideologically contaminated cultural theory, a pseudo-traditionalism in the service of rampant exploitation.

The ambiguities of Nakane's social theory are similar to those we encountered in *The Master of Go*. In both cases a quasi-feudal deference is joined to the rational manipulation of a formal system (economics, Go). But if anything, the novelist is a more provocative observer than the social theorist. He delineates clearly the unique formal rationality that is already present in traditional Japanese culture. This raises the question of whether values and practices linked to that rational dimension of the traditional culture might survive the disappearance of the old deference and accommodate themselves to modern conditions.

This is not a question that occurs to Kawabata, but I would like to consider whether the logic of place may not be independent of traditional authoritarianism. It seems to be built into the structure of Japanese culture and language at a much more basic level than differences in prestige or power and signifies a far wider range of distinguishing attributes. Perhaps, like Western individualism, it is a cultural form in the broad genealogical sense, capable of reproducing itself across epochal institutional changes, including changes in the distribution and exercise of authority.

There is considerable evidence for this interpretation. For example, speakers of the Japanese language (like several other Asian languages) must choose pronouns, verb forms, and forms of address that reflect differences in age, gender, and status that might be signified only tacitly—for example, by dress—in the West. There is a clear enough dis-

14. See Nishida (1958a and 1990); Abe (1988); Watsuji (1987); Berque (1986).

tinction between the way in which men and women speak—one of the most important differences of place—that some grammar books actually offer dialogues in both male and female versions. Masculine and feminine speech no doubt reflect gender hierarchy, but they are experienced as exemplifying the whole range of connotations of masculinity and feminity, not merely an authority relation. A similar observation applies to formal language, which persists despite the rapid softening of distinctions in social rank (Miller 1971).

Linguistic coding appears to add tremendous force to social differences or perhaps reflects their unusual force in social reality. The Japanese belong to a culture in which you have to know your place in the social setting in order to open your mouth. This can be quite inhibiting when they first arrive in the West and speak a language like French or English that does not offer any obvious way of signifying place.

The notion of place does not imply unquestioning submission to the authority of social superiors. In institutions such as companies and government agencies, a good deal of attention is paid to building consensus through group discussion. While things go smoothly, such consensus building is a two-way street that constrains the authorities as well as subordinates. Naturally, things do not always go smoothly. Self-assertion is often necessary, and while it is typically more restrained than it would be in the West, the Japanese certainly did not have to await the arrival of Western individualism to learn it. It is already present in their own culture, but qualified and concretized by the demands of place rather than conceived in universal terms as role transcendence as it would be in the West. Place is thus not about whether one plays one's own game, but about who one is and how, accordingly, that game must be played.

Place not only shapes everyday speech and social relations but also religion and art. As we have seen, Japanese martial arts have evolved into spiritual disciplines in part under the impact of this concept, reinterpreted through the Buddhist concept of no-mind. The combatants are trained to concern themselves less with winning than with immediately and swiftly interpreting their place in the system of moves so as perfectly to fulfill its situational requirements. In aesthetic terms, each gesture of combat is part of a pair, the other part of which must be and can be supplied only by the adversary. Every move in the game is in some deeper sense an element of a larger pattern produced through the collaborative competition of the players. In these artistic and religious applications of place, it is especially clear that traditional authority relations overlay a more fundamental cultural form that could perhaps survive without them.

PLACE AND ALTERNATIVE MODERNITY

Something like this martial approach to place is at work in Kawabata's depiction of the traditional game of Go, with its emphasis on the values of self-realization and aesthetics. He contrasts a way of life based on playing out of one's position in a larger system with the Western focus on fairness and winning. The difference between the two is not that one is tradition-bound while the other concentrates on the logic of play. Both are totally involved in the logic of play; both are therefore "rational" in the broad sense, although one emphasizes aspects of play most relevant to a culture of place and the other aspects that complement an individualistic culture.

The novel shows us two alternative ways of playing Go constructed around different *formal* dimensions of the game. Both ways aim at victory but under different aspects. The Western emphasis on equality stems from the equivalence of "sides" in the game, which does indeed conflict with traditional deference. But the Japanese concern with aesthetics is not opposed to the formal rationality of the game; it realizes another immanent dimension of it, the essential dependence of the players exemplified in the thrust and parry of struggle.

The aesthetic values that predominate in traditional Japanese play are thus not extrinsic to the essence of the game but rather represent dimensions of it that only appear clearly in a non-Western context. Nor are these values merely particularistic. Aesthetics is usually understood as a matter of subjective taste, but mathematical and technical systems have well-known aesthetic qualities rooted in objective rationality. A glance at any Go textbook immediately shows this to be true of games as well. The aesthetics of Go flow from the conditions of formally rational action just as rigorously as the values of the young challenger, while fulfilling a very different cultural agenda. Kawabata reestablishes the symmetry between tradition and modernity by showing that success as such is no more rational than deference. Both are external to the inner logic of play, differing primarily in the aspect of that logic they privilege.

In sum, certain traditional values possess at least as much "universality" as the supposedly modern value of fairness. In a sense, what the novel describes, perhaps without entirely intending to, is two alternative types of rationality, each of which is a candidate for modernity, although only one is triumphant, only one actually organizes a modern society.

We have here a model for thinking about alternative modernity. Japan is a good test case because it combines a very alien culture and a very familiar technology and institutional framework. Technologies, markets, and democratic voting, as rational systems, resemble the game of Go: they too can be practiced differently in different cultural settings. In this context, Japanese culture is not an irrational intrusion but rather emphasizes different aspects of technical rationality which, as we have seen, includes self-realization and aesthetics as well as the narrow pursuit of success ethnocentrically identified with it in the West.[15]

In Kawabata's match each move obeys the same rules but has a different significance in the different systems that invest it. Different cultures inhabit the board and influence its pattern of development. Perhaps all modern institutions and modern technology itself are similarly layered with cultural meanings. Where a vigorous culture, whether it be old or new, manages to take hold of modernity, it can influence the evolution of its rational systems. Alternative modernities may emerge, distinguished not just by marginal features such as food culture, style, or political ideals but by the central institutions of technology and administration.

Perhaps Kawabata's elegy was premature and something like this is already beginning to occur in Japan. A number of experts have attempted to show that the Japanese economy draws on unique cultural resources to achieve extraordinarily high levels of motivation and effectiveness (Dore 1987). They point to the importance in Japan of ideals of belonging, service, quality, and vocation by contrast with which the individualistic West appears ethically handicapped.

Unlike certain forms of deference which seem to be in the sort of steep decline Kawabata deplored, these ideals are not survivals doomed by the process of modernization; rather, they are the specific forms in which Japanese culture invests modernity. Indeed, the prevalence of these values may account for both the strengths and the weaknesses of the Japanese model. Industrial societies too can use a maximum of vocational commitment, attention to the whole, collaborative competition.

15. For more on the different moments of technical rationality, see Feenberg (1991: chap. 8).

But modern political systems function best when they rid themselves of the conformism that still characterizes the essentially bureaucratic ethos of the Japanese state. Hence the peculiar combination of effective economics and mediocre politics that characterizes this model (Van Wolferen 1989).

What remains to be seen is how far the process of culturally specific modernization will go and how much transformation the Western technical heritage will suffer as Japan liberates itself more and more from its original dependency on the Western model of modernity.

Conclusion

Culture and Modernity

THE CRITIQUE OF MODERNITY

Rational systems such as technology play a privileged role in modern societies. This is what distinguishes modernity from premodernity. That distinction is usually interpreted temporally, as progress beyond merely contingent and particular local customs through discovery of universal and necessary truths.

Rationality appears to be independent of the social world that surrounds it, and even determining for that world. This appearance of autonomy is not accidental. It stems from the abstraction, precision, and decontextualization of rational systems, as we have seen in the previous chapter. Yet beginning with Marx, critical theory and sociology have uncovered the social basis and bias of one rational system after another—the market, bureaucratic administration, law, science, technology. Today postmodernism and constructivism confirm that "technoscience" is not the independent infrastructure of society postulated by traditional Marxism and modernization theory, but a dependent variable, intertwined with other social forces.

These observations do not obliterate the distinction between modern and premodern societies as a shallow relativism pretends. How without that distinction could we explain or even signify the planetary triumph of Western civilization? But we cannot rely on the old idea of autonomous rationality any longer to make the distinction. Modernity is characterized not by the actual autonomy of reason but by a necessary illusion of autonomy. That illusion appears full blown in technocratic and dystopian fantasies of total administration. Here too is the source of Habermas's ambition to bound technical rationality in order to reestablish communication in its rightful place. But if the technical and the social are essentially interconnected, then we must abandon both the fear of dystopia and the hope in a purified communicative sphere.

Despite the very real changes introduced by modernity, rational coherence and cultural embeddedness are not alternatives but analytic layers of technology in modern as in premodern societies. There is no such thing as a "pure" technology, anymore than there is a "pure" grammar. Technical competence, like linguistic competence, is realized only in concrete forms. Rationality in the most abstract sense is neither a neutral means nor is it specifically Western; like linguistic structure, it is a dimension of behavior and artifacts in every culture.

But how then are we to describe modernity, what are its distinguishing features?

One approach to answering this question that has become increasingly popular in recent years is simply to deny the existence of the "great divide" between modern and premodern societies (Latour 1987: 211ff.; Bloor 1991: 138ff.). Constructivism, for example, argues that reasoning processes are similar in all societies and rational beliefs are relative to social interests like any others. Thus modern science would not be *fundamentally* different from the supposedly prerational beliefs of premodernity.

This line of argument appears to be motivated less by sympathy for tribal peoples accused of irrationality by anthropologists than by a concern to save the richness and diversity of experience and culture from naturalistic reductionism. I share this motivation, and accordingly have argued above that aesthetic and ethical experience give access to dimensions of reality that the natural sciences do not comprehend. It is a matter for speculation in what way science might someday illuminate these phenomena, at least until actual research has something to offer. The arrogant insistence on universal reductionism in advance of the data is in any case far removed from the intimate convictions of many scientists, and serves primarily in the public relations campaigns of such funding initiatives as the Human Genome Project or research in artificial intelligence. Relativism can be useful in fighting against these pretentious claims, but it jousts with a simulacrum of science and technology, not the real thing.

Furthermore, the relativist approach achieves its victories at the risk of collapsing the distinguishing features of rationality. One might wish to deny that scientific-technical rationality is inherently superior to every other mode of thought and cultural experience without assimilating it indiscriminately to nonrational social practices. Can we mitigate the ethnocentric implications of the great divide without denying the specificity of scientific-technical rationality, which is after all not merely another ideology but one of the essential contested terrains of modernity (Harding 1993: 14)?

Marcuse and Nishida interest me because they relativize not the content of rational beliefs but the form of rationality as such. They are too conscious of the immense and problematic social consequences of rationalization to ignore the discontinuity between reason and the rest. Yet they reject the ontological conclusions usually drawn from this recognition and refuse to see the triumph of the modern as proof that its representation of nature provides the last word on being and nothingness. They would agree with Whitehead that it is a "fallacy of misplaced concreteness" to identify our theories with an underlying reality that would presumably explain the presence of the world. We cannot, for example, reduce that world to an external combination, operated unconsciously by the brain, between natural phenomena represented in sensations and subjective feelings. Rather, theories about nature must be understood as abstractions from experience, abstractions that have a special but not a unique role to play in our dealings with the world.

As Hegelian praxis philosophers, Marcuse and Nishida understand rationality as an activity rather than as a passive reflection of what is. That activity has specific traits that distance it from ordinary experience, but it is also significantly bound up with other practices structuring the social and cultural world. Rationality thus arises on a practical background it can never entirely transcend and to which it necessarily returns in the form of rationalized institutions and technical achievements. Its reentry into the world involves specific recontextualizing practices because abstractions are not fully "real" apart from some sort of social concretization. Critique consists in deciphering this network of practice and theory so as to grasp the historicity and the potential of the given rational framework of experience.

These theories treat experience as ontologically fundamental. Naturalism is rejected, but so is nostalgia for a pure immediacy of the phenomenological sort. Instead, experience is interpreted as both *irreducible* and *historical*. This is a paradoxical view. How can a product of human action serve as an ontological foundation? How can a foundation be culturally conditioned and therefore local in space and time? How can multiple cultural actors enter into communication with each other without reference to an unconditioned nature shared by all? These puzzles of a philosophy of finitude need not detain us here; the difficulties may explain why this Hegelian approach has given way to Habermas's neo-Kantianism and postmodern relativism.

However, the paradoxes have returned recently in France in the work of several decidedly non-Hegelian students of modernity. In the writings of Michel Serres (1987), Bruno Latour (1991), and Augustin Berque (1990), experience is treated as an irreducible "hybrid" of natural and cultural moments. They do, of course, retain the distinction of nature and culture, but they reject both naturalistic and sociological reductionisms. Instead, they reverse the usual relation between the terms of the distinction and the experiential substratum it cuts across. Experience forms a whole that is more basic than the "parts" which compose it, and which are only identified after the fact through what Latour calls a practice of "purification." It is an interesting question whether this reformulation of experiential ontology can solve the problems praxis philosophy left in suspense.

HYBRID REALITIES

This is a book on technology and modernity, not ontology, so rather than pursuing these deep problems I would like to return to the question with which this chapter began regarding the difference between modern and premodern societies. Perhaps a look at the premodern way with rationality will help to reconstruct that difference without ethnocentric self-congratulation.

Premodern societies do not need a praxis philosophy or a constructivist sociology to tell them that the uses of rationality are always social at bottom. By contrast with modern societies, they invariably encompass each rational element, whether it be a game, a production method, an exchange, in symbolic systems, myths, and rituals that highlight social dependencies. Their technical processes seamlessly abstract natural objects from their original contexts, incorporate them under causal principles into some sort of device, and embed them in new social contexts. Abstraction from nature and social recontextualization do not appear to be separate in these societies, as they do in modern ones, but are so intimately bound up with each other as not to be easily distinguished. This intermingling of practices we would distinguish is not merely a limitation of simpler times, a "lack of differentiation" in Habermas's terms. On the contrary, it reveals an important truth about technical objects, that they too are human products, aspects of social life like any other, and that they inevitably vehiculate cultural meanings.

Every society produces a world of artifacts which, in addition to their simplest practical functions, support social roles and symbolize mythic or ritual forces. So long as artifacts remain relatively simple and technically independent of each other, as they generally do until modern times, they are culturally encoded by embedding them individually in a nontechnical symbolic framework (Lévi-Strauss 1955: chap. 22; Guillaume 1975: chap. 2). Craft and art are joined in a practice that simultaneously transforms the world and the producer. Artifacts acquire symbolic connotations supported by design features, ornaments, and ritual links to other nontechnical practices. Making an artifact is not merely "work" in our modern sense; it is an act of self-production and a ritual performance. A house is a house, but it is also a symbol of the cosmos, and building it defines the builder as a member of the community; an axe is an axe, but it is also the totem of a social group, and making it defines the maker as the head of a household, and so on (Bourdieu 1972: chap. 3; Sharp 1952: 69ff.).

I call this *symbolically expressive design* because here a cultural system speaks through its artifacts. The case of the stone axe in the Australian Yir Yoront tribe offers a particularly illuminating example of this kind of design. The Yir Yoront were a Stone Age people whose technology was as simple as can be, yet whose adaptation to their desert environment was remarkably sophisticated. Their principal tool, the stone axe, was used to cut brush, prepare food, and build shelter. Only adult males could make and own the axes, which they lent out to their dependent women and children. The axe was also the center of a trade circuit that brought them into contact with other tribes and a totem that played a certain role in their understanding of the cosmos. Here we have a single simple artifact that mediated not only technical tasks, but authority, gender, social relations, and belief systems (Sharp 1952).

The Yir Yoront's axe is a "hybrid" in the sense defined above. The hybrid status of such tribal artifacts is perfectly clear to those who make and use them. They have no problem discoursing intelligently on both their technical and symbolic features. But unlike us, they never wonder how nature and culture came to be joined in a unique and contingent configuration. Their technical world appears necessary to them in a way ours does not, and so they experience their hybrids as fundamental realities instead of decomposing them into abstract natural and cultural constituents as we do.

It is paradoxical that we moderns, who are so culturally self-conscious and who have organized practically everything around technologies, find it far more difficult to perceive the hybrids we have made. According to Bruno Latour (1991: 23ff.), this is due to the "Modern Constitution," that is, the basic self-understanding of modernity that separates technical rationality from social meaning. Artifacts are not grasped as unities from which these two dimensions are abstracted as they would be in any premodern society, but instead are seen as an external combination of two independent orders of phenomena: means and ends, facts and values, function and form, nature and culture, and so on. Under this dispensation rationality involves perfecting the first term of each pair regardless of the consequences for the second term.

So conceptualized, modern artifacts seem radically different from premodern ones, when really, Latour contends, they are quite similar in nature. The difference, such as it is, consists not in achieving a higher order of rationality, but in breaking with traditional taboos in order to draw ever more nonhuman objects into the social process: "the extension of the spiral, the breadth of the enrollments it brings about, the greater and greater lengths it goes to to recruit these beings," in sum, the construction of technology in the form of a system or network (Latour 1991: 147). This process requires a tolerance for social and symbolic change without common measure with the premodern mentality. The daring with which the moderns have shattered the symbolic order is thus worthy of note, but it is not evidence of a great epistemological divide.

TYPES OF DESIGN

Much of Latour's argument is persuasive, but I wonder if he has not overcompensated for the tendency to attribute uniqueness to the West at the risk of obscuring real differences. These become clearer when the focus is shifted to the design process. From that standpoint, it is clear that the "Modern Constitution" includes a new way of investing technology with cultural significance that largely replaces the old practice of expressive design. My hypothesis is that modern technology only appears "pure" to us because we view it in the old way while delegating values to it in this new one.

How in fact do technologies acquire broad cultural meaning and significance? There are three chief means: (1) rhetorical procedures that invest them with symbolic meaning, such as myths or advertising; (2) design features that embed values in the artifact; (3) interconnections with other technologies in a network that imposes a specific way of life.

First, rhetorical investments are too familiar to need much elaboration. There is, however, a significant difference between the way in which premodern peoples situate artifacts in a mythic framework and modern advertising. Traditional symbolic systems are relatively rigid and embrace discursive and material productions indifferently in a tight network of inherited significations. Advertising, on the other hand, belongs to the realm of the "imaginary," to arbitrary associations between words and things subject to organizational control or individual innovation, and in any case to a chaotic process of change such as that described in chapter 3. In premodern societies, the symbolic system structures the imaginary, and technical rationality as well, to contain their potential for disorder (Guillaume 1975: 29). As that system broke down in the transition to modernity, the imaginary took over many of its functions. The Yir Yoront's axe and masculine authority formed a symbolically inseparable unity, but steel axes arrived uncoded and available for multiple and manipulable significations.

Second, the incorporation of values in artifacts through intrinsic design features takes two different forms. Most obviously, it involves what we think of as ornamention, for example, designs symbolizing desirable attributes such as prestige or personal strength. However, an "ornament" is an aesthetic supplement to an original function, and this type of supplementarity is characteristically modern. The unity of production and ornamentation in premodern societies reflects the rigorous and exhaustive symbolic coding of artifacts and of the rituals of their production. The artifacts themselves do not therefore appear as "basically" functional but as symbolically embedded in a web of social relations that crosses all the boundaries of our "differentiated" society. The concept of aesthetics, at least in its application to design, is our impoverished version of this radical social embeddedness.

In addition to the aesthetic encoding of artifacts, a bias toward hegemonic practices can be designed into them. This bias may only become clear through comparisons between competing techniques. Then one begins to understand why specific technical choices were necessary given the practices encouraged by the symbolic framework of the society.

The story of the remarkable withering of firearms in Japan from the seventeenth to the nineteenth centuries illustrates this process. Once the country was unified, killing was no longer primarily a matter of numbers and a wider variety of practices and values could influence technical decisions about weaponry. The Japanese aristocracy was faced with a choice between two very different technologies of killing, guns and swords. They preferred the latter to the point of gradually abolishing firearms. Guns were a democratic weapon requiring little training and so might possibly have shifted the class balance of the society. But perhaps more significant, shooting was impersonal in a world where combat was supposed to represent the valor of a family tradition through the individual champions who bore its crest on the battlefield. Even the physical postures associated with polite behavior were incompatible with those required to use a gun (Perrin 1979). Thus the failure of the gun in this environment reflected the tight constraints of a system of practices in which it simply had no place.

The third way in which values are realized in technologies is far more difficult for us to perceive because it is both privileged and masked by our modern "Constitution." Modern technology lacks much of the symbolic richness imparted to premodern artifacts by traditional craft because aesthetic and ethical norms are no longer systematically embedded in the individual devices themselves. This is why it seems as though our machines are technically innocent, rational, stripped down to a bare causal nexus. But the peculiar exactitude and precision of modern technique, which allows it to be organized as a system, means that design consists largely in adjusting each artifact to its "fit" in the whole. It is the system that embodies values, not the individual devices. The meaning of complex modern technologies is in the connections. I will call the work of making those connections *system-congruent design*.

The intricately interlocking network or system of technologies appears value-free but in fact inducts us into a normative framework as we adapt to it in our daily activities. The unending chains of dependencies arising out of everything we use, from ballpoint pens to automobiles, from canned chili to computers, include us too. Our way of life, our very gestures are programmed by our artifacts with a rigidity that has no precedent in premodern societies. Indeed, in such societies only the symbolic system can determine a way of life, while techniques are fairly flexible and therefore available for use in a multiplicity of cultural systems.

I discussed the political dimension of this third relation of values and technologies in chapter 4. The automobile can serve here as an exemplary reminder of the characteristics of this type of design. The interlocking requirements of cars, urbanism, the petrochemical industry, production and consumption systems, and, as we have recently seen, the defense industry, all form a system dictating a specific lifestyle. One seeks in vain a precise place where valuative elements can be found intruding on this smoothly oiled machinery. Yet the system undoubtedly locks in a way of life and even a sort of worldview reflecting the practices enabled by these technologies.

These three ways of signifying and designing technology are not mutually exclusive. They usually function together to assign relatively univocal meanings to technical objects. Technologies are always already invested with aesthetic, ethical, and cultural values through a combination of rhetorical procedures, intrinsic features of devices and systems, and network congruences. What changes with the emergence of modernity is the proportions between these determinants.

Something rather like this analysis of design is mythologized in Heidegger's critique of modern technology. Heidegger contrasts the pious work of the Greek craftsman making a chalice with the destructive appropriation of the Rhine by a modern dam. The craftsman brings out the "truth" of his materials through the symbolically charged reworking of matter by form. The modern technologist obliterates the inner potential of his materials, "de-worlds" them, and "challenges" nature to fit into his methodically planned and controlled system (Heidegger 1977: 7–17). Not man, but pure instrumentality, holds sway in this "enframing" (*Ge-stell*); it is no merely human purpose, but a specific way in which being reveals itself, a way that obscures the entire problematic to which Heidegger's work is addressed, namely, the coming to presence of being in a world.

What I think Heidegger is pointing out is the transition from a cultural system based on expressive design to one based on congruent design. That transition has costs; indeed, it involves the destruction of a world. It was just this process of destruction which the Japanese nobility knew to resist on time. The Yir Yoront were less fortunate. Lauriston Sharp describes how the free distribution of steel axes by missionaries undermined their way of life. Males lost their social role as women and children received axes from the mission; intertribal relations broke down; the tribe's totemistic worldview collapsed in the face of the unclassifiable steel axe. A simple tool without symbolic significance in itself struck down an entire culture by enrolling its members on the periphery of the industrial system (Sharp 1952).

Like Habermas, Heidegger seems to find in technology a universal instrumental essence that would exhaust its social meaning. No doubt they would find that meaning in the story of the Yir Yoront. But that seems to me a rather ethnocentric interpretation. The Yir Yoront were not victims of "progress" in instrumental control of nature; they had achieved such a high degree of instrumental control of their particular branch of nature, the Australian desert, that no Westerner could hope to compete with them. For example, they could survive for weeks without carrying water. But of course this Aboriginal form of control was primarily individual. To show the Westerners' advance one must shift the criterion of control from the individual to the technically mediated group. That shift is of course defining for modern Western culture but it can claim no universality. Once the notion of control of nature is relativized, it becomes clear that this is a story about the triumph of one quite specific culture over another. This would have been the result of the introduction of guns in Japan too; indeed, that is what happened there at a later date.

Concrete social study of technology does not discover the grand narrative of pure instrumentality forcing its way through the barriers of ignorance and tradition. Rather, it finds congruent design everywhere accomplishing much the same work that premodern societies accomplished through expressive design; that is, the technical object is fully accommodated to a particular culture, the culture of the West. The planetary triumph of that culture results not so much from superior rationality as from the fantastic accumulation of political and military power in the long networks built by congruent design. Here a real asymmetry exists which no relativism can discount. Absolute criteria measure victory and defeat in the struggle for control over human beings. Colonialism has taught us to know those criteria: the loss of national and cultural independence, of identity, of time and resources.

FROM UNITY TO DIVERSITY

If this is true, Western capitalism is not the rational universal modernization theory takes it to be, not the untranscendable horizon of technical possibilities. Yet it does have what might be called a "practical universality" that has imposed itself on a planetary scale. No modern society can forego basic technical discoveries such as antibiotics, plastics, or electricity, and none can withdraw from worldwide communication networks. The cost of an entirely independent path of development is just too high (Rybczynski 1983: chap. 5). But significant innovations are possible with respect to what has been the main line of development up to now.

The terrain of practical universality is accessible from many standpoints for many purposes. It first emerged in the West around a particular panoply of technologies and rational systems. Today, as Western hegemony weakens, the different requirements of the various cultures that have adopted modern technology may provide contexts within which to reopen lost roads to progress or to discover new ones in the search for locally adapted alternatives.

The scope and significance of such change is potentially enormous. Technical choices establish the horizons of daily life. These choices define a "world" within which the specific alternatives we think of as purposes, goals, uses, emerge. They also define the subject who chooses among the alternatives: we make ourselves in making the world through technology. Thus fundamental technological change is interactive and self-referential. At issue is *becoming*, not *having*. The goal is to define a way of life, an ideal of abundance, and a human type, not to obtain more goods in the prevailing socioeconomic model.

But are new and diverse directions technically possible? One commonplace view holds that as modern technology becomes more complex, its structure constrains future developments more and more, eventually approximating a deterministic system (Ellul 1964). This is not what the evidence shows. In fact, new degrees of freedom open up inside the system at critical junctures and points of passage. Public interventions sometimes succeed in bringing advancing technologies to a halt or changing their direction of development. Fatalism is wrong because technology is essentially underdetermined, crisscrossed by a variety of demands and restrictions to which new elements are constantly added in unpredictable evolutionary sequences.

Technologists themselves discuss these matters in a language that has social implications of which they are not generally aware. In everyday technical usage, realized multiplicities of purpose are called "elegant" by contrast with designs that are restricted to a single function. Gilbert Simondon (1958: chap. 1), the French philosopher of technology, defined this notion more precisely as "concretization." Technology is "concrete" in Simondon's sense when a single cleverly conceived structure in the object corresponds to many different functional requirements. Simondon offers apparently neutral examples such as the elimination of spark plugs in the diesel engine, which uses the energy of combustion not only for power but also to reignite itself from cycle to cycle.

So long as functions are traced back to human nature or some other nonsocial source, this observation is of narrow technical interest. But constructivism has now shown that social groups stand behind functions. Thus in uniting many functions in a single structure, concretizing innovations do not simply offer technical improvements, they gather many social groups around artifacts or systems of artifacts. "Elegance" and "concretization" refer not merely to improvements in efficiency, but also to the positioning of technologies at the point of intersection of multiple standpoints and aspirations. Efficiency may in fact increase, but new social constellations also develop in tandem with technical changes.

The examples of experimental medicine and videotex discussed in this book illustrate this process. In each case, the technical system was conceived and implemented by a scientific-technical elite in response to a rather technocratic set of functional requirements. That starting point constituted an initial functional layer that sooner or later encountered resistance from a public with other ideas in mind. The resistance took the form of incorporating the technical system into another set of functional requirements through concretizing innovations on its margins. Thus a second layer was added to the first, not substituted for it, through reconciling several different types of functions in the same structures. Experiment and treatment, information and communication, were united in multifunctional systems. There is no limit in principle on the extension of such concretizing strategies in the democratic reconstruction of the technical base of modern societies.

Technological creativity is a form of imaginative play with alternate worlds and ways of being. A multicultural politics of technology is possible; it would pursue elegant designs that reconcile several worlds in each device and system. To the extent that this strategy is successful, it prepares a very different future from the one projected by social theory up to now. In that future, technology is not a particular value one must choose for or against, but a challenge to evolve and multiply worlds without end.

References

Abe, Masao. 1988. "Nishida's Philosophy of 'Place.'" *International Philosophical Quarterly*, vol. 28, no. 4.

ACT UP. 1989. *A National AIDS Treatment Research Agenda*. New York: ACT UP.

Adler, Herbert M., and V. B. O. Hammett. 1973. "The Doctor-Patient Relationship Revisited: An Analysis of the Placebo Effect." *Annals of Internal Medicine*, vol. 78, no. 4.

Amin, Samir. 1989. *Eurocentrism*. Trans. R. Moore. New York: Monthly Review Press.

Arisaka, Yoko. 1993. "Haiku, Nishida, and Heidegger: Toward a New Metaphysics of Experience." Manuscript.

Arnason, Johann. 1992. "Modernity, Postmodernity and the Japanese Experience." Manuscript.

Asimov, Isaac. 1972*a*. *The Caves of Steel*. New York: Fawcett Crest. Originally published 1953.

———. 1972*b*. "The Dead Past." In *Beyond Control*, ed. R. Silverberg. New York: Dell. Originally published 1956.

Attali, Jean, and Yves Stourdze. 1977. "The Birth of the Telephone and Economic Crisis: The Slow Death of the Monologue in French Society." In *The Social Impact of the Telephone*, ed. Ithiel de Sola Pool. Boston: MIT Press.

Avina, Robert, and Lawrence Schneiderman. 1978. "Why Patients Choose Homeopathy." *Western Journal of Medicine*, vol. 128, no. 4.

Bainbridge, William. 1986. *Dimensions of Science Fiction*. Cambridge: Harvard University Press.

Baltz, Claude. 1984. "Grétel: un nouveau média de communication." In *Télématique: promenade dans les usages*, ed. Marie Marchand and Claire Ancelin. Paris: Documentation française.

Barinaga, Marcia. 1988. "Placebos Prompt New Protocols for AIDS Drug Testing." *Nature*, vol. 335, no. 6.

Bates, Harry. 1975. "Farewell to the Master." In *Adventures in Time and Space*, ed. R. F. Healy and J. F. McComas. New York: Ballantine Books. Originally published 1940.

Baudrillard, Jean. 1968. *Le Système des objets*. Paris: Gallimard.

Bell, Daniel. 1973. *The Coming of Post-Industrial Society*. New York: Basic Books.

Benedetto, André. 1966. *Urgent Crier*. Basses-Alpes, France: R. Morel.

Benedikt, Michael. 1968. "*Alphaville* and Its Subtext." In *Jean-Luc Godard*, ed. T. Mussman. New York: Dutton.

Benjamin, Walter. 1969. "The Work of Art in the Age of Mechanical Reproduction." In *Illuminations*, ed. Hannah Arendt, trans. Harry Zohn. New York: Schocken Books.

————. 1978. "Paris, Capital of the Nineteenth Century." In *Reflections*, ed. P. Demetz, trans. E. Jephcott. New York: Harcourt Brace Jovanovich.

Berman, Marshall. 1982. *All That Is Solid Melts into Air: The Experience of Modernity*. New York: Simon and Schuster.

Bernard, Jean. 1978. *L'Esperance ou le nouvel état de la medecine*. Paris: Buchet/Chastel.

Bernstein, Jay. 1984. *The Philosophy of the Novel: Lukács, Marxism and the Dialectics of Form*. Minneapolis: University of Minnesota Press.

Berque, Augustin. 1986. *Vivre l'espace au Japon*. Paris: Presses Universitaires de France.

————. 1990. *Médiance: de milieux en paysages*. Paris: Reclus.

Bertho, Catherine. 1981. *Télégraphes et téléphones: de Valmy au microprocesseur*. Paris: Livre de Poche.

Bester, Alfred. 1956. *The Stars My Destination*. New York: Ballantine.

Bidou, Catherine, Marc Guillaume, and Véronique Prévost. 1988. *L'Ordinaire de la télématique: offre et usages des services utilitaires grand-public*. Paris: Editions de l'Iris.

Bijker, Wiebe, Thomas Hughes, and Trevor Pinch, eds. 1990. *The Social Construction of Technological Systems*. Cambridge: MIT Press.

Bijker, Wiebe, and John Law, eds. 1992. *Shaping Technology/Building Society*. Cambridge: MIT Press.

Bloor, David. 1991. *Knowledge and Social Imagery*. Chicago: University of Chicago Press.

Borges, Jorge Luis. 1964. "The Theologians," trans. J. E. Irby. In *Labyrinths*, ed. D. A. Yates and J. E. Irby. New York: New Directions.

Borgmann, Albert. 1984. *Technology and the Character of Contemporary Life*. Chicago: University of Chicago Press.

Bourdieu, Pierre. 1972. *Esquisse d'une théorie de la pratique*. Geneva and Paris: Librairie Droz.

————. 1981. "La Representation politique: elements pour une théorie du champ politique." *Actes de la Recherche en Sciences Sociales*, no. 36/37.

Branscomb, Anne. 1988. "Videotext: Global Progress and Comparative Policies." *Journal of Communication*, vol. 38, no. 1.

Bridgman, P. W. 1948. "Scientists and Social Responsibility." *Bulletin of the Atomic Scientists*, vol. 4, no. 3.

Briole, Alain, and Adam-Franck Tyar. 1987. *Fragments des passions ordinaires: essai sur le phénomène de télésociabilité.* Paris: Documentation française.

Brody, Howard. 1980. *Placebos and the Philosophy of Medicine.* Chicago: University of Chicago Press.

Brossat, Sylvia, and Patrice Pinell. 1990. "Coping with Parents." *Sociology of Health and Illness,* vol. 12, no. 1.

Bruhat, Thierry. 1984. "Messageries electroniques: Grétel a Strasbourg et Teletel a Vélizy." In *Télématique: promenade dans les usages,* ed. Marie Marchand and Claire Ancelin. Paris: Documentation française.

Buchanan, Denton. 1975. "Group Therapy for Kidney Transplant Patients." *International Journal of Psychiatry in Medicine,* vol. 6, no. 4.

———. 1978. "Group Therapy for Chronic Physically Ill Patients." *Psychosomatics,* vol. 19, no. 7.

Burke, John. 1972. "Bursting Boilers and the Federal Power." In *Technology and Culture,* ed. M. Kranzberg and W. Davenport. New York: New American Library.

Caillois, Roger. 1955. "Les Jeux dans le monde moderne." *Profils,* no. 13.

Cambrosio, Alberto, and Camille Limoges. 1991. "Controversies as Governing Processes in Technology Assessment." *Technology Analysis and Strategic Management,* vol. 3, no. 4.

Carter, Robert. 1989. *The Nothingness Beyond God: An Introduction to the Philosophy of Nishida Kitarō.* New York: Paragon House.

Cassileth, Barrie R., E. J. Lusk, D. S. Miller, and S. Hurwitz. 1982. "Attitudes toward Clinical Trials among Patients and the Public." *Journal of the American Medical Association,* vol. 248, no. 8.

Caufield, Catherine. 1989. *Multiple Exposures.* London: Secker and Warburg.

Chabrol, J. L., and Pascal Perin. 1989. *Usages et usagers du vidéotex: les pratiques domestiques du vidéotex en 1987.* Paris: DGT.

Chafetz, Morris, N. Bernstein, W. Sharpe, and R. Schwab. 1955. "Short-Term Group Therapy of Patients with Parkinson's Disease." *New England Journal of Medicine,* vol. 253, no. 22.

Charles, Allan G., K. L. Norr, C. R. Block, S. Meyering, and E. Meyers. 1978. "Obstetric and Psychological Effects of Psychoprophylactic Preparation for Childbirth." *American Journal of Obstetrics and Gynecology,* vol. 131, no. 1.

Charon, Jean-Marie. 1987. "Teletel, de l'interactivité homme/machine à la communication médiatisée." In *Les Paradis Informationnels,* ed. Marie Marchand. Paris: Masson.

Charon, Jean-Marie, and Eddy Cherky. 1983. *Le Vidéotex: un nouveau média local: enquete sur l'experimentation de Vélizy.* Paris: Centre d'Etude des Mouvements Sociaux.

Clarke, Arthur C. 1956. *The City and the Stars.* New York: Harcourt, Brace and World.

———. 1967. *Voices from the Sky.* New York: Pyramid Books.

———. 1972. *Childhood's End.* New York: Ballantine Books.

Condon, Edward U. 1969. *Scientific Study of Unidentified Flying Objects.* New York: Bantam Books.

Crowley, James. 1971. "Intellectuals as Visionaries of the New Asian Order." In *Dilemmas of Growth in Prewar Japan,* ed. J. Morley. Princeton: Princeton University Press.

Cummings, Bruce. 1989. "Japan's Position in the Postwar World System: Regionalism, the Korean War, and the Dawning 'Post-Postwar' Era." Manuscript.

Curran, William J. 1969. "Governmental Regulation of the Use of Human Subjects in Medical Research: The Approach of Two Federal Agencies." *Ethical Aspects of Experimentation with Human Subjects. Daedalus: Journal of the America Academy of Arts and Sciences,* vol. 98, no. 2.

Dale, Peter. 1986. *The Myth of Japanese Uniqueness.* New York: St. Martin's Press.

Darnovsky, Marcy. 1991. "Overhauling the Meaning Machines: An Interview with Donna Haraway." *Socialist Review,* vol. 21, no. 2.

de Certeau, Michel. 1980. *L'Invention du quotidien.* 2 vols. Paris: Union generale d'editions.

Derrida, Jacques. 1972. "Signature evènement contexte." In his *Marges de la philosophie.* Paris: Editions de Minuit.

Détienne, Marcel, and Jean-Pierre Vernant. 1974. *Les Ruses de l'intelligence: la mètis des Grecs.* Paris: Flammarion.

Dick, Philip K. 1973. *Ubik.* Frogmore, St. Albans: Panther.

Dordick, Herbert S., Helen G. Bradley, and Burt Nanus, eds. 1979. *The Emerging Network Marketplace.* Norwood, N.J.: Ablex.

Dore, Ronald. 1987. *Taking Japan Seriously: A Confucian Perspective on Leading Economic Issues.* Palo Alto: Stanford University Press.

Eco, Umberto. 1984. *The Role of the Reader.* Bloomington: Indiana University Press.

Ellul, Jacques. 1964. *The Technological Society.* Trans. J. Wilkinson. New York: Vintage.

Endo, Shusaku. 1980. *When I Whistle.* Trans. V. C. Gessel. New York: Taplinger.

Epstein, Steven. 1991. "Democratic Science? AIDS Activism and the Contested Construction of Knowledge." *Socialist Review,* vol. 21, no. 2.

Ettema, James. 1989. "Interactive Electronic Text in the United States: Can Videotex Ever Go Home Again?" In *Media Use in the Information Society,* ed. J. C. Salvaggio and J. Bryant. Hillsdale, N.J.: Lawrence Erlbaum.

Ewen, Stuart. 1976. *Captains of Consciousness.* New York: McGraw-Hill.

Feenberg, Andrew. 1988a. "Fetishism and Form: Erotic and Economic Disorder in Literature." In *Violence and Truth,* ed. P. Dumouchel. Stanford: Stanford University Press.

———. 1988b. "Technique or Praxis: The Question of Organization in the Early Marxist Work of Lukács." In *Lukács Today,* ed. T. Rockmore. Amsterdam: D. Reidel.

———. 1989a. "A User's Guide to the Pragmatics of Computer Mediated Communication." *Semiotica,* vol. 75, no. 3/4.

———. 1989b. "The Written World." In *Mindweave: Communication, Computers, and Distance Education,* ed. A. Kaye and R. Mason. Oxford: Pergamon Press.

————. 1991. *Critical Theory of Technology.* New York: Oxford University Press.

————. 1992. "Subversive Rationalization: Technology, Power, and Democracy." *Inquiry,* vol. 35, no. 3/4.

Feenberg, Andrew, and Yoko Arisaka. 1990. "Experiential Ontology: The Origins of the Nishida Philosophy in the Doctrine of Pure Experience." *International Philosophical Quarterly,* vol. 30, no. 2.

Fischer, Claude. 1988a. "'Touch Someone': The Telephone Industry Discovers Sociability." *Technology and Culture,* vol. 29, no. 1.

————. 1988b. "Gender and the Residential Telephone, 1890–1940: Technologies of Sociability." *Sociological Forum,* vol. 3, no. 2.

Fletcher, R. H., M. S. O'Malley, J. A. Earp, T. A. Littleton, S. W. Fletcher, M. A. Greganti, R. A. Davidson, and J. Taylor. 1983. "Patients' Priorities for Medical Care." *Medical Care,* vol. 21, no. 2.

Florman, Samuel. 1981. *Blaming Technology.* New York: St. Martin's Press.

Forty, Adrian. 1986. *Objects of Desire.* New York: Pantheon.

Foucault, Michel. 1977. *Discipline and Punish.* Trans. A. Sheridan. New York: Pantheon.

————. 1980. *Power/Knowledge.* Trans. C. Gordon. New York: Pantheon.

Fox, Renée. 1959. *Experiment Perilous.* Philadelphia: University of Pennsylvania Press.

Freedman, Benjamin. 1975. "A Moral Theory of Consent." *Hastings Center Report,* vol. 5, no. 4.

Freidson, Eliot. 1970. *Profession of Medicine: A Study of the Sociology of Applied Knowledge.* New York: Harper and Row.

Freud, Sigmund. 1961. *Civilization and Its Discontents.* Trans. J. Strachey. New York: W. W. Norton.

Gibson, William. 1984. *Neuromancer.* New York: Berkeley Books.

Giraud, Alain. 1984. "Une Lente Emergence." In *Télématique: promenade dans les usages,* ed. Marie Marchand and Claire Ancelin. Paris: Documentation française.

Giraudoux, Jean. 1935. *La Guerre de Troie n'aura pas lieu.* Paris: Grasset.

Glaser, Barney, and Anselm Strauss. 1972. "Awareness of Dying." In *Experimentation with Human Beings,* ed. Jay Katz. New York: Russell Sage.

Goffman, Erving. 1961. *Encounters: Two Studies in the Sociology of Interaction.* New York: Bobbs-Merrill.

————. 1982. *Interaction Ritual.* New York: Pantheon.

Goldman, Eric. 1961. *The Crucial Decade.* New York: Vintage.

Gossman, Lionel. 1971. "Literary Education and Democracy." *Modern Language Notes,* vol. 86, no. 6.

Goyan, Jere. 1988. "Drug Regulation: Quo Vadis?" *Journal of the American Medical Association,* vol. 260, no. 20.

Greenberg, Daniel. 1967. *The Politics of Pure Science.* New York: New American Library.

Guillaume, Marc. 1975. *Le Capital et son double.* Paris: Presses Universitaires de France.

————. 1982. "Téléspectres." *Les Rhetoriques de la technologie. Traverses,* no. 26.

————. 1989. *La Contagion des passions.* Paris: Plon.

Habermas, Jürgen. 1970. *Toward a Rational Society.* Trans. J. Shapiro. Boston: Beacon Press.

————. 1984. *Theory of Communicative Action.* Vol. 1. *Reason and the Rationalization of Society.* Trans. Thomas McCarthy. Boston: Beacon Press.

————. 1987. *Theory of Communicative Action.* Vol. 2. *Lifeworld and System: A Critique of Functionalist Reason.* Trans. Thomas McCarthy. Boston: Beacon Press.

————. 1991a. *The Structural Transformation of the Public Sphere.* Trans. T. Burger. Cambridge: MIT Press.

————. 1991b. "A Reply." In *Communicative Action,* ed. A. Honneth and H. Joas, trans. J. Gaines and D. Jones. Cambridge: MIT Press.

————. 1992. "Further Reflections on the Public Sphere," trans. Thomas Burger. In *Habermas and the Public Sphere,* ed. C. Calhoun. Cambridge: MIT Press.

Hamamoto, Darrell. 1989. *Nervous Laughter: Television Situation Comedy and Liberal Democratic Ideology.* New York: Praeger.

Haraway, Donna. 1991. *Simians, Cyborgs, and Women: The Reinvention of Nature.* New York: Routledge.

————. 1992. "The Promise of Monsters: A Regenerative Politics for Inappropriate/d Others." In *Cultural Studies,* ed. L. Grossberg, C. Nelson, and P. Treichler. New York: Routledge.

Harding, Sandra. 1993. *The "Racial" Economy of Science: Toward a Democratic Future.* Bloomington: Indiana University Press.

————. 1994. "Is Science Multicultural? Challenges, Resources, Opportunities, Uncertainties." In *Multiculturalism: A Reader,* ed. D. T. Goldberg. London: Basil Blackwell.

Harootunian, H. D. 1989. "Visible Discourses/Invisible Ideologies." In *Postmodernism and Japan,* ed. Masao Miyoshi and H. D. Harootunian. Durham, N.C.: Duke University Press.

Hartings, Michael, M. Pavlou, and F. Davis. 1976. "Group Counseling of MS Patients in a Program of Comprehensive Care." *Journal of Chronic Disease,* vol. 29.

Heidegger, Martin. 1977. *The Question Concerning Technology.* Trans. W. Lovitt. New York: Harper and Row.

Herf, Jeffrey. 1984. *Reactionary Modernism: Technology, Culture, and Politics in Weimar and the Third Reich.* Cambridge: Cambridge University Press.

Herrigel, Eugen. 1960. *Zen in the Art of Archery.* Trans. R. F. C. Hull. New York: Pantheon.

Hiromatsu, Wataru. 1990. *<Kindai no Chokoku> Ron* (Theories on 'Overcoming Modernity'). Tokyo: Kodansha.

Hiromatsu, Wataru, Akira Asada, Hiroshi Ichikawa, and Kojin Karatani. 1989. "*<Kindai no Chokoku> to Nishida Tetsugaku*" ('Overcoming Modernity' in Nishida's Philosophy). *Kikanshicho,* vol. 4.

Honneth, Axel. 1991. *The Critique of Power: Reflective Stages in a Critical Social Theory.* Trans. K. Baynes. Cambridge: MIT Press.

Horkheimer, Max, and Theodor W. Adorno. 1972. *Dialectic of Enlightenment.* Trans. John Cumming. New York: Herder and Herder.

Hoyle, Fred. 1968. *Ossian's Ride*. New York: Berkeley Books. Originally published 1959.

Huh, Woo-Sung. 1990. "The Philosophy of History in the 'Later' Nishida: A Philosophic Turn." *Philosophy East and West*, vol. 40, no. 3.

Ihde, Don. 1990. *Technology and the Lifeworld*. Bloomington: Indiana University Press.

Illich, Ivan. 1976. *Medical Nemesis*. New York: Pantheon.

Ingelfinger, F. J. 1972. "Informed (but Uneducated) Consent." *New England Journal of Medicine*, vol. 287, no. 9.

Iwaasa, Raymond-Stone. 1985. "Télématique grand public: l'information ou la communication? Les cas de Grétel et de Compuserve." *Le Bulletin de l'IDATE*, no. 18.

James, William. 1943. *Essays in Radical Empiricism and a Pluralistic Universe*. New York: Longman's, Green.

―――. 1952. *The Principles of Psychology*. Great Books of the Western World, vol. 53. Chicago: Encyclopedia Britannica.

Jameson, Frederic. 1973. "Generic Discontinuities in SF: Brian Aldiss' *Starship*." *Science Fiction Studies*, vol. 1, no. 2.

Jonas, Hans. 1969. "Philosophical Reflections on Experimenting with Human Subjects." *Ethical Aspects of Experimentation with Human Subjects. Daedalus: Journal of the America Academy of Arts and Sciences*, vol. 98, no. 2.

Jouet, J., and P. Flichy. 1991. *European Telematics: The Emerging Economy of Words*. Trans. D. Lytel. Amsterdam: Elsevier.

Kane, Robert L., D. Olsen, C. Leymaster, and F. R. Woolley. 1974. "Manipulating the Patient: A Comparison of the Effectiveness of Physician and Chiropractor Care." *Lancet*, no. 7870.

Katz, Elihu. 1980. "Media Events: The Sense of Occasion." *Studies in Visual Communication*, vol. 6, no. 3.

Kawabata, Yasunari. 1969. *Japan, The Beautiful and Myself*. Trans. E. Seidensticker. Tokyo: Kodansha.

―――. 1981. *The Master of Go*. Trans. E. Seidensticker. New York: Perigree.

Kazashi, Nobuo. 1993. "Four Variations on the Phenomenological Theme of 'Horizon': James, Nishida, Merleau-Ponty, and Schutz." Ph.D. dissertation, Yale University.

Kevles, Daniel. 1979. *The Physicists*. New York: Vintage.

Kolata, Gina. 1989. "AIDS Researcher Seeks Wide Access to Drugs in Test." *New York Times*, June 26.

Korschelt, Oscar. 1965. *The Theory and Practice of Go*. Ed. and trans. S. King and G. Leckie. Rutland, Vt.: Charles E. Tuttle.

Koyama, Iwao. 1935. *Nishida Tetsugaku*. Tokyo: Iwanami Shoten.

Kutner, Nancy G. 1978. "Medical Students' Orientation toward the Chronically Ill." *Journal of Medical Education*, vol. 53, no. 2.

Ladd, John. 1980. "Medical Ethics: Who Knows Best?" *Lancet*, no. 8204.

Latour, Bruno. 1987. *Science in Action*. Cambridge: Harvard University Press.

―――. 1991. *Nous n'avons jamais été modernes*. Paris: La Découverte.

―――. 1992. "Where Are the Missing Masses? The Sociology of a Few Mundane Artifacts." In *Shaping Technology/Building Society: Studies in Sociotechnical Change*, ed. W. Bijker and J. Law. Cambridge: MIT Press.

Lavelle, Pierre. 1994. "The Political Thought of Nishida Kitarō." *Monumenta Nipponica*, vol. 49, no. 2.

Le Guin, Ursula. 1971. *The Lathe of Heaven*. New York: Avon Books.

Lem, Stanislaw. 1974. *The Futurological Congress*. New York: Seabury Press.

———. 1984. *Microworlds*. New York: Harcourt Brace Jovanovich.

Lévi-Strauss, Claude. 1955. *Tristes Tropiques*. Paris: Plon.

———. 1963. "Réponse à quelques questions." *Esprit*, vol. 31, no. 322.

———. 1968. *Structural Anthropology*. Trans. C. Jacobsen and B. G. Schoepf. New York: McGraw-Hill.

Lidz, Charles W., A. Meisel, M. Osterweis, J. L. Holden, J. H. Marx, and M. R. Munetz. 1983. "Barriers to Informed Consent." *Annals of Internal Medicine*, vol. 99, no. 4.

Löwy, Ilana. 1987. "Choix scientifiques et choix ethiques dans le traitement de la maladie renale terminale." *Information sur les Sciences Sociales*, vol. 26, no. 3.

Loy, David. 1988. *Nonduality: A Study in Comparative Philosophy*. New Haven: Yale University Press.

Lukács, Georg. 1965. *Theorie des romans*. Neuwied and Berlin: Luchterhand.

———. 1968. *The Theory of the Novel*. Trans. A. Bostock. Cambridge: MIT Press.

Lyotard, Jean-François. 1979. *La Condition Postmoderne*. Paris: Editions de Minuit.

———. 1991a. *The Inhuman*. Stanford: Stanford University Press.

———. 1991b. *The Postmodern Condition: A Report on Knowledge*. Trans. G. Bennington and B. Massumi. Minneapolis: University of Minnesota Press.

MacIntyre, Alasdair. 1981. *After Virtue: A Study in Moral Theory*. Notre Dame: University of Notre Dame Press.

Mackillop, William, and Pauline Johnston. 1986. "Ethical Problems in Clinical Research: The Need for Empirical Studies of the Clinical Trial Process." *Journal of Chronic Disease*, vol. 39, no. 3.

Macpherson, C. B. 1973. *Democratic Theory*. Oxford: Clarendon Press.

Marchand, Marie. 1984. "Conclusion: vivre avec le Videotex." In *Télématique: promenade dans les usages*, ed. Marie Marchand and Claire Ancelin. Paris: Documentation française.

———. 1987. *La Grande Aventure du Minitel*. Paris: Larousse.

———. 1988. *A French Success Story: The Minitel Saga*. Trans. Mark Murphy. Paris: Larousse.

Marcuse, Herbert. 1964. *One-Dimensional Man*. Boston: Beacon Press.

———. 1966. "The Individual in the Great Society." *Alternatives Magazine*, March–April.

———. 1968. *Negations*. Trans. J. Shapiro. Boston: Beacon Press.

———. 1969. *An Essay on Liberation*. Boston: Beacon Press.

———. 1972. *Counter-Revolution and Revolt*. Boston: Beacon Press.

———. 1992. "Ecology and the Critique of Modern Society." *Capitalism, Nature, Socialism*, vol. 3, no. 11.

Marin, Louis. 1978. *Le Récit est un piège*. Paris: Editions de Minuit.

Marwick, Charles. 1987. "Proposal to Make Investigational New Drugs Available Without Clinical Trial Participation in Certain Cases Is Receiving Mixed Responses." *Journal of the American Medical Association*, vol. 257, no. 22.

————. 1988. "FDA Seeks Swifter Approval of Drugs for Some Life-Threatening or Debilitating Diseases." *Journal of the American Medical Association*, vol. 260, no. 20.

Marx, Karl. 1906. *Capital.* Trans. E. Aveling. New York: Modern Library.

Mayntz, Renate, and Volker Schneider. 1988. "The Dynamics of System Development in a Comparative Perspective: Interactive Videotex in Germany, France and Britain." In *The Development of Large Technical Systems*, ed. Renate Mayntz and Thomas Hughes. Boulder: Westview Press.

McCarthy, Thomas. 1991. "Complexity and Democracy: Or the Seducements of Systems Theory." In *Communicative Action*, ed. A. Honneth and H. Jonas, trans. J. Gaines and D. Jones. Cambridge: MIT Press.

McLuhan, Marshall. 1964. *Understanding Media: The Extensions of Man.* New York: McGraw-Hill.

Merrill, Judith. 1971. "What Do You Mean? Science? Fiction?" In *SF: The Other Side of Realism*, ed. T. Clareson. Bowling Green: Bowling Green University Popular Press.

Miller, Roy Andrew. 1971. "Levels of Speech (*Keigo*) and the Japanese Linguistic Response to Modernization." In *Tradition and Modernization in Japanese Culture*, ed. D. Shively. Princeton: Princeton University Press.

Miyoshi, Masao. 1989. "Against the Native Grain: The Japanese Novel and the 'Postmodern' West." In *Postmodernism and Japan*, ed. Masao Miyoshi and H. D. Harootunian. Durham, N.C.: Duke University Press.

Morley, James. 1971. "Introduction: Choice and Consequence." In *Dilemmas of Growth in Prewar Japan*, ed. J. Morley. Princeton: Princeton University Press.

Morone, Joseph, and Edward Woodhouse. 1989. *The Demise of Nuclear Energy?* New Haven: Yale University Press.

Najita, Tetsuo, and H. D. Harootunian. 1988. "Japanese Revolt against the West." In *The Cambridge History of Japan*, vol. 6, ed. P. Duus. Cambridge: Cambridge University Press.

Nakamura, Yujiro. 1983. "Nishida: le premier philosophe original au Japon." *Critique*, vol. 39, no. 428/429.

Nakane, Chie. 1970. *Japanese Society.* Berkeley: University of California Press.

Nietzsche, Friedrich. 1969. *On the Genealogy of Morals and Ecce Homo.* Trans. W. Kaufmann. New York: Vintage.

Nishida, Kitarō. 1958a. "The Problem of Japanese Culture." In *Sources of the Japanese Tradition*, vol. 2, ed. and trans. W. T. de Bary. New York: Columbia University Press.

————. 1958b. *Intelligibility and the Philosophy of Nothingness.* Trans. R. Schinzinger. Honolulu: East-West Center Press.

————. 1965a. *Zen no Kenkyu* (An Inquiry into the Good). In *Nishida Kitarō Zenshu*, vol. 1. Tokyo: Iwanami Shoten.

————. 1965b. "Rekishi Tetsugaku ni Tsuite" (On the Philosophy of History). In *Nishida Kitarō Zenshu*, vol. 12. Tokyo: Iwanami Shoten.

———. 1965c. "Sekai Shin Chitsujo no Genri" (The Principle of New World Order). In *Nishida Kitarō Zenshu*, vol. 12. Tokyo: Iwanami Shoten.

———. 1965d. "Nihonbunka no Mondai" (The Problem of Japanese Culture). In *Nishida Kitarō Zenshu*, vol. 12. Tokyo: Iwanami Shoten.

———. 1965e. "Nihonbunka no Mondai" (The Problem of Japanese Culture). In *Nishida Kitarō Zenshu*, vol. 14. Tokyo: Iwanami Shoten.

———. 1965f. "Watakushi no Tachiba Kara Mita Hegel no Benshoho" (My Standpoint Toward Hegel's Dialectic). In *Nishida Kitarō Zenshu*, vol. 12. Tokyo: Iwanami Shoten.

———. 1965g. "Shokanshu" (Collection of Letters). In *Nishida Kitarō Zenshu*, vol. 19. Tokyo: Iwanami Shoten.

———. 1970. *Fundamental Problems of Philosophy*. Trans. D. Dilworth. Tokyo: Sophia University Press.

———. 1987. *Last Writings: Nothingness and the Religious Worldview*. Trans. D. Dilworth. Honolulu: University of Hawaii Press.

———. 1990. *An Inquiry into the Good* (Zen no Kenkyu). Trans. Masao Abe and Christopher Ives. New Haven: Yale University Press.

Nishitani, Keiji. 1982. *Religion and Nothingness*. Trans. J. Van Bragt. Berkeley: University of California Press.

———. 1991. *Nishida Kitarō*. Trans. Y. Seisaku and J. Heisig. Berkeley: University of California Press.

Nora, Simon, and Alain Minc. 1978. *L'Informatisation de la société*. Paris: Editions du Seuil.

Norman, Donald. 1988. *The Psychology of Everyday Things*. New York: Basic Books.

Nuckolls, Katherine, J. Cassel, and B. Kaplan. 1972. "Psychosocial Assets, Life Crisis and the Prognosis of Pregnancy." *American Journal of Epidemiology*, vol. 95, no. 5.

Ohashi, Ryosuke. 1990. *Die Philosophie der Kyoto-Schule: Texte und Einfürhung*. Freiburg: Karl Albers Verlag.

———. 1992. *Nihonteki na mono, Yoroppateki na mono* (What Is Japanese, What Is European). Tokyo: Shincho Sensho.

Ong, Walter. 1971. "The Literate Orality of Popular Culture Today." In his *Rhetoric, Romance, and Technology*. Ithaca: Cornell University Press.

———. 1977. "From Mimesis to Irony." In his *Interfaces of the Word*. Ithaca: Cornell University Press.

Oppenheimer, J. Robert. 1955. *The Open Mind*. New York: Simon and Schuster.

Parkes, Graham. 1992. "Heidegger and Japanese Thought: How Much Did He Know, and When Did He Know It?" In *Heidegger: Critical Assessments*, ed. C. Macann. New York: Routledge.

Parsons, Talcott. 1964. *The Social System*. New York: Free Press.

———. 1969. "Research with Human Subjects and the 'Professional Complex.'" *Ethical Aspects of Experimentation with Human Subjects. Daedalus: Journal of the America Academy of Arts and Sciences*, vol. 98, no. 2.

Perrin, Noel. 1979. *Giving Up the Gun*. Boston: David R. Godine.

Petersen, Gwenn. 1979. *The Moon in the Water: Understanding Tanizaki, Kawabata, and Mishima*. Honolulu: University of Hawaii.

Pigeat, Henri, et al. 1979. *Du téléphone a la télématique: rapport du groupe de travail.* Paris: Documentation français.

Pilarcik, Marlene. 1986. "Dialectics and Change in Kawabata's Master of Go." *Modern Language Studies,* vol. 16, no. 4.

Pinch, Trevor, and Wiebe Bijker. 1984. "The Social Construction of Facts and Artefacts: or How the Sociology of Science and the Sociology of Technology Might Benefit Each Other." *Social Studies of Science,* vol. 14, no. 3.

Pippin, Robert. 1991. *Modernism as a Philosophical Problem.* Cambridge: Basil Blackwell.

———. 1995. "On the Notion of Technology as Ideology: Prospects." In *Technology and the Politics of Knowledge,* ed. A. Feenberg and A. Hannay. Bloomington: Indiana University Press.

Poster, Mark. 1990. *The Mode of Information.* Chicago: University of Chicago Press.

Powles, John. 1973. "On the Limitations of Modern Medicine." *Science, Medicine and Man,* vol. 1, no. 1.

Rabinowitch, Eugene. 1960. "Pushing Back the Clock of Doom." In *The Atomic Age,* ed. M. Grodzins and E. Rabinowitch. New York: Simon and Schuster.

Reidenberg, Marcus. 1987. "Should Unevaluated Therapies Be Available for Sale?" *Clinical Pharmacology and Therapeutics,* vol. 42, no. 6.

Report of the National Commission on Orphan Diseases. 1989. Office of the Assistant Secretary for Health, U.S. Department of Health and Human Services.

Ricoeur, Paul. 1979. "The Model of the Text: Meaningful Action Considered as a Text." In *Interpretive Social Science: A Reader,* ed. P. Rabinow and W. Sullivan. Berkeley: University of California Press.

Riesman, D., N. Glazer, and R. Denney. 1953. *The Lonely Crowd.* New York: Doubleday.

Rybczynski, Witold. 1983. *Taming the Tiger.* New York: Penguin.

Saint-Just, Louis-Antoine de. 1968. *Oeuvres choisies.* Paris: Gallimard.

Sakai, Naoki. 1989. "Modernity and Its Critique: The Problem of Universalism and Particularism." In *Postmodernism and Japan,* ed. Masao Miyoshi and H. D. Harootunian. Durham, N.C.: Duke University Press.

Santayana, George. 1926. *Winds of Doctrine.* New York: Scribners.

Schivelbusch, Wolfgang. 1988. *Disenchanted Light.* Trans. A. Davies. Berkeley: University of California Press.

Schudson, Michael. 1984. *Advertising: The Uneasy Persuasion.* New York: Basic Books.

Serres, Michel. 1987. *Statues.* Paris: François Bourin.

Shapiro, Arthur, and Louis Morris. 1978. "The Placebo Effect in Medical and Psychological Therapies." In *Handbook of Psychotherapy and Behavior Change,* ed. S. L. Garfield and A. E. Bergin. New York: John Wiley.

Sharp, Lauriston. 1952. "Steel Axes for Stone Age Australians." In *Human Problems in Technological Change,* ed. E. Spicer. New York: Russell Sage.

Shimomura, Torataro. 1966. "The Modernisation of Japan, with Special Reference to Philosophy." *The Modernisation of Japan. Philosophical Studies of Japan,* vol. 7.

Simak, Clifford. 1952. *City*. New York: Ace Books.

Simondon, Gilbert. 1958. *Du mode d'existence des objets techniques*. Paris: Aubier.

Slater, Philip. 1970. *The Pursuit of Loneliness*. Boston: Beacon Press.

Smith, Rebecca. 1989. "AIDS Drug Trials" (letter). *Science*, vol. 246.

Sontag, Susan. 1969. "The Imagination of Disaster." In her *Against Interpretation*. New York: Dell.

Soviak, Eugene. 1971. "Journal of the Iwakura Embassy." In *Tradition and Modernization in Japanese Culture*, ed. D. Shively. Princeton: Princeton University Press.

Stover, Leon. 1973. "Science Fiction, the Research Revolution, and John Campbell." *Extrapolation*, vol. 14, no. 2.

Sturgeon, Theodore. 1971. *More Than Human*. New York: Ballantine Books. Originally published 1953.

Sugita, Genpaku. 1969. *Dawn of Western Science in Japan*. Trans. R. Matsumoto and E. Kiyooka. Tokyo: Hokuseido Press.

Suzuki, D. T. 1970. *Zen in Japanese Culture*. Princeton: Princeton University Press. Originally published 1959.

————. 1973. *The Zen Doctrine of No-Mind*. New York: Samuel Weiser.

Swann, Thomas. 1976. "The Master of Go." In *Approaches to the Modern Japanese Novel*, ed. K. Tsuruta and T. Swann. Tokyo: Sophia University Press.

Szasz, Thomas S., and Mark H. Hollander. 1956. "A Contribution to the Philosophy of Medicine: The Basic Models of the Doctor-Patient Relationship." *A.M.A. Archives of Internal Medicine*, vol. 97, no. 5.

Szilard, Leo. 1961. *The Voice of the Dolphins*. New York: Simon and Schuster.

Tanizaki, Jun'ichiro. 1977. *In Praise of Shadows*. Trans. T. J. Harper and E. G. Seidensticker. New Haven, Conn.: Leete's Island Books.

Teng, Ssu-yu, and John K. Fairbanks. 1954. *China's Response to the West*. Cambridge: Harvard University Press.

Thompson, Paul. 1983. *The Nature of Work*. London: Macmillan.

Treichler, Paula. 1991. "How to Have Theory in an Epidemic: The Evolution of AIDS Treatment Activism." In *Technoculture*, ed. C. Penley and A. Ross. Minneapolis: University of Minnesota Press.

Ure, Andrew. 1835. *The Philosophy of Manufacturers*. London: Charles Knight.

Van Wolferen, Karel. 1989. *The Enigma of Japanese Power*. New York: Random House.

Vattimo, Gianni. 1991. *The End of Modernity*. Trans. J. Snyder. Baltimore: Johns Hopkins University Press.

Warshow, Robert. 1964. *The Immediate Experience*. New York: Anchor Books.

Watsuji, Tetsuro. 1987. *Climate and Culture: A Philosophical Study*. Trans. G. Bownas. Westport, Conn.: Greenwood Press.

Weber, Max. 1949. *The Methodology of the Social Sciences*. Trans. E. Shils and H. Finch. New York: Free Press.

————. 1958. *The Protestant Ethic and the Spirit of Capitalism*. Trans. T. Parsons. New York: Scribners.

Weckerlé, Christian. 1987. *Du téléphone au Minitel: acteurs et facteurs locaux dans la constitution des images et usages sociaux de la télématique.* 2 vols. Paris: Groupe de Recherche et d'Analyse du Social et de la Sociabilité.

Whitehead, Alfred North. 1925. *Science in the Modern World.* New York: Macmillan.

Whitfield, Stephen. 1991. *The Culture of the Cold War.* Baltimore: Johns Hopkins University Press.

Williamson, Jack. 1949. *The Humanoids.* New York: Lancer Books.

Winner, Langdon. 1992. "Citizen Virtues in a Technological Order." *Inquiry,* vol. 35, no. 3/4.

———. 1993. "Social Constructivism: Opening the Black Box and Finding It Empty." *Science as Culture,* vol. 3, part 3, no. 16.

Yusa, Michiko. 1991. "Nishida and the Question of Nationalism." *Monumenta Nipponica,* vol. 46, no. 2.

Zimmerman, Michael. 1990. *Heidegger's Confrontation with Modernity: Technology, Politics, Art.* Bloomington: Indiana University Press.

Index

Designer: U.C. Press Staff
Text: 10/13 Sabon
Display: Sabon
Compositor: Prestige Typography
Printer and Binder: Haddon Craftsmen, Inc.